1ST EDITION

PRACTICAL MARKETING ESSENTIALS

DENNIS E. SMITH, MBA

Practical Marketing Essentials

Copyright © 2021 Dennis E. Smith

Published by Dennis E. Smith / Association of Marketing Leadership & Rigor

ISBN 978-1-7378777-0-7

eBook ISBN 978-1-7378777-1-4

About the author

Dennis E. Smith, MBA received his B.S. degree in Business Administration from the University of Delaware and his Master's in Business Administration from Arizona State University. He has a variety of business experience ranging from accounting, finance, to sales and marketing across several industries including SAAS, CPG, and consumer durables. He has gained experience at both mid-size businesses and multiple global enterprises, including Stanley Black & Decker, Inc., Henkel AG & Co KGaA, and most recently is director of marketing at GoDaddy, Inc.

Beyond his passion for marketing, Dennis is an avid sports enthusiast, welder, and carpenter. While at the University of Delaware, Dennis was a member of the nationally ranked Division I lacrosse team. He continues to stay active by participating in club lacrosse and hockey. When not on the field or ice, you can often find Dennis in his garage building furniture or completing his latest DIY project.

This book is dedicated to Dennis' mother Doris and late father Donald F. Smith, DVM, DACVS
for their enduring support and inspiration.

Contents

Part 1: The foundation for success

Part 1 chapters:

1. Marketing basics
2. Marketing & human nature
3. Market & customer segmentation
4. Supply & demand
5. Branding
6. Brand strategy
7. Brand preservation
8. Product & service marketing

CHAPTER 1: MARKETING BASICS

In this chapter we will do a brief overview of essential concepts that marketing professionals must know as they are the foundation for success. The fact is that marketing is not an exact science but a combination of science and art. We will discuss the marketing 4 Ps, 4 Es, and 3 Cs.

Marketing 4 Ps	Marketing 4 Es	Marketing 3 Cs
• Product	• Experience	• Customer
• Price	• Exchange	• Company
• Promotion	• Evangelism	• Competitors
• Place	• Everyplace	

The Ps and Cs of marketing that have been taught and used for many years, and more recently the 4 Es were developed as an evolution of the 4 Ps. These categorizations are basic tenets of marketing, so as various topics are covered throughout this book they will be rooted in these principles.

1.1 Marketing: Science and art

Marketing is a dynamic and multifaceted profession that requires the ability to bridge customer insights, product development, design, analytics, and strategy. To some, marketing professionals have the reputation as the people who work with colors and designs or figure out how to best dupe customers into making a purchase. While there is a hint of truth to this reputation (duping excluded), marketers are commonly held responsible to answer complex analytical questions such as, "Was the discount we ran incremental?" or "How much do we expect to grow if we launch product 'X' next year?"

The beauty and curse of marketing is that it requires the use of both sides of the brain—the mathematical and analytical side as well as the creative side. The business questions posed earlier produce the opportunity to solve a mathematical question. However, they will almost always leave a degree of uncertainty due to the fact that the marketplace is so dynamic. To be an effective marketer requires the understanding of the market to assess the level of uncertainty. In the example of the discount, there will always be "noise" in the analysis. That noise may come from an endless number of sources such as direct competitors, indirect product promotion gaining a share of wallet that day, or the impact of a sunny day versus a rainy day. If marketers could perfectly predict market growth, they should switch to a career in finance and become the most successful stock traders of all-time.

An interesting and understated aspect of marketing is the need to intimately know your customers. A marketer will be required to act as a psychologist, sociologist, and anthropologist. Without an in-depth understanding of the customer and consumer, it is difficult to develop products to meet a need, and then just as importantly craft messaging that will effectively generate demand for your products.

Lastly, marketing has a degree of art associated with it. Knowing the customer, and understanding the business, will steer the creativity of a good marketer. Imagery, tonality, and brand essence are all created from the profound knowledge of the marketer.

1.2 The 4 Ps

Product

A product can take shape in different forms—a tangible product or a service. It may also be the combination of both such as a restaurant. At a restaurant you receive a tangible product, the food, as well as a service experience. As a marketer, you should have extensive knowledge about the consumer with the ability to help guide product decisions and innovation.

The product is at the foundation of many strategic marketing frameworks. This is because while terrific marketing campaigns may get shoppers to buy a product, their experience must live up to the expectations set forth by the brand. If a brand promises great quality and performance, but the product fails to deliver, the brand reputation will falter and most likely result in a struggling business.

Price

Price in the most basic sense is what a customer pays for your product; however, in marketing the considerations are wide-ranging. Pricing strategy is critical to success. It significantly impacts key business facets such as product position, demand, revenue, unit sales, and margin. Price doesn't just entail the price that a consumer pays to purchase the good or service. Price considerations extend throughout the supply chain. For example, in a business-to-business transaction, a manufacturer may sell to a retailer at a certain price. Then the retailer will sell the product to its customers for a different price. At both of those levels, you as the marketer of the product are responsible for the strategic decisions regarding the price and its implications to the business and brand. For instance, a prestige brand may charge higher prices and sacrifice sales volume in order to maintain a sense of exclusivity.

Price refers to all of the direct actions taken that affect what the customer pays for your goods or services. This extends to offers where a discount or a coupon may be applied to the purchase, which affects the price paid.

Promotion

Promotion is the act of creating awareness and disseminating information related to your brand or product. Often the role of the marketing professional is thought of synonymously with the promotional responsibilities of the profession. As you may already know and will learn in this text, the role of a marketer is wide-ranging.

Promotion may be done in a vast number of ways. In a basic sense it may be categorized as organic (unpaid) or paid, such as advertisements. Examples of organic promotions are press releases, word of mouth, and unsolicited endorsements. Examples of paid promotions include television advertisements, events, and social media advertisements.

The word *promotion* is often used to describe an offer or pricing promotion, tactics that alter the price a customer pays for your product. In this text the use of *promotion* will adhere to the definition stated previously and not be used to refer to price-related tactics.

Place

Place refers to multiple aspects of both brand and product placement. Most commonly, we think of place as the location in which the product is available for purchase. These are the sales channels such as e-commerce, brick and mortar retailers, or telemarketing. Within a given channel, place remains a consideration at a more granular level. For example, within a brick and mortar retailer your product may be merchandised (placed) in an aisle with related products as well as merchandised on a display at the checkout counter.

Place also considers where a brand is seen and its associations, such as places where the brand is advertised and where it is being used. Event sponsorships or social media influencer channels are just a couple examples of the types of places a product or brand may be encountered.

Included in the discussion of place is the consideration of geographical location. These considerations are wide-ranging, from differences among expansive regions around the world to differences between adjacent neighborhoods such as Little Italy and Chinatown in Manhattan, New York. Preferences among these locations may differ drastically, and as a marketer you must understand and adapt to the difference in customer preferences.

Time is an important facet of place. Timely advertising to capture a person browsing the internet to make a purchase, can mean targeting them with a banner ad. Or if you ever walk through New York City during a rain storm, you will immediately encounter the concept of time as the street vendors shift from selling trinkets to selling umbrellas.

1.3 The 4 Es

The 4 Es were recently introduced as one-for-one replacements of the 4 Ps. The 4 Es has appealed to many, as its approach is perceived to be more customer engagement and response focused.

Experience

Experience replaces *product*. When a customer purchases a product or service, there is more to consider than whether or not the customer need was met. There is an experience associated with how that need was met. Customers will often come away with a sense of emotion such as satisfaction, frustration, or delight. The term *experience*, provokes marketers to focus on the customers' emotional connection to the solution. A greater connection to the solution, in turn creates a bond to the brand, which will ultimately develop into loyalty and evangelism.

Exchange

Exchange replaces *price*. Exchange extends beyond price, and considers the value that the customers derive from your product or service. Value encompasses the entire experience with the brand, including rewards programs and benefits. Additionally, customers can derive value and a sense of ownership from the ability to provide feedback, or from the exchange of information either directly with the brand, or with the brand's community. Lastly, the exchange and use of customer data may be used to improve experiences. This benefits the customer in the form of a better experience, and benefits the brand, in the form of greater customer loyalty and advocacy.

Evangelism

Evangelism replaces *promotion*. Traditional marketing was focused on pushing a message out to customers. The availability of information, such as reviews, has evolved with the advent of the internet and social media. Customers have become increasingly skeptical of push marketing, and have become more reliant on third-party information that they perceive as more objective. The shift to the term *evangelism* emphasizes the importance of vocal advocates for your product or service, who will provide referrals and word of mouth support.

Everyplace

Everyplace replaces *place*. The change in terminology promotes a focus on the customers' places, versus a focus on where the product or service is merchandised, sold or rendered. Marketers must understand where customers spend time, both offline and online, as well as where the customers are receptive to marketing messages or influence. *Everyplace* also refers to the need for consistent delivery of the brand experience, regardless of time or place.

1.4 The 3 Cs

Customer

Customer is a term commonly and incorrectly used synonymously with the term *consumer*. Understanding the difference between the two may be confusing, but it is vital. Without a proper understanding of the differences, marketing efforts, including product development and product positioning, can be misguided because it can cause you to focus on the wrong group or miss the need to address both groups.

Let's clearly define the difference between a customer and a consumer. A consumer is the person or entity who uses the product or service. The customer purchases the product or service, and they may also use the product, so they would, by definition, also be a consumer. Therefore, a person or entity may start as a customer but then eventually be a consumer as well. Let's take, for example, cereal. The customer may be a retailer that buys the cereal from the cereal manufacturer. The retailer will not use or consume the product, so it is not a consumer. The person who buys the cereal from the retailer and actually eats the cereal is both a customer and consumer. If the cereal is, for instance, purchased by a parent but the cereal is eaten by her children, the parent becomes exclusively a customer and the children are exclusively the consumers.

Your task as a marketer is to understand the customer and consumers, their relationship, and how to generate differentiation for your product or service. As you work to understand and develop marketing messages, there is a common mistake nearly all marketers make. That mistake is to judge the messaging through your eyes and say "I like it." STOP. Recognize that the message is not created for you or what you like. What you like is irrelevant. What matters is, what will the customer or consumer think?

Company

In the realm of marketing, the company can make a significant impact in several ways. First, a company may be synonymous with the brand and fully represent the brand in every action that it takes. For example, Apple® is both the company name and the brand name used to identify many of its products and services. Second, the company mission or strategy may dictate the type of positioning a brand or product may have. An example would be the difference between a company that is focused on small batch high-end production of premium products, versus a bulk low-cost overseas manufacturer. The former company would support a high-end innovative brand, whereas the latter would be better suited for a less reactive, more stable brand and industry. Third, a company with multiple brands and product categories will prioritize each, determining growth expectations and resource allocation. Lastly, the company will have a strategy regarding its financial investment into its marketing department. This will impact the availability of various marketing tactics and could impact the investment levels into marketing research.

Competitors

As a marketer it is very likely that understanding competitors will be a core function of your role. When discussing competitors there are some guidelines to help ensure success.

Understand your placement in the market relative to the competition. One common method to visualize and document the market is via a perceptual map. Later in this text we will discuss perceptual maps in greater depth.

Don't mimic your competition. A mistake consistently made by marketers is to benchmark against competitors, assume they are doing things well, and then feel the need to copy them. Before you copy them, ask yourself, why do you think what they are doing is the optimal solution? Are they actually doing a better job than you? In addition, ask, how is copying my competitors going to help us beat them? How will copying them help me achieve anything beyond parity?

Be vigilant and recognize that competition may come from outside your immediate competitive set and industry. Particularly in the age of rapidly changing technology, new competitors may emerge without warning.

Take, for instance, Uber and its impact on the taxi industry. Or Dollar Shave Club® and its impact on the razor market. It's not easy to anticipate these threats, but as we review various frameworks to understand customers and how to meet their needs, these frameworks are intended to help uncover disruptive innovation.

———————————

CHAPTER 2: MARKETING & HUMAN NATURE

Before delving into an examination of the stereotypical marketing functions such as branding, product, sales, and design, we will first examine the core of any successful marketing effort. Effective marketing starts with an understanding of the customer and consumer. In many aspects of marketing it is necessary to play the role of a psychologist or a sociologist. In this chapter we will review two well-established frameworks for understanding consumers as well as introduce the concept of rational versus real customers.

2.1 Maslow's hierarchy of needs

Maslow's hierarchy is a framework that helps us to understand the human thought process. There are five levels in Maslow's framework, which are depicted in the form of a pyramid. The pyramid helps to represent that the lower levels are foundational and required in order to build up to the higher levels. It is important to note that Maslow's hierarchy of needs assumes rational human behavior (Maslow, 1970).

As you review the five different needs levels, think of the marketing implications of each. In a marketing context there may be opportunities to leverage any of the five levels to increase the sense of need for your product or service.

Figure 2.1.1 Maslow's hierarchy of needs pyramid

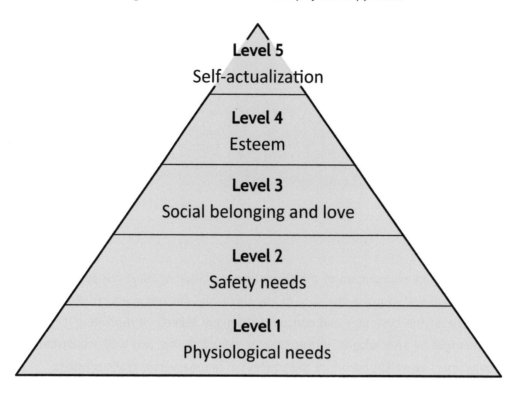

Level 1: Physiological needs

These needs are the most basic necessities for survival such as food, water, and air. As the foundation of the needs pyramid, a person must have these fulfilled prior to advancing to a higher level.

Level 2: Safety needs

These needs not only refer to personal physical safety but also refer to emotional and even financial safety. If humans are feeling threatened, they will be preoccupied with attaining the feeling of safety and thus are unable to advance to the next level.

Level 3: Social belonging and love

The feeling of belonging or acceptance is a need that may extend from a person's immediate family to outside social groups. The importance of this need may vary tremendously by person as part of their personality characteristics.

Level 4: Esteem

Esteem can also be viewed as respect, and it can manifest itself in two forms. The first is self-respect and the amount of self-worth a person feels. The second considers other people and the amount of respect and value they attribute to a person.

Level 5: Self-actualization

This is when a person achieves their maximum potential, or at least what they perceive to be their maximum potential. This is also known as reaching total self-fulfillment.

Two examples of how marketing can capitalize on human needs:

A car commercial that touts five-star safety ratings and claims its brand is the safest on the road. This commercial simply focuses on the level 2 safety need of Maslow's hierarchy. It addresses the customer's feeling of threat that is caused by the risk associated with driving.

A luxury car brand that focuses on building a reputation of prestige. This may fulfill multiple levels of the needs pyramid. The driver may feel a better sense of social belonging (level 3), a higher sense of self-esteem (level 4), and may even be so much as to make the person feel that they've made it in life because they have their dream car (level 5).

2.2 Aristotle's seven causes of human action

The core goal of marketers is to create a compelling reason for a customer to take an action such as to make a purchase. Aristotle identified seven causes of human action, which provide us with an excellent framework to understand customer motivations and how we may drive customer action.

Chance

By definition, chance can't be predicted or modeled, so you may wonder, how do I as a marketer capitalize on this cause of human action? While you may not be able to predict exact action, you can create favorable circumstances that increase your likelihood for success. By researching and understanding your customer, you may discern unique ways to reach your customer so that when chance occurs, you're prepared.

Nature

People are inclined to make decisions and act based on their gut instincts. This means customers may take certain actions because they are drawn in by something, something as simple as a certain design or color because it instinctually feels better. Testing and optimizing concepts, messages, and creative assets are ways in which you can increase your marketing effectiveness.

Compulsion

People are irrational and often impulsive. Marketing may capitalize on compulsion in several ways from product placement near a checkout line, using display ads to stay top of mind, and creating urgency by using tactics such as flash sales.

Habit

Humans are creatures of habit. People feel comfort and are attracted to things that are familiar. This desire for familiarity leads to the importance of consistency in marketing. Top brands have been able to command fierce loyalty that even transcends generations. For example, Apple with its consistent simplistic designs and experiences, or Coca-Cola® with its unchanged red color.

As a marketer of a challenger brand, you must discover key milestones when habits may be malleable. At those milestones there is an opportunity to challenge loyalty and become the new preferred product or brand.

For instance, a customer has been loyal to the same shampoo for years. If that customer is on a shopping trip and her preferred brand is out of stock, now is an opportunity for a challenger to enter and win.

Reason

While people are often irrational, there are purchases in which customers make decisions based on reason. In high-involvement purchases, where extensive research and consideration are done, reason has more prominence. A high-consideration purchase may be the purchase of a new car. The customer takes her time, conducts research, completes multiple test drives, and shops around for the best price. To effectively target rational customers, the brand and product must be differentiated with a strong value proposition, which we will discuss in greater detail later in the text.

Passion

Passion can trump all rational thought and cause people to act purely based on emotion. In marketing, the ability to create a passionate bond between your brand and the customer can reap incredible loyalty and advocacy. To achieve this, marketers must understand the target customer's interests and psychographics.

Many brands attempt to capitalize on customer passion through methods such as cause marketing. A simple example is the hundreds of brands who use pink ribbons in their advertising and on packaging during Breast Cancer Awareness month.

An example of a brand with truly passionate consumers is Southwest Airlines. Customers feel that they are taken advantage of by other airlines that subject them to bag fees and change fees. Prior to the Covid-19 pandemic, Southwest® differentiated itself by foregoing these fees and gained a passionate response from customers. They've won fierce loyalty and have created a brand with great advocacy as evidenced by its exceptionally high net promoter score.

Desire

Desire is another emotional cause of action. Desire can manifest itself as an appeal to a customer's aspirations. Brands can appeal to customers by providing a heightened social status, or perhaps by providing a heightened sense of lust or romance. Alternatively, a brand may help the customer achieve the desired reputation as someone who is environmentally friendly.

2.3 The rational vs. real customer

Marketing research is completed with the aspiration to gain a thorough understanding of the customer. That understanding is utilized for many purposes, such as product and message development. The research may provide amazing insights, which can lead to a terrific product concept, and a smooth product launch, but then the launch results underperform. This example of failure could be due to the difference between the rational and the real customer.

Research can often take the real-world element out of the customer's thought process, causing them to state more rational thoughts than they would encounter in real-life situations. The idea of the rational versus the real customer helps us to understand the difference between what we expect as an action versus the actual action taken by a customer. The rational customer is a hypothetical customer who may effectively serve as a decoy to marketers. The real customer should be your focus as it better represents how customers act in real-world situations.

Rational customer	Real customer
• Perfectly defines the problem and need	• Both emotional and rational thoughts impact decisions
• Is aware of all possible solutions	• Is influenced by biases
• Researches and is aware of all relevant information	• Likely lacks motivation
• Accurately evaluates all of the information according to their goals	• Will take shortcuts
• Accurately assesses each possible solution based on the information	• Does not have complete information
• Accurately calculates the value of each solution and selects the highest value option	

CHAPTER 3: MARKET & CUSTOMER SEGMENTATION

The development of market and customer segments is a critical responsibility of marketing professionals. Segmentation is where a set of customers is placed into an identifiable group based on various characteristics. These groups help you to hone in on and study their unique characteristics so that you may then appeal to their needs in a more precise and authentic way. This precision will theoretically result in greater sales and loyalty for that target customer segment.

3.1 The need for segmentation

As stated, segmentation helps you, the marketer, to gain a greater understanding of the customer. This will help you find unique and innovative solutions to their needs, it will help you calculate the size of the sales opportunity, and it will help you to find ways to build a connection with the customer. One of the key performance indicators (KPIs) a brand should maximize with their target customer segment is the percentage of customers who agree with the statement, "Brand 'X' is a brand for me." The ability to authentically communicate and appeal to the customer is critical to raising this KPI.

Three reasons for segmentation:

- Customers differ in their needs and wants

- A brand cannot expect to appeal to all customers

- A successful value proposition and benefit statement need to be tightly focused to deliver appeal and relevance

3.2 Segmentation criteria

The concept of customer segmentation is fairly simple; however, effectively building segments can be a daunting task. Companies spend tens if not hundreds of thousands of dollars conducting research that is intended to develop the perfect set of customer segments. With this knowledge, they hope to gain critical insight into what each segment desires and how they can connect to them.

Characteristics of good segments

Good customer segments meet a set of criteria that ensure they can provide value to the business. Segments that are poorly defined or lack certain characteristics may, in fact, not be real segments or may be segments of limited to no value. In order to ensure usefulness, customer segments should be able to meet these criteria:

- **The segments are distinct** - The customers within the group should be similar, and there should be little overlap with other groups.

- **The segments are operational** - The segment should be identifiable and accessible in marketing channels.

- **The segments are engaging** - Marketing communication to the segment should be able to connect with the customers in an impactful and engaging manner.

- **The segments are substantial** - The segment is large enough to be compelling from a revenue and / or profit perspective.

Customer variables of interest

When segments are drawn, a large number of variables may be used to differentiate the groups. The following examples of variables show how customers may be clustered together, meeting the four characteristics stated previously.

- **Descriptors ("who")** - Demographic information such as age, income, education, family status, and profession.

- **Bases ("why")** - Psychographic and anthropological information such as needs, preferences, and lifestyle.

- **Behaviors ("what")** - Actions such as product experience, sources of information, loyalty, or offer seeking.

- **External ("where")** - Factors driven by location such as country, community, terrain, or weather.

- **Time ("when")** - Life stages and timeliness such as graduating from college, having a baby, or launching a business.

The necessity of research

In nearly all cases, marketing research is necessary to properly define segments. These research studies are best left to experienced researchers who have the ability to utilize statistical tools to complete cluster and other forms of analysis. Later, we will discuss both the research as well as frameworks commonly used to better understand segments.

Segment straddling

Straddling is a term used to describe when a brand or product is targeted at more than one customer segment. It is commonly cited as a marketing best practice to focus solely on one customer segment. There is a marketing cliché: "You can't be everything to everyone."

While this may be true in many cases, the ability to effectively straddle multiple segments can open the door to new growth opportunities. When straddling, a key to success is to avoid alienating or confusing one segment as you attempt to appeal to another.

Facebook is a great example of the pitfall of trying to become everything to everyone. Facebook began as a website specifically targeted to college students, at one time even requiring a .edu email address to join. As Facebook desired to grow, it opened the door to all users. As time went on, younger users have become alienated by Facebook and have begun seeking other forms of social media such as Instagram and Snapchat. In 2018, it was expected that Facebook would lose two million users under the age of 24 (Berr, 2018).

An example of effective straddling is in the case of the Ford® F-150 truck. This truck is commonly advertised to two distinct segments. The first, is the weekend user who has the truck as a toy to haul boats and go on adventures. The second, is the construction worker who needs a workhorse truck that lives up to the challenge of the jobsites. Effectively reaching these two segments has helped solidify the status of the F-150 as the reason the Ford F-series trucks are the bestselling trucks for 43 years (Johnson, 2020).

CHAPTER 4: SUPPLY AND DEMAND

A basic principle of economics is the balance between supply and demand. To illustrate that relationship, supply and demand curves are commonly utilized. This chapter will help explain the underlying basis for price and volume sales changes as they are impacted by supply side or demand side drivers. Price elasticity is also rooted in the supply and demand curves, and we will go in-depth on the topic of price elasticity later in the text.

4.1 The supply and demand curves

Figure 4.1.1 Supply and demand curves

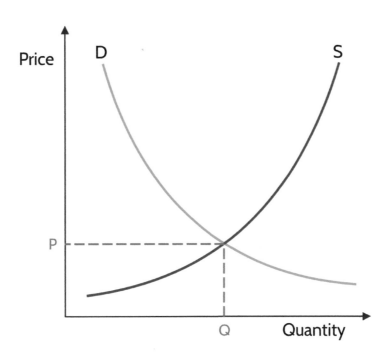

The standard graphical representation of a supply and demand curve has price along the Y (vertical) axis and quantity along the X (horizontal) axis. There are two types of curves: a downward-sloping demand curve and an upward-sloping supply curve. In figure 4.1.1 there is a demand curve "D" and a supply curve "S."

Where the demand curve and supply curve intersect is called economic equilibrium because it is where the market forces are balanced so demand and supply match. At that equilibrium point, a certain price "P" will coincide with a certain quantity of sales "Q."

4.2 Shifts in supply and demand

For various reasons, the demand or supply for a certain product may shift. This shift will cause the equilibrium point to move. For instance, in figure 4.2.1 demand was represented by curve "D1". Let's say that all of a sudden, the product represented by "D1" increased in demand due to a discovery that the product lowered the chance of heart disease. The demand curve will then shift to the right, to the position "D2." The equilibrium point changes and is now located as a higher quantity and price. More people are buying and demanding the product, and they are also willing to pay a higher price

Figure 4.2.1 Demand curve shift

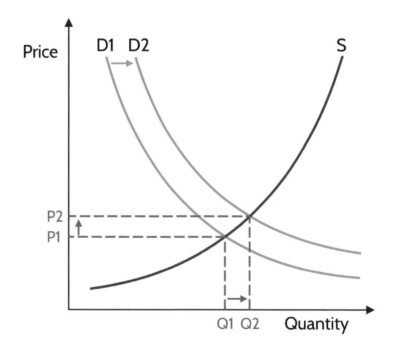

If an event occurred shifting the supply of a product or service, then the supply curve would shift to the left or right as the demand curve remains static.

4.3 Drivers of supply and demand shifts

Now that we've seen how the shift in a demand or supply curve can affect the equilibrium price and quantity, let's discuss what the drivers of shift are. The drivers of demand shifts are placed into five classifications; supply drivers fall into four classifications.

Demand drivers	Supply drivers
• Consumer income	• Production costs
• Price of substitutes	• The number of suppliers
• Tastes and preferences	• Producers' expectations of future prices
• Consumers' expectations of future prices	• Resource and labor availability
• The number of competing consumers	

Bear in mind that a shift is the movement right or left of a demand or supply curve; it is not the change in the shape of the curves. The shape of the demand curve and the supply curve indicates the level of elasticity, the elasticity of demand and the elasticity of supply.

4.4 Price elasticity

In the comparison figure 4.4.1, inelastic demand versus elastic demand, the shape of supply curves "S1" and "S2" are the same. The difference between the two charts is the angle of the demand curve "D." These different demand curves reveal the effect that elasticity has when there is a shift in the supply curve. In both charts the supply curve has shifted lower from "S1" to "S2," thus causing price to increase and quantity to decrease.

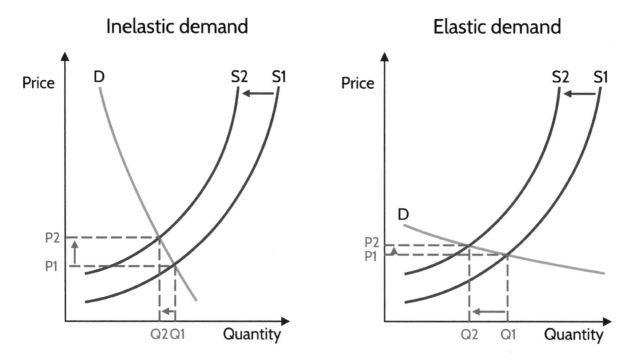

Figure 4.4.1 Inelastic versus elastic demand

For inelastic demand, the quantity demanded decreased slightly, while the price increased dramatically. This means that the amount of demand for this product is resilient to change. Even despite a substantial increase in price, the quantity demanded is minimally impacted, and is considered inelastic.

For elastic demand, the shift in supply caused a small increase in price. This small increase in price reduced the quantity of products sold tremendously. Therefore, the amount of product demanded reacted significantly to a small price change and is highly elastic.

Price elasticity has a profound effect on the pricing and offer strategies that marketers employ. The use of branding to create differentiation, value, and loyalty will potentially boost demand, but also importantly, reduce price elasticity.

———————

CHAPTER 5: BRANDING

A core function of the marketing profession is to create and cultivate brands. Brands can be extremely powerful, with the ability to drive differentiation and consumer preference between two products that are otherwise exactly the same. In this chapter we will define what exactly a brand is and discuss the benefits a strong brand provides.

5.1 The definition of brand

In marketing, a brand is an identifying mark that carries a meaning. Examples of identifying marks are words, logo designs, and unique product designs. Brands should elicit emotions and carry expectations, and the ability of a brand to deliver these emotions can be valued at billions of dollars in what's known as brand value.

There is a widely used quote by Jeff Bezos, the former CEO of Amazon.com, where he insightfully explains the influence a brand has. "Your brand is what other people say about you when you're not in the room."

Many people are familiar with this quote and commonly repeat it, but without thinking of the significance. Understanding this in the most direct sense, think about the many times you've been at a restaurant and negatively discussed the food or service with your dining companions. The server or manager walks up and asks, "How is your meal?" Rather than give an honest response, you just nod and say, "Good."

Think...is there a better way to get real feedback? The power of this quote extends to another marketing trend that has emerged over the last many years, which is the fact that the customer's voice has never been louder. The internet has created countless ways for customers to voice their opinions and have them heard. This dissemination of information about companies, brands, and products via the internet has amplified customer voices. These voices are commonly trusted more than the voices of the companies themselves, thus shrinking the control companies and brands used to enjoy.

To ensure your brand's success you'll need to advocate for your consumers and deliver an experience that exceeds their expectations. Your advocacy may be rewarded with satisfied vocal consumers, who are fiercely loyal and, in return, advocate for your brand. Marketing research will help you understand how to deliver an exceptional experience.

5.2 Sub-brands

A sub-brand is a brand that fits under a higher-level, primary brand. The primary brand will command the overall vision, mission, and position. The sub-brand should nest below, following and supporting the guidance set forth by the primary brand. Sub-brands can be a powerful way to differentiate and help a brand focus on specific segments or benefits.

For example, under the Degree® deodorant brand there are multiple sub-brands. Underneath the primary Degree brand, the sub-brand Odor Protect is for consumers who want lasting odor protection, but do not want aluminum in their product. The Clinical Protection sub-brand is built using a unique formula designed to stop sweat better than the other sub-brands. These two sub-brands focus on differentiated benefits to meet the needs of consumers while supporting the primary Degree brand promise of confidence and protection that won't let you down.

You should be aware of the pitfalls that misuse or overuse of sub-brands may cause. Sub-brands that are not carefully constructed can easily diminish the consistency, meaning, and awareness of the primary brand. They may even attract new customer segments to the brand which may alienate the brand's primary customer segment. These issues may not only cause the sub-brand to fail, but also irreparably damage the primary brand. You will need to ensure that the sub-brand supports and does not conflict with the primary brand's vision, mission, and position.

5.3 The importance of brand loyalty

Building brand loyalty should be one of your top priorities as it can result in several competitive advantages. The ability of a brand to drive these competitive advantages can carry a significant tangible value. According to Forbes, in 2019 the world's most valuable brand was Apple, which was valued at $205.5 billion (Badenhausen, 2019). Here are some of the advantages created by a strong brand.

Stronger consideration versus the competition

A brand with fierce loyalty is less vulnerable to competitive pressures. Loyalty increases brand purchase intent and creates a mental barrier that is difficult for competitors to break through. Habits are formed so purchases occur with less research and consideration.

Higher margins

A strong brand can enjoy higher margins due to a couple of different drivers.

- **Higher prices** - A strong brand that has loyalty may be able to command higher prices because its customer base perceives the brand as the one for them regardless of the price.

- **Higher market share** - A strong brand may own a large share of the market. The higher the market share, the higher number of products being produced. This high level of production volume can increase scale and result in a lower cost per unit produced.

Third-party support

Partners and third parties such as retailers, advertisers, and complementary brands recognize brand strength. Their recognition of your brand's strength will drive their desire to associate with your brand. It can offer benefits such as partnership opportunities, negotiation leverage, and preferential treatment.

Communication efficiency

Brand strength can help your brand spend less on advertising or help you make your advertising dollars stretch further.

- **Free promotion** - A strong loyal brand can help reduce the need for a high level of advertising investment. Advocacy, referral, and word of mouth can be highly efficient free forms of promotion.

- **Brand scale** - A brand carries value and expectation. If that value and expectation is able to extend across product categories, there is an opportunity to develop a master brand.

An example of a master brand is Dove personal care products. According to its website, Dove products are "designed to make you feel beautiful" (Unilever, 2020). This statement transcends across product categories that Dove sells products in, such as body wash, deodorant, and hair care. These products deliver the same beauty benefit, which supports the master brand. Advertising for a single product category will have a halo effect on the other product categories under the master brand.

Category expansion, line extension, and licensing

The loyalty to a brand can open a number of opportunities, such as the expansion of product lines or licensing rights.

- **Category expansion** - The previous Dove example illustrates how a strong brand saw the opportunity to expand its product offerings into additional categories. After gaining traction in cleansing products, Dove extended its line to deodorant, skin care, and even hair care products. The proliferation of product categories increases the scale of the brand.

- **Line extension** - For Dove, its brand strength and loyalty within a single category may offer the opportunity to expand its product line. This could allow them to create additional product variants that appeal to shoppers who had not previously purchased Dove products.

- **Licensing** - Licensing or selling the rights to use your brand's mark is a way to increase profit and value. A great example of licensing is found with baby strollers. A review of strollers available for sale may lead you to encounter Ferrari and Jeep® strollers. These strollers are obviously not manufactured by the car brands. The car brands allow the stroller manufacturer to use their brand marks in exchange for compensation. The strength of the Ferrari and Jeep brands motivated the stroller manufacturer to use the car brand names as a way to boost its product appeal.

CHAPTER 6: BRAND STRATEGY

The ability to build and maintain a strong brand can deliver a multitude of business benefits as we had reviewed in chapter 5. In this chapter, we will discuss proven methods available to help define your brand and shape its strategy. As we progress through the chapter, you may notice that there is overlap between methods. This overlap is intentional. These methods are the output of years of various research and strategic brand work. Take time to understand the different methods and think about which resonates best with you. Throughout your career in marketing, you will find that organizations differ in their choice of methods. Over time, familiarity with these will serve you well.

6.1 Brand vision and mission

The brand vision is what you want your brand to stand for in the long term; it is what you want the brand to represent. IKEA is a brand that provides a great example of a brand vision: "to create a better everyday life for the many people" (IKEA, 2020). The brand vision should serve as guiding principles for product development as well as the message that you communicate to the public. As a long-term vision, these statements should infrequently change and should act as a set of goal posts that help you stay focused and consistent from the inception of the brand out to the horizon.

Comparing a brand vision to a brand mission, the brand vision may be altruistic in nature, whereas the brand mission defines why and how you work to produce products or render services. Again, IKEA offers a great example: "to offer a wide range of well-designed, functional home furnishing products at prices so low that as many people as possible will be able to afford them" (IKEA, 2020).

A simple way of thinking about a brand vision versus a brand mission is, the vision is where the brand aims to be in the future. The mission is focused on the present and describes how to achieve the vision.

When crafting a brand vision statement, answering these questions can help guide the process:

- Where do we want to go?
- When do we want to get there?

- How do we want to get there?

When crafting a brand mission statement, answering these questions can help guide the process:

- What do we do?

- Who are we doing it for?

- Why do we do it? In other words, what's the benefit of our work?

6.2 Brand promise

Some marketers may prefer to create a brand promise that aligns with the vision and mission, or possibly in lieu of those statements. A brand promise is a statement developed to set expectations of what the product or service will provide. The statement should explain what the brand does, and for whom it does it. The statement should include a key benefit(s), which may be functional and tangible or emotional and intangible. The promise must be realistic and credible. It's a promise that must be kept in order to build brand trust. A brand promise is not always a public-facing statement, but if powerful and compelling may be used as part of marketing communication. An example of a good brand promise is that of the Nike brand: "To bring inspiration and innovation to every athlete in the world" (Power Reviews, 2019).

6.3 Brand manifesto

A brand manifesto is a different spin on a brand vision, mission, or promise. A brand manifesto differs by its focus on emotional appeal. Manifestos describe what the brand stands for, similar to a vision statement, and it can describe how the brand will progress toward that vision, much like a mission statement. The manifesto is, however, rooted in emotion and action. It is meant to inspire people both internal and external to the company, driving a deep-rooted connection. Manifestos do not have a standard format, but they should be concise and written in an inspirational tone.

6.4 Brand positioning

Brand positioning is defined as an "act of designing the company's offering and image to occupy a distinct place in the mind of the target market" (Kotler, 2006). It is the brand's place in the market relative to substitutes and its perception by consumers. The position of a brand is not a statement, but rather a placement within the market. For example, a brand may be positioned in the market as a luxury, trendy brand for young professional American men.

Often marketers confuse taglines with a brand position. Taglines such as the Coca-Cola brand's tagline "open happiness" may espouse the brand's essence, but is not a declaration of the brand's position. A brand position should be well thought out from the onset, as the ability to shift a product position once it is established will be extremely expensive and difficult, if not impossible.

To demonstrate the strength of a brand position, take for instance BLACK+DECKER power tools. At one time, BLACK+DECKER power tools were commonly known as high-quality, professional-grade tools. Over time the brand earned the reputation as a value brand that is for homeowners who infrequently use power tools. In the mid-2000s, BLACK+DECKER attempted to build a higher quality sub-brand named FireStorm® that was targeted to light-duty professional work. Due to the strength of the BLACK+DECKER brand's position as a homeowner's brand, its association with the FireStorm brand hindered the new sub-brand's acceptance by professionals. Just a few years after its initial launch, the Firestorm sub-brand was discontinued.

An example of a brand that has been uniquely and successfully positioned is Southwest Airlines. Its positioning is one of delighting customers and being their advocate through friendly service and by limiting fees. In 2008, American Airlines was the first airline to announce charging fees for checked luggage (Seaney, 2017). Soon after nearly all other airlines followed suit with the exception of Southwest. Prior to the Covid-19 pandemic, you would be hard-pressed to find an airline that didn't charge fees to change flight reservations, but Southwest chose not to. Southwest firmly maintained its brand position as a customer advocate. By solidifying its position and by differentiating itself, Southwest has attained a passionate and loyal customer base.

Brand architecture

As a company grows, it may present the opportunity to launch sub-brands or expand into additional brands. To best manage this scenario, you should develop a brand architecture. A brand architecture provides a framework to appropriately segment and position brands relative to each other. It should help with delivering brand consistency and leveraging brand loyalty where desired. There are four types of brand architectures listed below. Please note that in each example the brands listed are a sample of each company's brands, not a complete list.

Branded house

The branded house is an architecture where the company brand is primary and is connected to various sub-brands. In figure 6.4.1, UPS is the company brand and as a branded house, The UPS Store, UPS Capital, etc. are each branded with the company brand name. This approach leverages the company's brand name to capitalize on its awareness, credibility, and loyalty.

Figure 6.4.1 Branded house

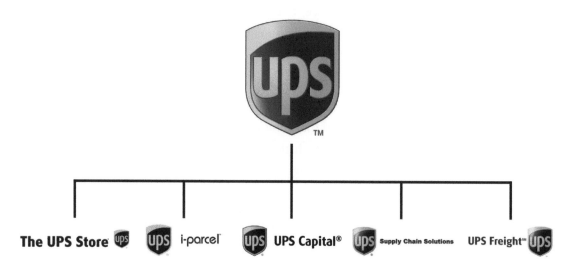

House of brands

A house of brands is an architecture where the company brand is separate from the brands that it owns. The brands are communicated separately from the company brand name, as shown by the Unilever brands in figure 6.4.2. This increases the individuality of each brand, allowing the company to target different customer segments and offer different brand visions.

Figure 6.4.2 House of brands

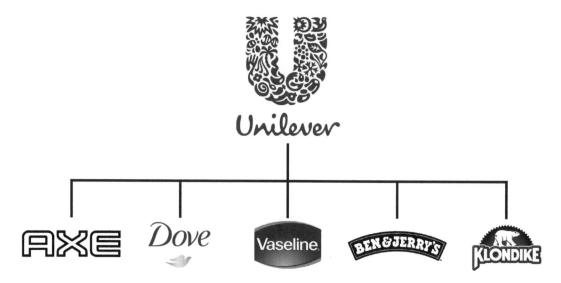

Endorsed brands

An endorsed brands architecture is a structure in which the company brand name is used in conjunction with the other company brands as a way to build trust and credibility. In the example of Best Western® (figure 6.4.3), you will see that Best Western owns several brands and links itself to those brands by adding "by Best Western" to their logos.

Figure 6.4.3 Endorsed brands

Hybrid

A hybrid brand architecture is just as described; it is any combination of two or more of the aforementioned architecture types. Hybrid architectures are common. Hilton provides a great example of a hybrid architecture with examples of a branded house and endorsed brands as shown in figure 6.4.4.

Figure 6.4.4 Hybrid

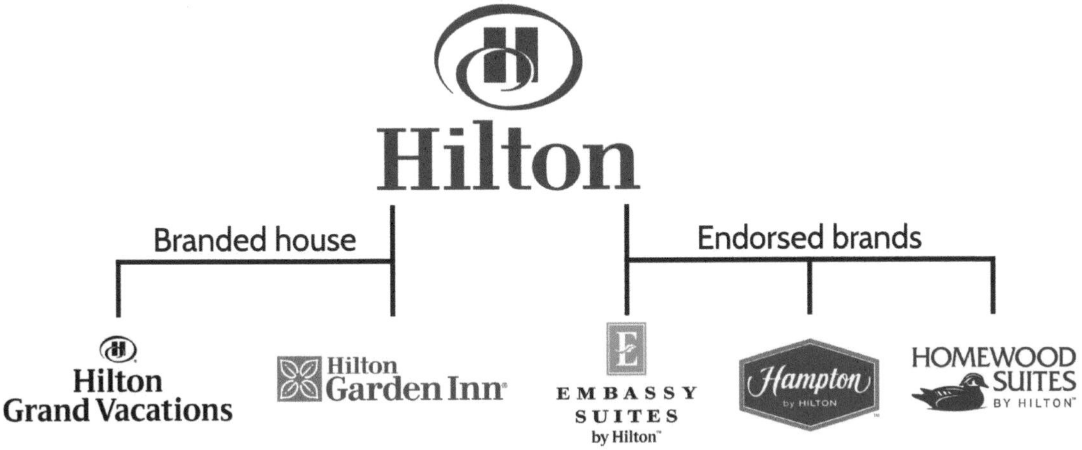

6.5 Brand character and personality

Brand character is the personification of a brand by bringing it to life through a set of human characteristics. The goal of creating a brand character is to build brand uniqueness so that the target customers better identify and engage with the brand. Creating this character comes through several means:

- **Vision or values** - What you want your brand to stand for in the long term. It is what you want the brand to represent.

- **Mission** - Why and how you work to produce products or render services.

- **Stories** - The experiences people have encountered and shared about the brand.

- **Position or image** - The brand's place in the market relative to substitutes and its perception by consumers.

Brand personality can be seen in a good example from Old Spice. The personification was particularly strong during the 2010 Isaiah Mustafa campaign where you could see him, the spokesperson, riding a horse backwards. In 2020, Isaiah Mustafa continues to be utilized as a spokesperson for the brand.

The personality exhibited by Mustafa and Old Spice is that of a suave jokester or class clown. This created a unique personality that customers were drawn to and continue to associate with. When the campaign launched, it was so engaging that it grew body wash sales by over 107% (Maynard, 2010). Over the subsequent years, Old Spice continued to embrace this new-found characterization and saw substantial market share growth in all personal care products.

Figure 6.5.1 Old Spice ad

Source: (Business Wire, 2021)

6.6 Brand frameworks

In this section we will review a few common frameworks used by marketers to assess a brand. There are two brand pyramids: the first is the brand pyramid, and the second is the brand resonance pyramid. There are similarities between the two, but in particular the brand resonance pyramid provides a framework for deeper brand examination.

The third framework we will review is the perceptual map. This framework offers a simple way to visualize where brand positions are relative to each other, as well as reveal potential "white space" opportunities.

The brand pyramid

A comparison between the two pyramids will reveal that the brand pyramid is a more basic representation of the brand and its attributes. At the foundation are the products or services offered by the brand, and as you move up the pyramid, the emotional connection to the consumer is explained.

As a marketer, a primary goal of yours is to deliver on the intended brand essence. Delivery of this can generate loyalty and lasting emotional connections with customers, which may span generations. Here is a look at the brand pyramid and an explanation of its various levels.

Figure 6.6.1 Brand pyramid

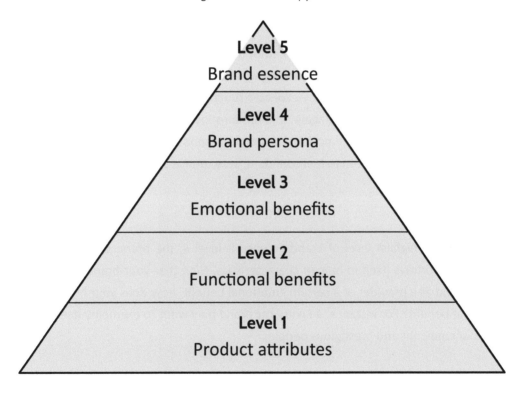

Level 1

The foundation is set in the actual product or service. Some examples of these product attributes include:

> Price
> Specifications
> The value proposition
> Manufacturing quality or precision

> Source, such as "locally-made" or "German-engineered"

When thinking of the products and how they relate to a brand, determine what are the consistent aspects that tie all of the products and services together so that they fit within the brand.

Level 2

The next level higher is the assessment of the functional benefits that the products deliver. In other words, what does the product or service do that directly and tangibly solves the need of the customer? Here are some examples:

> Reduced cost

> Increased efficiency or time savings

> Increased comfort

> Higher durability

> Easier to use

Level 3

The third level of the brand pyramid is emotional benefit. A product is built in a certain way (level 1) to deliver a benefit (level 2) with the goal of eliciting a positive emotional response (level 3). You want your product to provide the expected functional benefit in such a way that a customer develops trust, intends to purchase again, and remains loyal. When shaping a brand and its product, determine what the desired emotional customer response is. As customers or consumers use your products, do you want them to feel confident, sexy, smart, accomplished, efficient, or perhaps something else?

Level 4

Just below the highest level of brand essence is level 4, the brand persona. This persona is how the brand portrays itself in human characteristics. Now that your brand is connected to the customer's mind as a provider of a certain emotional benefit, how does your brand exemplify and reinforce that benefit? For instance, a luxury car brand may want to exemplify itself with the characteristics of confident and prestigious people.

Level 5

The brand essence is also commonly referred to as the brand idea. It is similar to a brand vision and mission. It is the distilled notion of what the brand represents to customers. It should also clearly indicate your brand's positioning. Each of the lower levels should complement each other to support the brand essence.

Brand resonance pyramid

The brand resonance pyramid (Keller, 2012) offers a methodology to help you understand the various considerations to build a strong brand. As you review the pyramid, you will notice that it evaluates the rational and the emotional aspects of the brand. This construct helps marketers to separate the tangible and functional requirements of a product from the feeling and perception that is created through brand and experience. Here is the brand resonance pyramid and an explanation of its various elements.

Figure 6.6.2 Brand resonance pyramid

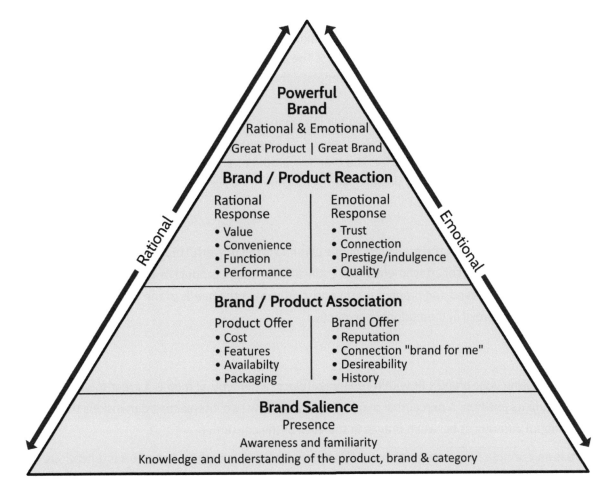

Brand salience

The first level and foundation of the pyramid is brand salience. Salience refers to the presence or the awareness of the brand. Along with awareness, salience also includes any preconceptions regarding the product or brand.

Brand / product association

The second level is the associations with the product or brand. These associations can have a profound effect on customer shopping behavior and in particular for first-time customers.

> **Rational:** The tangible information available about the product or brand such as the cost, performance metrics, appearance, and qualifications.

> **Emotional:** The intangible information available about the product or brand such as the reputation, supporters, endorsers, and meaning.

Brand / product reaction

The third level is the customer reaction to the product or brand. In this level, the information regarding what is offered in the association level is further internalized by customers, allowing them to develop a response. These responses may affect first-time customers or it may influence the likelihood of a repeat purchase based on their prior experience.

> **Rational:** Based on the tangible information available, customers determine how well the product or brand meets their needs. The customers will make an assessment on criteria such as the product's ability to complete the task, its level of performance, its value, and its ease of use.

> **Emotional:** Based on the intangible information available, customers determine how well the product or brand meets their needs. The customers assess their emotional needs, and compare it to what they feel the brand or product signifies. Some examples of these emotional needs are trust, prestige, and belonging.

Powerful brand

The highest level in the brand resonance pyramid is the powerful brand. At this level customers determine their level of attachment and identification with the product or brand. To create a strong attachment, the brand and product must consistently meet the needs of the customers at all levels from both a rational and emotional perspective.

Perceptual map

When assessing your brand's fit within the marketplace, a perceptual map is a great tool that allows you to simply diagram its position. A perceptual map will typically show two intersecting dimensions that are able to depict meaningful differences between brands in the eyes of the consumer.

Here is an example of a perceptual map of common automobile brands. Note, this is a fictitious example and not based on data.

Figure 6.6.3 Perceptual map

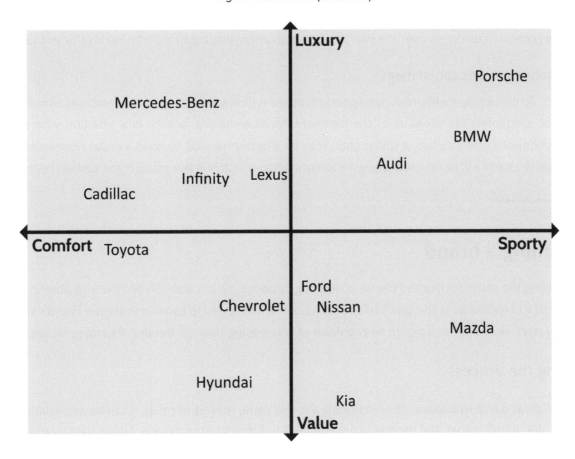

A potential downside of perceptual maps is that dimensions may be an oversimplification of what matters to consumers. To limit that downside, there may be perceptual maps built using a third axis that utilizes three-dimensional visualization tools, but maps such as these are generally rare.

As you work on building a perceptual map, do so utilizing data rather than gut feeling. Often, marketers who are familiar with their industry and consumers build maps based on existing knowledge. This can be a situation where bias overtakes reality, thus causing poor understanding of the brand's position relative to others.

The value of perceptual maps

Perceptual maps are terrific tools to visualize your brand's placement in the market. An output of this visualization is the ability to identify "white space" or open areas in the market where a need is potentially unmet. In figure 6.6.3, there is white space in the lower left where there is comfort and value. Before concluding this is a great place to move a brand or build a new brand, you must investigate the desirability of owning a brand in that space. It may be an area where there is little market opportunity or no profit to be made.

An additional layer of information that may be added to a perceptual map is the location of customer segments. In the bottom left area of the perceptual map (figure 6.6.3) you may find there is no customer segment, and that is why no brands exist in that space.

Additionally, perceptual maps may bring a desire to move one's brand from one area to another. Before making this movement a goal of yours, you must be realistic in the ability of the brand to shift perception. Most often brands that attempt to shift their position fail. It is a monumental task, particularly for established brands. The transition may cost millions of dollars in advertising and can confuse customers over the course of the transition, leading to a decline in loyalty and sales.

Limitations to perceptual maps

As previously mentioned, perceptual maps are typically limited to two dimensions, which may not adequately represent all of the pertinent decision-making factors. In a situation where two dimensions won't suffice, a spider chart may be a better method to build a visual representation. Spider charts will be covered when we discuss differentiation in the product marketing chapter.

6.7 Naming a brand

Choosing the name for a brand can be an exciting opportunity, but also can be ripe with potential pitfalls. The choice of a brand name is an opportunity to be creative, find a way to communicate the brand's vision, and offer a new start. Here are a few tips to be cognizant of when going through the brand naming process:

Managing the process

- **Clear decision makers** - While creating a brand name may be exciting, it can be excruciatingly painful. Brand names and naming in general tend to bring strong opinions. Utilize data where possible, but ensure that at the onset of the project the proper decision-making process is known.

- **Set and maintain boundaries** - At the start of a naming project a set of requirements should be created. Examples may be items such as the name must be literal and descriptive or the name must be two syllables or less. Names are brainstormed and suggested. Biases and emotions often enter naming discussions, so to avoid wasted time, fearlessly maintain the project's boundaries.

- **Conduct and trust research** - As previously stated, opinions and biases will exist. Conduct research, learn what the customers want and trust that research to guide the correct naming decision.

Name ideation

- **International implications** - Many brands expand to find themselves viewed in international regions and other languages. As you vet potential brand names, take into consideration the meaning of the name around the world.

- **Longevity** - Having a trendy brand may be great and it may facilitate immediate customer adoption, but what happens when the trend wears out? Is your brand name one that can live on, or is it one that will go the way of the trend?

- **Expandability** - Maybe the most important consideration in this list is expandability. A mistake that is made over and over again is to name a brand after a specific flagship product. Plan ahead. Plan for growth. Ask yourself, does this brand name allow for expansion into related or new product categories?

For example, IHOP®, the International House of Pancakes, had a perception issue and will continue to have a perception issue due to its brand name. The company and brand are about pancakes, a single product. In 2018, recognizing people don't realize they sell burgers, IHOP cleverly created a social media campaign asking people to guess what its new company name IHOB stood for. The PR stunt worked well creating buzz, but long term, the brand is still stuck on pancakes.

6.8 Brand logo versus brand identity

A brand logo is a mark that is intended to quickly allow customers to identify the brand. It should consistently represent a brand and should trigger an emotional response with target customer segments. While the logo is a mark that triggers emotion and expectation, the brand identity extends beyond the logo. The brand identity creates familiarity through the consistent use of characteristics such as colors, typography, the logo, and tonality.

For example, The Home Depot logo is clear and impactful, but it's only a small part of what makes the brand identifiable. If you were dropped into a warehouse home improvement store and saw orange shelving, orange shopping carts, and associates with orange aprons you'd know exactly which store you were in—The Home Depot. The consistency of the brand identity drives familiarity and brings with it, expectations.

Figure 6.8.1 The Home Depot logo

Figure 6.8.2 The Home Depot store

Source: (The Home Depot, 2021)

6.9 Co-branding

Co-branding is a common marketing practice where two brands are linked in order to strengthen the value proposition of a brand or product. The two brands may be in the same product category or they may be significantly different products with different benefits that when combined, aim to offer a compelling solution. The co-branding may occur between brands within the same company or may be an agreement between separate companies. Co-branding may extend into all facets of marketing including products and promotion.

Procter & Gamble is well-versed in leveraging its powerful brands to cross different categories to co-brand. For example, the Tide brand is known in the laundry care category for its ability to fight stains. Another P&G brand, Febreze is in the air freshener category and is known for freshness. P&G saw an opportunity to reach a customer segment of laundry detergent consumers who desire a detergent that is effective against stains but also delivers freshness. P&G created a new line of detergent, Tide Plus Febreze, that leverages the known benefits of Tide, plus the freshness benefit of Febreze.

Figure 6.9.1 Tide Plus Febreze

Source: (Target, 2021)

Licensing

Licensing is a form of branding in which an organization pays another organization for the ability to use its owned brand or mark. Licensing can be paid for in a number of ways, but it is commonly done via a percentage royalty paid on each sale made or may be paid as a lump sum that grants use for a specific period of time or number of units produced.

Brands commonly use this tactic to gain favor with a certain customer segment. This is done by partnering with charitable organizations, that appeal to the customers. For example, the Brawny® paper towel brand had co-branded its packaging with the Wounded Warrior Project® to show its support for military veterans.

Figure 6.9.2 Brawny with Wounded Warrior Project

Source: (Butschli, 2021)

Retail store partners can also offer co-branding opportunities. Some retailers may run promotional campaigns where participating products are required to place supporting logos, messages, or colors on their packaging. Retailers use this co-branding to create better awareness and consistency for their campaigns. The manufacturer agrees to make these changes in an effort to gain access to ad space and additional merchandising space.

CHAPTER 7: BRAND PRESERVATION

We have discussed brands, their value, the expectations they create, and the need for consistency. In this chapter, we will discuss how you can ensure that your brand remains consistent and protected from misuse. We will also discuss the possible need to update a brand through what is known as a rebrand.

7.1 Protecting your brand

As a marketing professional, you will take on the responsibility to uphold your brand and ensure that it remains powerful. In chapter 6 we discussed various branding frameworks, and in the frameworks, it is evident that factors, both internal and external, need to coalesce to support brand strength.

As you consider factors that may impact your brand and what needs to be controlled, an analysis of the questions who, what, where, when, and how offer a good starting point. Here are examples of how those questions may be applied.

- **Who?** - Lululemon is a brand that consistently portrays a healthy and active lifestyle. The brand is consistent about who they allow to represent its brand. From advertisements, models, leaders of branded yoga events, to store associates—all embody the Lululemon brand and its associated lifestyle.

- **What?** - What occurs as people consume or are exposed to a brand that may have a profound effect on its value. The National Football League was recently on damage control following numerous players taking a knee during the national anthem. Due to what was happening, the NFL brand faced backlash and in 2017, became one of the top 15 most polarizing brands (Baker, 2017).

- **Where?** - DEWALT® is a brand that is proud of its toughness. Because of that desire to be tough in all situations, its brand guidelines stipulate where the brand logo is not permitted for use. Some of these forbidden places are on things that are soft and squishy or on balloons, since they may easily be popped.

Geography also plays an important role in brand consistency. Unilever has masterfully leveraged its ice cream Heartbrand logo to garner familiarity and trust. While the products and brands are uniquely named throughout the world, the Heartbrand logo remains consistent to transcend language barriers.

Figure 7.1.1 Unilever Heartbrand ice cream logos

Source: (Brtnická, 2021)

- **When?** - "When" may be applicable in a couple of ways. For example, when may be a time of day that a brand wants to associate with, such as Thomas'® English muffins and its association with breakfast. Another way when may be used is in an experiential setting. For instance, a brand that desires to be nostalgic may avoid placement in modern settings.

- **How?** - Protecting the representation of your brand can be difficult as how it becomes used proliferates. As an example, when using the brand on promotional materials, such as embroidery or stickers, the brand colors may be difficult to preserve. Additionally, the logo could become distorted as it is printed or stitched onto different surfaces. Any deviation from the brand identity could impact the consistency and even the respect people have for the brand. Something so simple may negatively impact brand equity.

Trademarks

Trademarks provide exclusive legal protection for a symbol, word, or words such as a brand logo or a tagline. The intent of this section is to provide a basic understanding of why marketers pursue trademarks and how to learn more about the process. This section is not intended to provide legal advice or fully explain the process of acquiring a trademark.

Marketers put great effort into the creation of unique names, tag lines, designs, identities, and logos. The result of this effort is called intellectual property, which can potentially be protected through the use of trademark registration. Connected to logos you often see the symbols ™ or ®. The former represents that the piece of intellectual property has been filed for trademark protection with the U.S. government and is pending registration. The latter symbol represents registration of the mark and is legally protected from infringement by other parties. Registration allows owners of the given intellectual property to legally prevent others from using the mark without consent.

Registration is done through the U.S. government via the USPTO, United States Patent and Trademark Office. The process of registration is commonly done with the assistance of legal counsel, but may be taken on by ambitious marketers. If registration is desired outside of the U.S., the World Intellectual Property Organization (WIPO) based in Geneva, Switzerland, is an international trademark registration body.

7.2 Brand book

A brand book is a document that is used to drive brand consistency by providing guidelines and examples of how the brand should come to life. The brand book should detail all of the pertinent information regarding the brand from the vision and mission to its character, and its identity.

The brand book should be utilized both internally as well as with partners, such as agencies who will complete work that involves the brand. It may contain confidential information but should be provided to trusted partners in an effort to maintain brand consistency.

In some instances, a style guide may be created as a truncated form of a brand book. The style guide will contain basic information such as typography, colors, logo use, etc. It should contain enough information for designers to build creatively within the brand's guidelines.

Here is an outline of a thorough brand book:

Elements of a brand book

- **Brand vision**

- **Brand mission**

- **Brand manifesto (if applicable)**

- **Brand pyramid**

- **Brand personality and tonality** - Include statements or keywords that will help exemplify how the brand should come to life. These statements should define what the brand is and what it is not. Examples:

    > **What we are:** Funny & clever; smart & sophisticated

    > **What we are not:** Silly & class clown; snobby

- **Logo**

    > **Use and variations:** Explain how and when different variations of the logo should be used, including colors.

> **Spacing:** State the required distance or buffer that needs to be between the logo and any other object in a design.

> **Scale:** State the minimum allowed size of the logo. Describe what elements of the logo may be shifted or resized.

- **Colors and combinations**

  > **Colors:** List the colors that will be consistently used to identify the brand. These colors are known as a palette. Typically, brands will have the most used colors in a primary color palette and then a secondary color palette for colors that are okay to use at a lesser extent.

  > **Color scaling:** Define the balance between the colors, meaning you should document the amount of use colors get relative to others. For example, at least 75% of any artwork design must be in primary colors and the remaining space may be filled with colors from the secondary palette. Notate any requirements that change based on the medium such as in advertising, on the branded website, or on the product itself.

  > **Color combinations:** From the color palettes, set parameters around which colors may be used together. This should help avoid the use of clashing colors and aid contrast.

  > **Overlays:** Overlays are design elements used in creative assets that can help define space and create dimension. For instance, many designs will take a rectangular space and split it in half using a diagonal line. On one side of the line the background is one color and on the other side a different color. Overlay guidance can define what the angle of the line must be. It can also define what the acceptable ratios of the two areas may be.

- **Typography**

  > **Font and font size:** Define the font and font size for various uses such as headlines and paragraph copy.

  > **Capitalization and emphasis:** State where and when to use capital letters, as well as where and when to use emphasis tools such as bold, italics, or underlines.

  > **Spacing:** Detail the use of indents, line and paragraph spacing.

  > **Hierarchy:** Establish the relationship or ratio between headlines, sub-headlines, and body copy.

- **Writing style** - Provide some examples of writing that demonstrate how the brand character comes to life. In this section you will want to define differences in writing style by medium. For instance, a webpage with product information is written in a formal and technical tone while the brand blog is written with an informal tone.

- **Photography**

  > **Color and tone:** Color and tone refer to the use of colors but also include the feel of the photographs. For example, should a photograph of a family in a park look natural and raw or should the family be posed and situated in the sunlight on a perfect day?

  > **Overlays**

- **Focal points** - Focal points in artwork are areas in a design that are intended to draw the most attention. For example, for advertisements, explain where the attention of viewers should be, on the product pictured in the ad or on the users of the product who are smiling because they are enjoying the product.

- **Illustrations and icons** - Explain general guidelines for and when to use as well as how to use in coordination with photography.

- **Associations** - Dictate where the brand may be used and who you'd like to represent the brand. For example, make the proclamation that the brand is only to be associated with professional athletes and not amateur athletes. State which associations are okay and those that are forbidden, for instance political organizations. Explain where the brand may be used or not used, such as the DEWALT® example discussed in section 1 of this chapter.

- **Channel guidelines** - Explain and show examples of how the brand should look across various mediums. The brand identity should remain consistent, but there may be some nuanced changes by medium in order to maximize effectiveness. For instance, a television ad will be able to show videos of people interacting with the brand by using the product. A magazine print ad may need to pick only one key moment of product use; perhaps the brand guidance is a single frame from the TV ad to feature. Here are some examples of mediums that a brand book may contain guidance for:

  > TV
  > Print
  > Social channels
  > Digital advertising
  > Product displays

7.3 Rebranding

It is a common occurrence in marketing to encounter a rebranding project. A rebrand is when the decision is made to update the brand identity and possibly the brand vision. The need to rebrand may be due to competitive pressures, changes in consumer preference, or sometimes the desire of new leadership to change direction.

The decision to rebrand should not be taken lightly. The amount of time and effort required to complete a rebrand project is enormous. Additionally, a rebrand will have a transition period, which will create brand inconsistency and customer confusion. The transition period may last months or even years as various marketing materials are updated and product inventory sells through.

If you are in the position to influence a rebrand decision, be clear about the need for the rebrand. Often a rebrand takes tremendous effort and no meaningful business outcome is achieved; it only results in wasted money and man-hours. Remove personal and leadership bias from the process and insert customer feedback and data to drive decision making. A minor brand update may take just as much organizational effort as a step-change to the brand. Therefore, ensure that the rebrand can create a meaningful business impact so that there is at least the potential for it to be worth the effort.

If a rebrand is to move the brand into a different area of a perceptual map, there must be customer data that supports the move. The market research should show that the brand has the ability to shift its perception. For instance, would it be realistic to think that the Kia automobile brand can shift perceptions to compete against Porsche in the luxury and sporty area of the perceptual map in figure 6.5.3?

In 2017, Gymboree® filed for chapter 11 bankruptcy, and as it reemerged from bankruptcy it relaunched the brand in 2018. This is a great example of a brand that attempted to shift its place in the perceptual map and faced a tough battle, which it eventually lost. Gymboree had shifted from a light-hearted children's brand to a trendier and "adult" style of clothing. This resulted in alienating much of its loyal customer base (Hanbury, 2018). In January of 2019, it was clear that the rebrand had failed as Gymboree once again filed for bankruptcy, closing all of its remaining 800 stores. It is worth noting that rights to the Gymboree brand were purchased later in 2019 by The Children's Place, and the brand is currently active once again (Thomas, Gymboree brand will stage a comeback in 2020 thanks to Children's Place, 2019).

CHAPTER 8: PRODUCT & SERVICE MARKETING

In chapter 6 we reviewed multiple brand frameworks, and in those frameworks, we saw that the foundation of a powerful brand hinges on the actual product or service that is provided. Product marketing is a role that requires expertise in the customers' needs with a precise understanding of the features and benefits that are best suited to meet those needs. The expertise of product marketers puts them in a position to look outside the existing set of solutions and drive innovation. Product marketing is the marriage of an intimate knowledge of consumer needs and how to meet those needs while delivering consistency with the brand's vision and mission.

In this chapter we will discuss the tenets of product marketing, how to deliver a compelling product or service, and fundamental knowledge of innovation. For simplicity, we will often use the term *product* as an encompassing term for both product and service.

8.1 Building a compelling product

Generating demand

You as a marketer are tasked with creating demand. In general, the creation of demand is thought to be driven by offers, promotion, and advertising. This is done with the intent to boost demand and is met with increases in supply, and thus resulting in a higher point of economic equilibrium. This view of demand creation is accurate in the majority of instances.

However, demand may also be driven by scarcity. Scarcity generates a high level of demand by limiting supply, in the form of time, quantity, or both. Thinking back to the supply and demand curves, if supply is kept constant and demand is increased, it allows for economic equilibrium to occur at a higher price. In some instances, this may be desirable, or may be necessary based on the availability of supply.

An example of scarcity is the McDonald's McRib® sandwich. This sandwich is not an everyday item on the McDonald's menu but for a discrete amount of time it is sold with high demand. Customers rush to McDonald's to buy a McRib sandwich before they are no longer available. This may be desired by McDonald's for a number of reasons. One may be that the McRib sandwich may be difficult to supply in perpetuity and is only feasible when met with extraordinarily high demand. The necessary high level of demand is only sustainable for short periods of time when customers feel supply is scarce.

Jobs to be done

The phrase "jobs to be done" is intended to instill a focus on the high-level need of what a customer is trying to accomplish, or otherwise stated the job they want to complete. The ideal of jobs to be done (JTBD) is that a customer wants a solution or an outcome rather than a product. As a product marketer this framework facilitates broader thought than within the confines of a product or set of products. You have more flexibility to envision solutions and thus innovate. Focusing on the solution or outcome that the consumer desires will also assist in the formation of a compelling benefit statement.

Here is a simple example of how the JTBD mind-set is put into practice. Consider the statement: A consumer needs to put a hole in a piece of wood.

Commonly people would assume using a drill is the best way to place a hole in wood. But notice in that statement, the word *drill* is not used and that is purposeful. If the word *drill* were used in the statement, the possible solutions are limited to drilling. If that solution is not assumed, you can think beyond the drill. It opens the possibility to step-change innovation rather than simply creating the next more powerful or easier to use drill.

The example just given takes a broad view of the customer. As solutions get ideated and vetted, your understanding of specific customer segments is imperative. For instance, you can create a new solution to put a hole in wood that is faster and easier than ever before. However, the solution will cost $10,000, whereas drills available to complete the work a little slower cost $30. Is there a customer segment that will spend the $10,000 to meet their need? As the product marketer you must understand the customer segments to smartly innovate. Maybe there is an industrial customer segment that is willing to pay $10,000 for the faster speed.

To illustrate this point, take as an example, two people want to get to work. The job to get done is to arrive at work on-time and safely. Both arrive at work safely every day, but one prefers a car as his solution while the other prefers a bike. The key question to answer is why? What motivates those two consumers with the same JTBD to seek different solutions. Research will help you understand what the motivation is, such as cost, exercise, avoidance of traffic, or to limit pollution.

Differentiation

To create demand for your product, you will need to communicate to customers how it is unique or differentiated from the other available solutions. Your ability to understand customer segments, develop differentiated solutions, and effectively communicate that differentiation will be what drives your business's success from a marketing perspective. As we discussed in chapter 6 and the brand pyramids, the product lays the foundation for the brand's success. The essence of the brand, its vision and mission may also help to differentiate products. In some instances, such as with commoditized products, the brand is responsible for the majority of the differentiation. The balance may differ by industry, but the combination of the products and brand will always mesh together in the formation of the brand pyramid.

In the discussion of product and brand differentiation, the granularity of the product should be considered. A product may be referenced as an individual product at the most granular level or product may be used to reference a product line that encompasses several tiers and variants. A sub-brand may also be relevant to help create a level of differentiation within a brand. These distinctions should be made, and there should be the recognition of how the brand, sub-brand, product, and product line match customer segments.

To illustrate the use of a brand, sub-brand, product line, and product we can look at the automobile industry. A brand such as Ford® is a brand that espouses a certain reputation and essence. Underneath the Ford brand is the sub-brand F150, which carries its own reputation and essence. A customer may have made the decision based on the sub-brand reputation that an F150 is right for them. From there the F150 sub-brand is further segmented in additional sub-brands (referred to as models on Ford.com) including "Limited," "Platinum," "LARIAT," "XLT," "XL," and "Raptor." At this level, many customers may or may not recognize these as brands, but rather as product tiers. An F150 Raptor offers a significantly differentiated set of features and style than an XLT; the Raptor sub-brand is discernible versus the XLT. However, a comparison between the XLT and the XL may show more nuanced differences. Because of the nuance, the sub-brand difference between the XLT and the XL may be lost on a number of customers and create unnecessary complexity in the product line. If a situation such as that of the XLT and the XL arises, the question should be raised as to the value of the granularity and the need to maintain the two sub-brands, or in this case models. (Note: This example is purely for illustrative purposes. There is no evidence that the XLT and the XL lack differentiation. They were purely chosen for comparison due to the similarity in name.)

The challenge for you as a marketer is to understand the amount of consideration the customer is willing to put into the purchase decision. Based on the amount of effort customers put into the research process, there will be a point at which the differentiation among sub-brands and product options may become incomprehensible to customers. Too many options may confuse or frustrate potential customers. This may be particularly true for products with lower consideration and price points, such as common household goods.

To learn the optimal level of brand and product variation, market research should be conducted. Intuition and gut feel may be the most expeditious, but proper market research may unveil new opportunities and help to avoid costly mistakes. Research doesn't just apply to new product launches; research is important to understand the current brand and product portfolio.

Measuring differentiation

Perceptual maps are a visualization tool that is commonly used to clearly display how a brand or product is differentiated. The limitation of traditional perceptual maps is the use of only two dimensions that are represented by an X-axis and Y-axis. Earlier in chapter 6 it was mentioned that three-dimensional visualizations are an option to add a third dimension, but these visualizations may be difficult to interpret and can't be put onto paper or a presentation slide. An alternative solution to compare more than two dimensions is to use a comparative table or a spider chart.

Let's fictitiously compare a car brand that offers three trim levels of the same brand, sub-brand, and model. The measurable and relevant dimensions are price, comfort, handling, power, and sound quality. Each dimension is rated by customers on a scale of 1 to 10 (lowest / worst to highest / best).

Figure 8.1.1 Table of feature dimensions

Feature dimension	Trim level		
	Trim A	Trim B	Trim C
Price	1.0	3.0	10.0
Comfort	9.0	3.0	2.0
Handling	9.0	10.0	4.0
Power	6.0	10.0	3.0
Sound quality	10.0	3.0	2.0
Total average	7.0	5.8	4.2

In the example figure 8.1.1, you are able to simply look across the rows and see how the trim levels differ. A review of the average total may give an indication of which trim level is the best. Trim A has the highest number so it possibly offers the most. However, you should be careful about making that conclusion. If this research was conducted with a customer segment that is highly sensitive to price, Trim "C" may be the best option for them despite having the lowest average. Therefore, understanding the customer and how much weight they place on each of these dimensions is critical.

The spider charts in figure 8.1.2 provide a great visualization tool to quickly see how the trim levels differ by simply scanning the purple shapes. In this example where a higher number is considered better, a larger shape indicates a better trim level. But as we discussed during the review of figure 8.1.1, these shapes must be considered in the context of the customer segment.

Figure 8.1.2 Spider charts

With spider charts you could potentially overlay the customer segment and the importance of each rating as you see in figure 8.1.3.

Figure 8.1.3 Spider chart with Trim "C" overlay

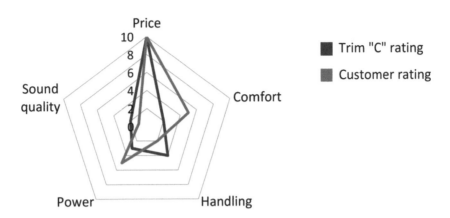

In figure 8.1.3 it's visually apparent that Trim "C" is a good match with the customer segment, due to the importance of price. If you were to overlay the customer segment onto Trim "A" (figure 8.1.4), it is easy to discern the lack of fit.

Figure 8.1.4 Spider chart with Trim "A" overlay

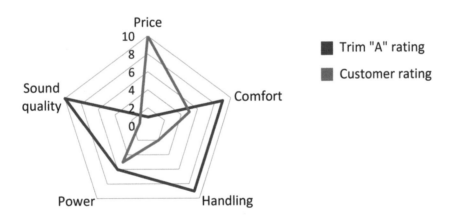

Benefit statement

A benefit statement is a concise way to define exactly how the product will meet a customer's needs. To properly craft a benefit statement, the target customer and specific need (job to be done) must be well defined. For the target customer of young professional women who struggle to get going in the morning, an example of a simple benefit statement is, "Uplift your day with new Expresso Martini bodywash." The benefit delivered to the consumer is to uplift their day.

Benefit statements should be singular in nature, with a focus on one benefit that a consumer can grasp in an instant. It is often the case that marketers want to combine multiple benefits into one statement. For instance, in the bodywash example above, a marketer may make the mistake of producing a benefit statement of "Uplift your day and smell great with Expresso Martini bodywash." Combining multiple benefits into the statement will dilute the most important benefit, and thus the message becomes muddled and less effective.

A benefit statement may be used to drive innovation or it may be an effort to better communicate an existing product. For benefit statements with the purpose of driving innovation, they should be aspirational and attainable. Partnering with R&D teams will help you understand whether or not a benefit is attainable, but the process of constructing innovative benefits should push the boundaries of the current constraints. In the previous example of the uplifting bodywash, the key question is: how does this bodywash functionally uplift the customer's day? The R&D team can investigate and provide different solutions. Maybe the uplift could be provided by a certain fragrance profile or perhaps an ingredient like menthol that provides an invigorating sensation as it's applied to skin.

While a benefit statement should be singular in nature, there are a couple of dimensions that may be brought into the statement. The first is the need, and the second is the method in which that need is met. For example, a customer is intending to build a website to support her business. The need she seeks to meet via the website is to gain awareness and sales, more simply put, to grow her business. She has never built a website before so ease of use is extremely important, so the method of her meeting that need must be easy. This can result in the benefit statement for a website product that is "the easiest way to grow your business."

Brand positioning vs. product benefit

It's important to understand the difference between a brand and a product and where the marketing of the two differ. A brand should stand for a broader or higher level of customer perception with the ability to cascade across a product portfolio. A product benefit should be more specific in nature and is able to fulfill the consumers' specific need. Each of the products that fit within a brand should provide benefits and product attributes that are consistent with the brand position.

For example, let's look at the clothing brand Lululemon. The brand is supported by and is expected to provide high-quality and comfortable athletic apparel. Lululemon gained notoriety for its yoga apparel, but has continued to expand its product line to include hats, jackets, and daily wear. In each new product line, Lululemon has remained true to the high quality and comfort expectations set by the brand. This consistent delivery of the brand position via its products has resulted in fierce customer loyalty and tremendous company growth.

Reasons to believe (RTB)

A reason to believe is a statement of fact that will give consumers reassurance that the benefit promised in the benefit statement will be fulfilled. Commonly, a benefit statement is supported by a set of two to five reasons to believe. RTBs are features, ideas, claims, or data points that help to shape customer-facing marketing messages. Similar to a benefit statement, an RTB should be simple and concise so that it may be understood quickly when it's communicated.

Reasons to believe should directly support the benefit statement by providing details about how the product meets the customer's need. Let's use a t-shirt as an example. The benefit the t-shirt provides is to be comfortable. The RTBs could be:

- The shirt is made with 100% premium cotton

- The shirt has flex stitching, which allows it to move with you better

- The shirt is tagless

- The shirt wicks away 70% more moisture

Each of the listed RTBs explains different ways in which the product was designed to be comfortable, thus demonstrating how the product delivers on the stated benefit.

In this example, the RTB "the shirt wicks away 70% more moisture" is a claim. Claims are statements that can be proven as fact. The proof, commonly called substantiation, should be documented so that you are prepared to defend the claim in the event it is challenged by a third party. Claims are a powerful way to create differentiation versus the competition.

Positioning statement

A positioning statement explains how a product or service solves a customer need. The statement should be crafted with differentiation versus competitors and other potential solutions. A good positioning statement is built with an understanding of the target customer and the need. Then introduce the product, the benefit the product provides, and the primary reasons why that target customer should believe that the product will provide the claimed benefit.

A positioning statement may be for a specific product or it may encompass a product line. It is the responsibility of marketers to understand the customer segments and how far the positioning statement should extend.

Here is the standard framework for a positioning statement, where you, the marketer, are responsible for filling in the bracketed information.

> For [target customer] who [statement of the need or opportunity], the [product name] is a [product category] that [statement of key benefit – that is, compelling reason to buy]. Unlike [primary competitive alternative], our product [statement of primary differentiation].
> (Moore, 1991)

The positioning statement should be concise and easy to understand. It will serve as the foundational guide for the product's marketing communication. Put your positioning statement to the billboard challenge by thinking through the following scenario: Your target customer is driving on the highway at 65 miles per hour and sees a billboard for your product—will they be able to understand it and the benefit it provides? This test doesn't just apply to billboard advertising but is a way to understand how effective the message may be as a display ad on a webpage, an ad on a social media platform, a newspaper ad, or a display in a department store.

In order to convey a strong consistent message, a product should have a one-to-one relationship between a customer segment and a product position. A product may have a different position for another customer segment, but to avoid confusion the relationship should be one-to-one and the likelihood of the positioning being communicated between segments should be minimized.

Unique selling proposition (USP)

A unique selling proposition is the key distinctive RTB, feature, idea, claim, data point, or benefit that a product delivers, which no competitors offer or may be unable to offer. The strength of the statement lies in its ability to create a significant level of differentiation, to increase purchase intent, and to maintain its status as a differentiating feature or benefit. A common USP used across industries is to claim the position as the #1 bestselling product in a given category. This provides customers reassurance that your product must be good because so many others have chosen it. Another example often used by mobile phone brands is to claim the number of hours a phone may continuously run without the need to be recharged.

8.2 Building a compelling product – frameworks

Value proposition

A value proposition is a succinct statement that defines the clear and measurable benefit a customer experiences through a product or service. The value proposition should differentiate the product or service from substitutes by communicating superior customer value. Value propositions may follow a number of formats such as a simple sentence and may also be supported through the use of a visual aid. The goal of a value proposition is to convey a message that can be understood and is compelling to customers in a matter of seconds (Lanning, 2000).

A simple yet effective example of a value proposition is that of Dollar Shave Club. "A great shave for a few bucks a month."

The value proposition canvas is a framework used to help develop a product or service for a specific customer segment. The tool was first developed by Dr. Alexander Osterwalder. In the canvas framework there are two larger sections, one focused on the customer and the other focused on the solution. Each of these sections is broken down into three sub-sections as shown in figure 8.2.1 (Osterwalder, 2014). Completing this canvas will help you create a cohesive product offering, but it is incumbent upon you to determine what aspect(s) of the product will drive differentiation and be the foundation for your value proposition.

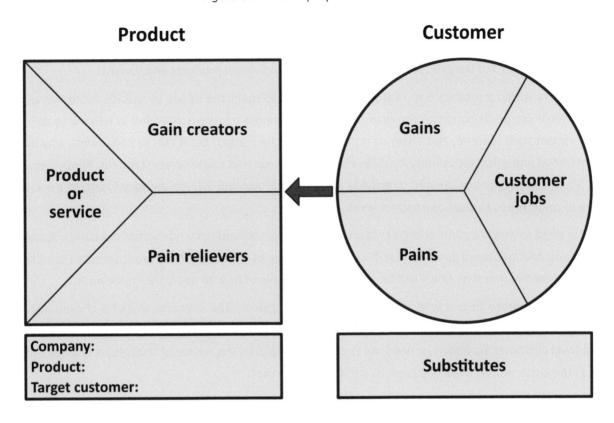

Figure 8.2.1 Value proposition canvas

Product sections		Customer sections	
Product / service	The actual product or service that will enable or facilitate the completion of the customer job.	Customer jobs	The task or need the customer is setting out to fulfill.
Gain creators	Features of the product or service that will help to create or enhance the customer gains.	Gains	The expectation of positive experiences the customer expects to encounter in the process of completing the job.
Pain relievers	Features of the product or service that will help to eliminate or minimize the customer pains.	Pains	The expectation of negative experiences the customer expects to encounter in the process of completing the job.

Smith's Hierarchy

Marketing tools such as the brand pyramid or value proposition canvas offer you an excellent framework to assess a product or product line. These frameworks, however, only consider high-level attributes and fail to adequately move beyond the product line and cascade into individual products and variants.

Products within a product line—variants—are critical to meet the needs of specific customer segments and thus maximize profit potential. For example, a brand pyramid may do a great job at helping to define how a cereal variant such as Honey Nut Cheerios is positioned in the market, but it fails to help define why there is a customer need and sales opportunity for different size boxes, such as single serve, standard, family size, or twin packs. Smith's Hierarchy was created to provide a framework that will include an assessment of the customer needs and preferences through the variant level.

The need to assess customer segments and build product variants extends across industries. Some examples are consumer packaged goods as just discussed. Software as a service (SAAS) products often use plan tiers, and the automotive industry, which will be used in this example of how to apply the framework.

Smith's Hierarchy begins with the target customer segment. The segment must be chosen in order to properly define and assess the hierarchy. Then the hierarchy follows the 'funnel of thought' starting with the highest-level customer aspiration or need. As the hierarchy follows the funnel of thought, it becomes more focused as the customer segment preferences are more tightly met.

In the framework, parallel to the funnel of thought, is the 'layers of differentiation'. These layers may be relevant at any stage of the hierarchy. To create a compelling product, you must consider how these items manifest themselves and create differentiation for your product offering.

Often, marketers will make the mistake of using excessively broad customer segments when they complete frameworks such as the value proposition canvas. Smith's Hierarchy is designed to challenge you to further define your segments so that you can understand and state why a certain customer will purchase the single serve size of cereal versus the customer who will buy the twin pack.

Recall the customer segmentation section, that a segment must be both operational and substantial. Disciplined segmentation will guide you in creating relevant product variants that can drive customer preference and can also help you understand when creating an additional product variant isn't prudent.

Figure 8.2.2 Smith's Hierarchy

Product name (variant):_____

Customer segment: _____

_____

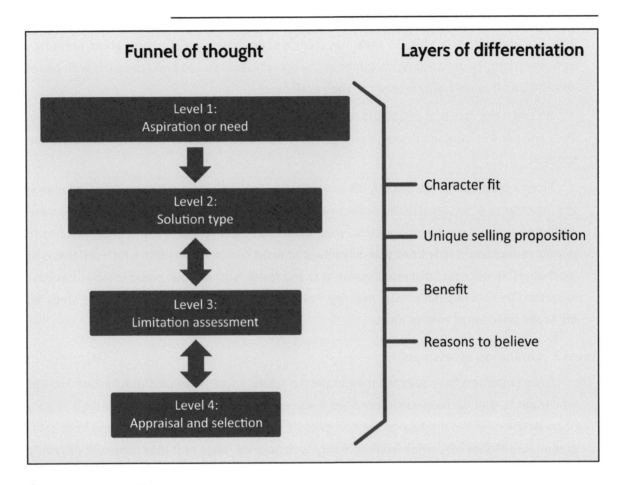

Customer segment

    Define the customer segment that the product is intended for. Use segment definitions that follow the guidelines discussed in chapter three. Ensure the segments are defined well enough that they will allow you to successfully determine the suitable product variants at the appraisal and selection level.

Level 1 - Aspiration or need

    The aspiration or need may manifest itself in a number of ways. The customer may have a clearly defined need such as a goal or a task that must be accomplished. Conversely, the need may be altruistic in nature where the customer may not be clear on if or what the solution may be but there is a longing for something. There may also be a need that isn't recognized where a customer is content with the status quo without the expectation that something better could or should exist, for example Uber disrupting the solution that taxis provided. In particular, the recognition of al-truistic and status quo needs can present transformative innovation opportunities. In the research section we will discuss some methods to uncover these needs.

Level 2 - Solution type

To illustrate solution type, think of a person who needs to get to work. This person has three viable options: drive a car, ride a bike, or take a bus. Each of these options demonstrates a solution type. In this scenario, it's likely that the person knows his or her preferred solution. Customer segments may prefer different solutions, and their rationale may also differ. For instance, a person who prefers to ride a bike to work may be in the segment focused on healthy living. However, a person who also prefers to ride a bike to work may choose to do so because she cares about reducing vehicle emissions. Understanding customer segments will allow you to build products with benefits and features that are highly relevant to their preferences.

It's often the case that customers don't know what solutions exist and which is best for them. They will need to conduct research and compare options in order to determine their preferred solution.

From a promotional standpoint, it's to your advantage to know your customer segments and the importance of this level in the decision-making process. If the solution is commonly known by customers without much consideration, your focus should not lie there. If the solution is one that requires education, it may be to your advantage to assist customers to learn which solution is best for them. This will help build brand awareness and foster trust as your brand is viewed as having expertise. This will hopefully result in giving your brand an advantage in the remaining steps leading to the selection of your product.

Level 3 - Limitation assessment

Once customers have selected their preferred solution type, they next must assess and apply limitations to that decision. Limitations are features or factors that are strongly desired. It's a yes or no decision—if the product or solution doesn't satisfy a limitation, it is removed from consideration. Limitations may come from necessity such as price range or it may come out of principle such as a hybrid drivetrain. A factor may not just be part of a product but part of the experience associated with the product or service. In a product purchase a sales person's lack of knowledge may be a limitation that leads a customer to remove the product from consideration.

Limitations are applied by customers to help reduce the number of viable options that are under consideration when they are ready to make their final purchase decision. Your goal as a marketer is to remove unwanted limitations that will reduce the number of potential buyers, while maintaining limitations that are desired. A desired limitation may be to only offer cars above a certain price point in an effort to maintain your brand's luxury position. Some examples of limitations for an automobile purchase may include:

> Budget constraints

> Financing availability

> Lease availability

> Rating of 3.5 or higher from a trusted review website

> A third row of seating

> 5-star safety rating

> Hybrid drivetrain availability

Level 4 - Appraisal and selection

Customers have narrowed their choices and feel prepared to make a purchase. At this level, a sale may close but there is the chance that customers may balk and return to a higher stage of the hierarchy. This could happen if customers realize the options available to them aren't desirable, so they must reassess their limitations or perhaps solution type.

Appraisal features or factors aren't as strongly held preferences as we saw in the limitations level. Here customers don't look at the features as a binary yes or no decision, but rather appraise each feature and apply a value to it. The customers place a value on a feature, and if the cost exceeds that value, they will prefer a different feature or go without. Take, for instance, the color of a vehicle. The base color white is included in the current price; however, for $500 the vehicle could be painted blue. A customer may think that $500 is well spent on the blue color and select that feature.

Depending on the customer segment, factors and features may fit into either level of appraisal or limitation. For a specific segment, maybe a blue color car is a deal breaker and needs to be available.

It is your duty as a marketer to understand the value and importance of each feature. This knowledge will allow you to build differentiated and appealing products where customers derive a high level of value. Here are some examples of possible features that fit into the appraisal and selection category of an automobile purchase.

> Color

> Chrome wheels

> Sun roof

> Leather seats

> Premium sound system

> Offer or discount

Layer of differentiation - Character fit

As a customer progresses in the hierarchy, each of the levels are both consciously and unconsciously impacted by character fit. Character fit accounts for the values or characteristics that determine a customers' aspirations as well as their desires that brands or products espouse. Some examples include, an American-made product, a luxury brand product, or an eco-friendly product.

Layer of differentiation - Unique selling proposition (USP)

For the stated customer segment, you must find a point of differentiation that will separate your solution from the competition. It may be the solutions' unique ability to match character fit, or perhaps related to the benefit or reasons to believe. In the scenario of the automotive industry, perhaps a USP is to provide a luxury automobile at an affordable price. This proposition would be differentiated from the rest of the luxury market that is premium priced.

Layer of differentiation - Benefit

The benefit provided to the customer must be considered during the conceptualization of a solution. If a customer does not recognize the ability of the solution to provide a benefit, the customer will not find a rationale to purchase the solution.

Layer of differentiation - Reasons to believe (RTBs)

Reasons to believe are often cited as points of differentiation. These are things such as efficacy claims, ingredients, materials, and manufacturing location. For an automobile, gas mileage, horsepower, towing capacity, rated #1 by a reviewing party, 5-star safety ratings, are all examples of reasons to believe that could create differentiation.

Customer journey map

The process of building a customer journey map is one that helps you to fully understand the experience a consumer encounters when using a product or service. Customer journey maps are created by tracking the various steps and milestones throughout the journey of using a product. Each of these steps is measured in two ways:

- The perception of the steps as positive, neutral, or negative.

- The level of impact the step has on the perception of the overall journey. The most important steps are deemed "moments of truth" where a failure at that stage is catastrophic or exceeding expectations results in delight.

The customer journey map we are discussing is not to be confused with a decision journey map, which we will discuss later in the promotion and advertising chapter. The primary difference between the two journey maps is the scope of the journey. A customer journey map focuses on the experience of the customer using the product or service, whereas a decision journey map focuses on the path the shopper took to become a customer. It is common, however, that both customer journey maps and decision journey maps are simply referred to as journey maps.

Customer journey maps are intended to portray the average experience and reactions by a customer segment as they use the product or service. The map itself is a high-level depiction of what the average customer within a segment perceives to be their experience. There are various sections to the customer journey map as depicted in figure 8.2.3:

- **Columns** - Represent stages in the journey. The titles for each stage are located in the purple area at the top of the journey map (e.g., enter & queue).

- **Linear steps** - The steps are represented as circles with a brief description of the step. A heart is used to depict the critical moment of truth steps in the experience. In some customer journey maps the diameter of the circle may differ to indicate varying levels of impact to the overall journey; larger circles indicate higher impact.

- **Drivers** - Located at the bottom of the customer journey, drivers summarize which functions of the product or service impact the experience rendered at each stage of the journey.

Here is a simple example of a customer journey map for dine-in customers at a quick service restaurant, also known as a fast-food restaurant.

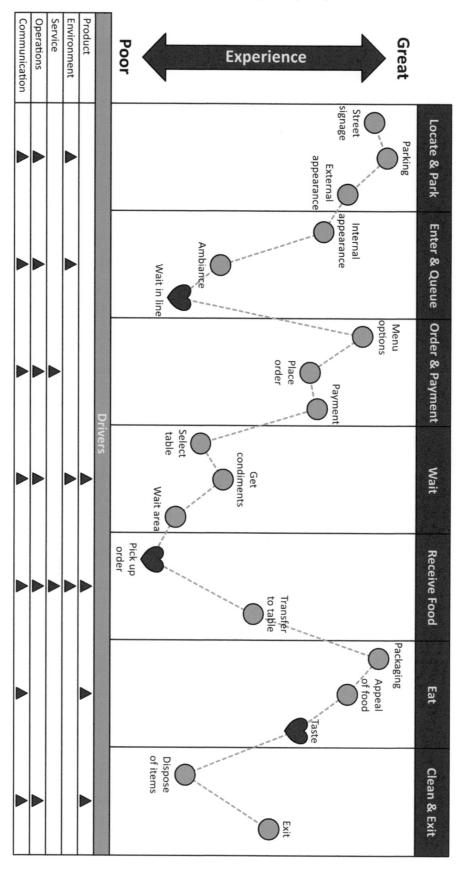

Figure 8.2.3 Customer journey map

In addition to the visualization of the journey map shown in figure 8.2.3, there should be documentation that explains why each step of the journey was placed in its location. This understanding will allow your cross-functional team and you to prioritize plans to improve the customer experience.

The best method to build a journey map is to conduct customer research, and we will cover some of those techniques in the research chapter. In the absence of time or budget for research, it is also possible to use your existing knowledge of the customer's experience to develop a journey map. However, it is always recommended to conduct research rather than use assumptions and institutional knowledge.

8.3 Product claims

Claims

Claims are statements that are used to create differentiation among products and brands. They are often used to support the position of a product or brand so that it will have a more convincing value proposition to customers. A claim most likely is used as a reason to believe, strengthening the believability that a product can deliver on its stated benefit. A simple example of a claim is "9 out of 10 doctors recommend product XYZ."

Claims are used in an attempt to differentiate and demonstrate superiority versus the competition. Due to the competitive nature of claims and the promises they make to consumers, you must take care to ensure that the claims are substantiated. In many organizations, legal counsel assists marketers by providing guidance on what is acceptable verbiage and adequate substantiation. In highly competitive markets it is tempting to become aggressive and make assertions or comparisons that are not easy to prove. Unsubstantiated claims can make your company vulnerable to legal challenges from both competitors and consumers. Claims that draw comparison versus competitors are highly sensitive. Highly regulated industries may have established criteria and approved methodologies for claim substantiation.

Claim categories

Claims may fall into one or more of several categories. Here is a list of common claim categories with examples:

Claim category	Explanation	Example
Guarantees	A steadfast promise that is backed up.	You'll lose 15 pounds in one month or your money back.
Torture test	An extreme demonstration of the product in use.	Someone wearing a coat through an Arctic snow storm and remains warm.

Claim category	Explanation	Example
Measurable claims	Tested and statistically proven results.	• 2x faster • 48-hour protection • 600 horsepower
Comparison to competition	Demonstrate superiority head-to-head.	A head-to-head blind taste test with random participants to demonstrate the preferred taste of the promoted product. Two different brands of paper towels shown cleaning up a liquid side-by-side to demonstrate the superior absorption of the promoted product.
Borrowed equity	Associate your product with something to make it seem better.	A laundry detergent co-branded "with Oxi technology."
Logic	Make a logical argument why the benefit is believable.	Never miss a customer because a website server has 100% uptime.
Analogy or Metaphor	Use a common understanding to explain a benefit more clearly.	This moisturizer will leave your skin as soft as a baby's butt.
Endorsement	Paid person who has the ability to influence. This person should have credibility.	Shaquille O'Neal endorses IcyHot® as the product he uses to relieve his back pain.
Testimonials	A positive review or statement from a credible source that is relatable.	A quote from a neighbor recommending a roofing company.
Social proof	A group agreement makes the benefit more credible.	• 9 of 10 dentists recommend product XYZ. • Join the millions who saved money by using product XYZ.

8.4 Product innovation

Product innovation cycle

The product innovation cycle refers to the cadence or timing at which a new version of a product or solution is released. The innovation cycle is not always predictable and is always subject to disruption as innovations are introduced as new ways to meet consumer needs. An example of an innovation cycle is mobile phones. Approximately once a year in October, new models of mobile phones are released. The innovation cycle can vary greater in duration. It could be as little as a couple of months for things such as software, but in the case of airplanes, it could be years to more than a decade before the next significant product release.

Innovation cycles are not simply a function of a company's preferred cadence for product development, as external factors may have a significant impact. In hypercompetitive industries, companies may need to innovate at an uncomfortably fast pace, thus increasing the opportunity for mistakes and failure. Innovation cycles may also be dictated by market demand. In the example of mobile phones, the fall season is targeted for innovation due to the upcoming Christmas sales surge. Retailers may also dictate innovation cycles as they reconfigure shelves and product placement on a consistent annual or semi-annual basis.

Adoption curve

Significant innovations that change the landscape of how consumer needs are met may follow an adoption curve or otherwise known as an innovation curve. The adoption curve depicted in figure 8.4.1 helps us to understand the mind-set of consumers and the rate at which interest builds for a new solution (Rogers, 1962). The adoption curve breaks consumers into five segments and numbers below the adoption curve indicate the percent of customers that fall into each group.

Figure 8.4.1 Adoption curve

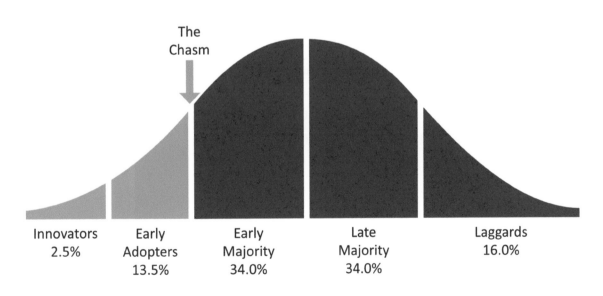

- **Innovators** - These are consumers who are enthusiastically awaiting new solutions and are eager to try new things. Often, this segment is more affluent or financially stable.

- **Early adopters** - Consumers who are open to new solutions, are actively engaged opinion leaders, and are more socially active.

- **Early majority** - Consumers who are open to change but need a reliable reason to change. This segment is often comprised of middle-class consumers and is more price-sensitive than the innovators and early adopters.

- **Late majority** - These are the generally older, more conservative consumers who prefer to rely on what they know works. They are skeptical of new solutions and are significantly price-sensitive.

- **Laggards** - These consumers are reluctant to change. They are skeptical of the need to change and may have a sense that they'll need help to use the new solution.

Along the top of the curve is a point in time referred to as "the chasm." The chasm is the point at which the consumer segments adopting the solution have a fundamental difference in mind-set (Moore, 1991). The innovators and early adopters segments want a new solution to change the way things are done, and are open to taking a risk on something that may not be perfect. The other segments want a proven solution where their motivation isn't to try something new, but is rather to increase the efficiency of what they need to do.

Minimum viable product (MVP)

A minimum viable product refers to a basic version of a product that the product development team believes will suffice consumer needs. The goal of an MVP version of a product is to gain real users in order to gather data and learn about their experience with the product. The idea of MVP product versioning is common within the SAAS (software as a service) industry. In particular, the SAAS industry embraces this product development methodology for a few reasons. SAAS products don't require inventory, there is no setup cost for production such as tooling, and the products are often built to be receptive to updates that require little to no consumer action. An MVP can increase the speed of innovation and help the company immediately gain adoption and market share while the product is further refined.

In your role as a marketer and an expert in consumer needs, you should advocate for the consumer and ensure that the MVP meets consumer needs and reinforces your brand's position. This is especially important for established brands where a high level of product quality is expected. A poor customer experience with an MVP version of a product can betray trust and break hard-earned loyalty.

Part 2: Business planning

Part 2 chapters:

CHAPTER 9: STRATEGY

In this chapter we will move outside the realm of marketing for a moment and briefly discuss broader business strategy. We will then review several methods to assess your business so that a sound strategy may be developed. Lastly, we will discuss how to write a marketing plan that is built to deliver on the determined business strategy.

9.1 Business strategies

For businesses there are three generic strategies that may be employed in an effort to gain a competitive advantage (Porter, 1980):

- Overall cost leadership

- Differentiation

- Focus

One of these strategies must be implemented and fully committed to without straying into the other strategies. Strength in any of the strategies builds over time as expertise and optimizations compound. Any deviance away from the strategy will weaken your position as they may diminish optimizations that were achieved over time.

Overall cost leadership

To achieve cost leadership, you must focus optimizing on all aspects of cost controls such as manufacturing, customer service, research and development, sales, advertising, and more. There must be the realization of economies of scale where high sales volume results in lower inputs and process costs. As costs are minimized, table stake levels of features, quality, and customer service must not be ignored. The cost leadership model is desirable as competition lowers prices to compete. They lose profitability whereas your firm maintains a healthy level of profit. To compete as a cost leader and achieve economies of scale that are advantageous compared to the competition, you should command a leading market share position.

Differentiation

A differentiation strategy is one that appeals to many marketers because it depends on their ability to effectively communicate what makes their brand different from the competition. It is a strategy in which the brand offers something that is perceived as unique within the industry. This can range from having the best customer service, to the fastest turnaround time, the freshest ingredients, or the best technology. Differentiation creates an advantage by building customer loyalty, thus creating habit and reducing price sensitivity.

Focus

This is a strategy where you select a segment of the market to focus on, such as a specific need, a certain geographical location, or a product segment. The prior two strategies span an industry-wide focus, whereas this strategy siphons off part of the industry where you will intently focus efforts in order to build an advantage. For the chosen focal segment, you will be able to use your focus to implement a strategy of differentiation or cost leadership. With your focus in place, you can develop unmatched expertise in that segment, besting the competition.

9.2 Business assessment

SWOT Analysis

SWOT analyses are intended to help guide strategy by offering a simple framework to summarize internal **Strengths** and **Weaknesses** as well as identify external **Opportunities** and **Threats**. A SWOT analysis can be completed at various levels within the business such as the brand level, product group level, or the business unit level. The key is to complete the analysis so that it is a useful tool to guide strategy and action plans. Here is an example of a SWOT analysis for a premium watch brand.

Figure 9.2.1 SWOT analysis

SWOT Analysis of XYZ premium watch brand	
Strengths	**Opportunities**
• High loyalty and advocacy • High profitability • Talented engineering team	• Premium watch market is growing 15% per year • 80% of watch buyers are willing to try a new brand
Weaknesses	**Threats**
• Lack of marketing and sales expertise • Manufacturing is at 98% capacity • Unaided brand awareness is only 9%	• 70% of sales are dominated by three brick and mortar retailers • Phones are making watches obsolete as time-telling devices • The chance for recession in the next 12 months is high and will reduce the demand for premium watches

From this example of SWOT analysis, several priorities may be discussed. If the company views this brand as a growth driver, there are weaknesses in marketing and the supply chain that will need to be addressed before the desired level of growth can be achieved. If the economy enters a recession, what is the action plan to mitigate losses and position the brand for success until the economy recovers? Is there a need or opportunity to prepare a sub-brand that is better positioned to meet the needs of a more price-conscious customer segment?

Guiding principles for completing a SWOT assessment:

- Be honest with yourself, avoid being overly optimistic or critical.

- For each quadrant focus on the top two to four items.

- Focus on the areas with the highest potential to make a business impact. The items identified should help guide strategic initiatives.

- When assessing external factors, look outside just your industry and be aware of the potential for disruption. Disruption may occur from competitors, but it may also occur from acts of God or other factors such as the 2020 Coronavirus pandemic and similar situations.

- Remember Strengths and Weaknesses are internal, whereas Opportunities and Threats are external.

- Review and update the SWOT analysis on a regular basis, at least once every 6 to 12 months.

Boston Consulting Group (BCG) matrix

The BCG matrix was developed as a framework to assess the current state of an individual business unit, brand, or product with the intent to direct future resource allocations. The matrix follows two axes measured from low to high. The X-axis is a quantification of the market share you command; the Y-axis is an assessment of the overall market growth. Each axis holds two designations, low and high, which yields a matrix consisting of four quadrants. Here is a pictorial view of the framework.

Figure 9.2.2 BCG matrix

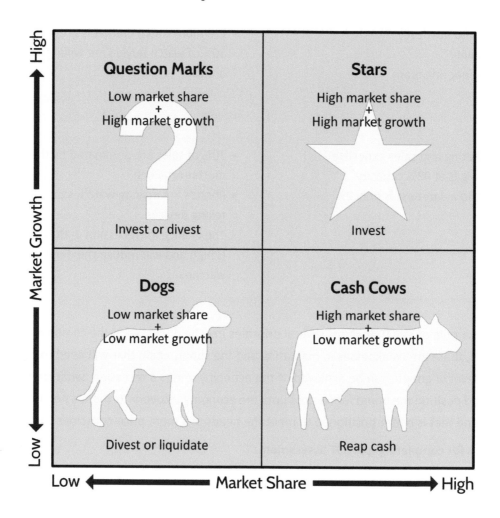

The four quadrants of the BCG matrix explained:

- **Stars** - The top right quadrant where the business commands high market share in a high-growth market. This quadrant should be invested in for aggressive growth and protected from external entrants.

- **Question marks** - The top left quadrant where the business has a low amount of share in a high-growth market. Business units that fall into this space require a choice—either invest in the business unit with the goal of transforming it into a star or choose to exit the business and divest it. The decision is based on a number of considerations such as:

  > Importance of the business unit to the company's overall portfolio
  > Competitiveness in the space

> Amount of market fragmentation

> Amount of investment required for success

- **Cash cows** - The lower right quadrant is where the business unit has high share in a low-growth or declining market. Cash cow is named as such because you should milk this business. The cash generated from the business units in this quadrant should be used to fund the business units located in the Question marks and Stars quadrants. Due to the low or declining market growth, the likelihood of new competitive entrants is lower, thus the need for investment is lessened.

- **Dogs** - The lower left quadrant is where the business unit has low share in a low-growth or declining market. These businesses are in a poor position and unlikely to deserve prioritization or investment by the organization. These business units should be divested or liquidated.

9.3 Game theory and the prisoner's dilemma

Game theory is a mathematical model that was developed to understand the psychology of human interaction and to predict the behavior of rational individuals. Game theory was originally demonstrated via the prisoner's dilemma. This is a story of two criminals who have been arrested and are separately being asked to confess to the crime. Each of the criminals knows the potential outcome he could face based on his response. The potential responses and the outcomes are captured in the following matrix.

Figure 9.3.1 Prisoner's dilemma

		Criminal A	
		Silent	Betrays
Criminal B	Silent	Both get 1 year in prison	A: walks away B: get 3 years in prison
	Betrays	A: gets 3 years in prison B: walks away	Both get 2 years in prison

Based on self-interested rational behavior, the criminals will betray each other in order to secure the best outcome for himself regardless of the decision the other criminal makes (von Neumann & Morgenstern, 1944).

In business, this thought process may be applied as a method to understand and anticipate the behavior of competitors. As an example, we can use this framework and apply it to advertising. The current state of the industry is that a group of competitors are not aggressive. They are choosing not to pay for ad placements on competitive brand search engine terms or keywords. In the current state, all of the companies are staying silent. It's likely they are not capturing the highest number of sales possible because they choose to be unaggressive.

One of the companies is weighing the opportunity to advertise on competitive brand search terms. This company will "betray" the others with the hope to gain a better outcome for itself. The reaction of competitors to this betrayal and the potential for retaliation is where the concept of game theory presents itself. The company will need to model competitive actions and measure the potential of the reward versus the risk.

The model may be built structured as a decision tree. A decision tree provides a method to outline different paths of actions and their probability to project the outcome. The results of the tree will provide an estimate for the expected outcome generated by the possible actions taken by both your company and those of your competitors. Here a simple example of a decision tree to assess the various scenarios brought by advertising on competitive search terms. The three metrics in the decision tree are:

- **Revenue** - The revenue generated by the advertising channel

- **Ad spend** - The dollars spent to advertise in the channel

- **Net** - The revenue minus the ad spend

Figure 9.3.2 Decision tree

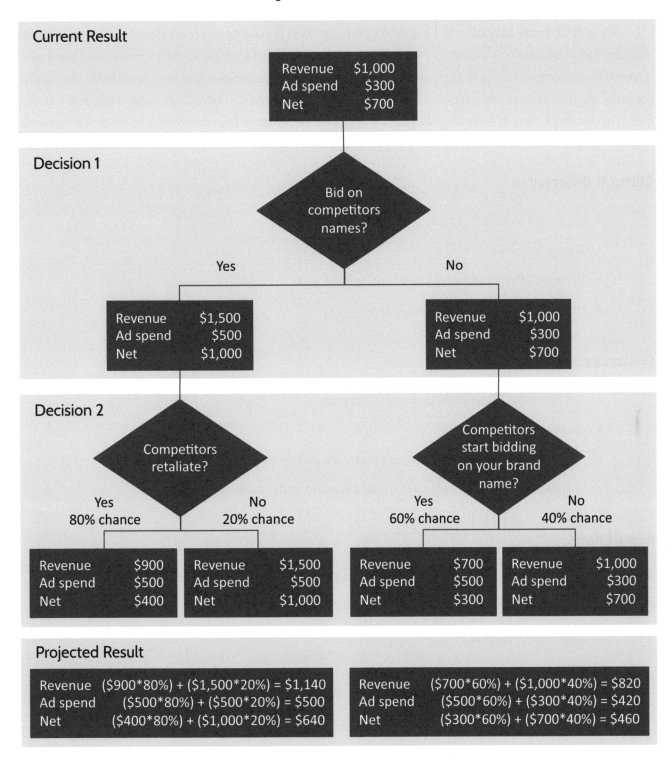

Current Result

Revenue	$1,000
Ad spend	$300
Net	$700

Decision 1

Bid on competitors names?

Yes

No

Revenue	$1,500
Ad spend	$500
Net	$1,000

Revenue	$1,000
Ad spend	$300
Net	$700

Decision 2

Competitors retaliate?

Competitors start bidding on your brand name?

Yes
80% chance

No
20% chance

Yes
60% chance

No
40% chance

Revenue	$900
Ad spend	$500
Net	$400

Revenue	$1,500
Ad spend	$500
Net	$1,000

Revenue	$700
Ad spend	$500
Net	$300

Revenue	$1,000
Ad spend	$300
Net	$700

Projected Result

Revenue	($900*80%) + ($1,500*20%) = $1,140
Ad spend	($500*80%) + ($500*20%) = $500
Net	($400*80%) + ($1,000*20%) = $640

Revenue	($700*60%) + ($1,000*40%) = $820
Ad spend	($500*60%) + ($300*40%) = $420
Net	($300*60%) + ($700*40%) = $460

Based on the decision tree example in figure 9.3.2, you may conclude that it is best to begin advertising on competitors' brand names. This is depicted as you follow the decision path to the left and bid on competitors names as the first decision, the end result has the best revenue and net dollar outcome.

9.4 International scale and complexity

Many firms aspire to grow, and a key driver of that growth is expected to come from the vast opportunity associated with international expansion. International expansion is not a simple endeavor and should be carefully considered prior to pursuing it. Even some of the largest, most established brands and firms fail in their quest. For instance, top retailers Walmart and the Home Depot have struggled to effectively expand into the E.U. and China, respectively. Here is a list of things to consider when evaluating the opportunity to enter international markets. This list is not exhaustive, but a sample of what needs to be considered prior to international expansion.

Cultural differences

- Local interpretation of symbols and colors
- Shopping norms
- Lifestyle differences such as likelihood to have a car
- Home size and amount of storage space

Customer segmentation

- The existence of the same customer segments
- Customer segment size
- The ability to use existing marketing materials and messaging
- The need for a dedicated local marketing team to understand customer needs

Regulations

- Trademark and intellectual property protection
- Product formulation and materials
- Safety requirements
- Taxes
- Tariff and importation regulations
- Payment and subscription service regulations

Operational complexity

- Office locations and time zones
- Supply chain and lead times
- The ability to transact in other currencies and manage fluctuations in foreign exchange rates

- Translation and adjustment of products as well as marketing materials to meet local requirements

International expansion may literally bring a world of opportunity. However, prior to expansion, careful consideration must be made to the points listed previously. The organization must be fully committed to expansion and have the ability to scale in size. Personnel, processes, and systems must be ready to support the added responsibility.

9.5 Marketing plan

A marketing plan is a strategic document that is created as a communications tool with the intent to gain broader organizational support. The plan will state your recommendations for the business and what your goals, strategies, and tactics are to support the realization of your plan. As the recommendations are developed, involvement from cross-functional teams such as sales, R&D, supply chain, finance, and operations are highly recommended. The format of the marketing plan may differ substantially by organization, but the purpose remains the same—to communicate the plan and gain organizational support. Plans are commonly created or revised on an annual basis.

There are four sections to a standard marketing plan:

1: Situation analysis

This section can be quite lengthy as it contains relevant information across a broad spectrum of information related to the industry, brand, and competitive landscape. Here are some items to consider:

> The 4 Ps (4 Es) and 3 Cs

> Analyses utilizing tools such as a SWOT analysis

> Historical and forward-looking trends

> Prior years financials including marketing investments

2: The plan

After fully understanding the situation, it's time to build and articulate a well-constructed plan. The plan does not include situational or historical information. It is rather a forward-looking recommendation with the objectives, strategies, and tactics to deliver on the plan. One of the objectives should be financial and most times focused on delivering profit.

It's common for even experienced marketers to confuse or combine objectives, strategies, and tactics. Here is an explanation of the three along with the recommended number of each to contain in a marketing plan. It is important to limit the number of items to facilitate focus and avoid an untenable number of priorities.

Group	Explanation	Example(s)	Recommended number
Goals (Objectives)	The goals for the business to achieve	• 10% revenue growth • Increase market share 5 points	1-2
Strategies	Broader initiatives or actions that will support the achievement of an objective	• Gain wider product distribution • Launch brand into a new product category	3-4 in support of each objective
Tactics	Specific actions that are taken to deliver on a strategy	• Offer retailer "X" higher margin in exchange for more distribution • Run a television campaign to support the launch of the brand in the new product category	3-4 in support of each strategy

3: Financials

A detailed financials section should forecast the expectations of the business's performance. It should estimate the expenditures such as the marketing advertising investment required to achieve the business performance objectives. Some of the common financial metrics to include are:

> Revenue

> Units

> Cost of goods

> Overhead and fixed costs

> CAPEX (capital expenditures)

> Margin

> Marketing spend by channel

> Trade spend

These projections should be broken down as deemed useful by classifications such as region, channel, brand, product line, or customer segment. In addition to the classifications, the projections should be measured in appropriate time horizons, such as monthly, quarterly, and annually.

4: Additional information

The additional information section is a place for any pertinent information that does not properly fit within the other areas of the document. Some of those items may be unquantified risks, assumptions, and required decision dates. Additionally, this section may include special initiatives that the marketing team may need to allocate resources to that satisfy organizational needs but do not directly support the defined marketing objectives.

CHAPTER 10: MARKETING RESEARCH

Marketing research is a diverse topic that encompasses a wide range of goals and methodologies. The ability of an organization to produce, understand, and implement insights gathered from research is vital to its sustained success. When companies, brands, and products are successful, people notice and competitors will arise mimicking what they see working in order to capitalize on market demand. As competition increases, marketers must be able to determine the best path forward to maintain differentiation and growth. Marketing research is the foundation to shaping that best path forward. In this chapter we will review the following:

- Research basics

- Common primary marketing research methodologies

- Common secondary marketing research sources

- Common marketing research goals

- Creating a research plan

- Delivering insights

- Statistical analysis

10.1 Research basics

Primary vs. secondary research

There are two overarching forms of marketing research. The first is primary research and what most people think of when they hear the term *research*. It refers to the first-hand gathering of proprietary research and insights. Secondary research is second-hand research, where the information comes from an outside source and is not specifically gathered and exclusive to you. A few examples of secondary research types are industry reports, white papers, and scientific articles.

The time and cost to complete primary research are usually higher than sourcing secondary research, but the advantage of primary research is the ability to customize and gain the exact desired insights. Conversely, secondary research is usually less expensive and quicker to gather, but gaining precise answers and insights may be difficult. Additionally, a downside to secondary research is its inherent lack of exclusivity. This type of research is commonly available to any researcher willing to pay for access. Therefore, the insights you gather may be the same as those gained by your competitors.

Qualitative vs. quantitative

Research may be categorized in one of two ways, either qualitative or quantitative. Qualitative research is research done to gather feedback without the expectation of completing numerical and statistical analysis. It typically involves fewer participants and often with the intent to deliver a deeper, even conversational understanding of the participants' responses. An example of a qualitative study is an interview. A benefit to some qualitative research methodologies is the opportunity to have a more fluid interaction with the participants. This allows for real-time adjustments as more is learned about the participant. A limitation to qualitative studies is that your sample will be smaller and thus care needs to be taken to not extrapolate the sample's responses as representative of the entire population.

Quantitative research is typically completed at a larger scale (based on the number of respondents) and utilizes statistical analyses to provide results. An example of quantitative research is a survey with questions such as "On a scale from 1-7, please rate the importance of product ease of use." Quantitative studies are unlikely to present the opportunity for direct researcher to participant interaction but do provide a better representation of the population.

Respondent fatigue

The opportunity to engage with customers and gather their feedback should bring excitement to any marketer. With this opportunity it's easy to become overzealous and expand the scope of a research study resulting in the addition of numerous questions.

If you've ever taken a survey, you know there is a line at which your patience and interest wane and your willingness to provide quality feedback dissipates. This is known as "respondent fatigue." In an effort to limit questions, challenge yourself and your research team to remain focused on answering the primary goal of the research.

In general, you will want to keep your studies, particularly surveys and similar quantitative studies, to about 10 minutes or less in duration. In the next section we will discuss determining research goals, scope, and key questions to help avoid this pitfall.

Validation approach

A marketing research best practice is to follow the validation approach. This approach is characterized by first completing smaller qualitative studies, and then moving to the larger quantitative studies. The qualitative study is completed first in order to discover potential participant responses and to hone in on the proper questions for the quantitative study. In addition, the insights generated from the qualitative study can then be validated by data and statistical analyses from the quantitative study.

Utilizing the validation approach offers two key benefits:

- **Accuracy** - During the qualitative studies, you will be able to find and learn more in-depth information about the participants' viewpoints. These learnings will help determine the best structure for the questions posed in less flexible quantitative studies. A simple example may be the writing of a multiple-choice question. Entering the research process, you may have an assumed set of answer choices for the multiple-choice question. Upon completing the qualitative research, you may discover that additional answer choices should be added to the question.

- **Cost** - Qualitative studies are generally less expensive than quantitative. Qualitative studies can help increase the effectiveness of quantitative questions as well as limit the length and cost of the quantitative study. Qualitative research can be scaled until you feel confident in the insights that will be utilized in building the quantitative study. Lastly, skipping the qualitative stage may yield less than optimal results in the quantitative study. This could require the need to run the study again, thus doubling the cost.

Sample size and statistical significance

A well-analyzed quantitative study will include the measurement of statistical significance. These analyses will allow you to know if the difference between responses was due to sheer chance or is in fact an outcome you should expect the population to exhibit. Marketers and researchers often make the mistake of foregoing the completion of statistical significance. They rely on relative numbers and eyeballing charts to judge the significance of results. This practice should be challenged.

In order to gain statistical significance, the sample size (which often equals the number of respondents) needs to meet a minimum size requirement. The minimum sample size differs based on the expected difference between responses and the size of the total population. These calculations may be confusing, so consulting with a researcher or statistician is recommended.

When determining the sample size, you should anticipate the ways in which the data will be segmented, also known as cross-tabulated. As the data is split among segments, the sample size is also split, yielding the possibility that statistical significance becomes unattainable. For example, you have a multiple-choice question that was answered by the desired sample size of 100 people. Now, let's say you want to compare the responses of males versus females to see if there is a difference between the two segments. There were 35 males and 65 females who responded. With the data split between these two segments, your ability to achieve statistical significance may be potentially lost.

Monadic vs. sequential monadic tests

Monadic tests are those in which a respondent is exposed to only one stimulus. Sequential monadic testing exposes a respondent to multiple stimuli.

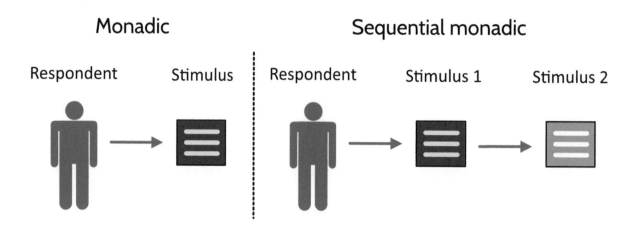

Figure 10.1.1 Monadic vs. sequential monadic test

The difference between these test methodologies is important to understand when calculating the number of respondents needed and selecting the questions. An example of a study where this methodology decision is relevant is product concept testing. Typically, you'd have multiple concepts to test, and you would need to decide whether or not you'd like the respondents to evaluate and provide feedback on one concept or many.

A monadic test is beneficial to use when you want to ask more questions and gain a more in-depth understanding of the stimulus while reducing the possibility of fatigue. It also removes the chance of relative bias that may occur when a respondent is exposed to a stimulus and then another stimulus. The bias occurs when the first stimulus impacts the way in which the subsequent stimuli are evaluated. Because a monadic test methodology only shows a single stimulus to each participant, the cost for the study can be multiple times that of a sequential monadic study.

A sequential monadic study is advantageous when cost is a concern. Because each respondent is exposed to at least two stimuli, the number of respondents and the cost may be drastically reduced. Another benefit is the speed at which you can gain the desired sample size. With fewer respondents needed, the study will be completed faster. For sequential monadic testing, it's best practice to randomize the order in which the stimuli are presented in order to limit the impact of relative bias.

10.2 Common primary research methodologies

The types of research conducted by and for marketers is boundless. There is the constant emergence of innovative ways to gather and test information. Primary research is research that is conducted by you or specifically on your behalf and built to achieve the goal you're trying to accomplish. In this section we will review some of the most common primary research methodologies that are proven to be useful to marketers.

Surveys

Surveys are what many people think of first when research is mentioned. Within the category of surveys there are numerous ways to ask questions that will provide their own unique results. As a general best practice, keep survey length to at most ten minutes. As the time goes up, the likelihood of completion and gaining quality responses greatly diminishes. Surveys should be used to provide quantitative and statistically significant results.

As mentioned, there is a multitude of ways surveys may be structured. Here are some of the most commonly used question types and formats:

Multiple choice

Ask questions and provide the respondent a list of options to select from. Depending on your question, you may want them to be able to select only one of the listed items or multiple.

Figure 10.2.1 Multiple choice

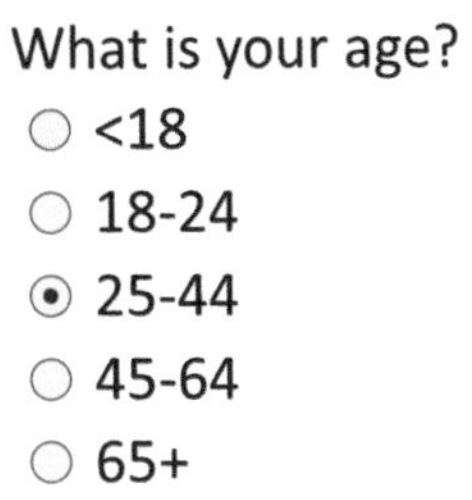

What is your age?
- ○ <18
- ○ 18-24
- ⦿ 25-44
- ○ 45-64
- ○ 65+

Open response

Open response poses a question and respondents are asked to write in their answer.

Figure 10.2.2 Open response

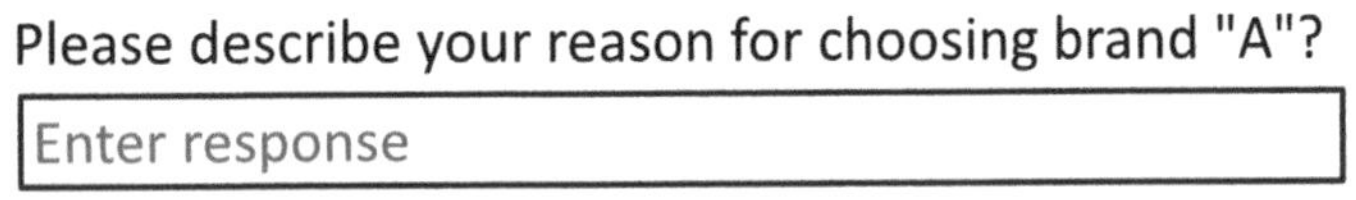

Please describe your reason for choosing brand "A"?

Enter response

Sentiment

Sentiment questions are those that give a prompt or a stimulus for the participant to respond to. For instance, you may show respondents a magazine ad and ask a set of questions regarding their perception of the ad.

Likert scale

A Likert scale may be more simply known as a rating scale. Respondents are asked to give a numerical rating that indicates their level of agreement.

Figure 10.2.3 Likert scale

Please rate the importance of the following features. (1-not at all important, 7-extremely important)

	1	2	3	4	5	6	7
Comfort	○	⦿	○	○	○	○	○
Sound	○	○	○	○	⦿	○	○
Handling	○	○	○	⦿	○	○	○
Price	○	○	○	○	○	○	⦿

Semantic scale

A semantic scale is similar to a Likert scale but with a key difference. A semantic scale question excludes the need for a level of agreement to the question statement. The scale in a semantic question uses a pair of adjectives that are opposites.

Figure 10.2.4 Likert versus semantic

Likert scale
Please rate your level of agreement with the statement: The store was clean. (1-Strongly disagree, 7-Strongly agree)

1	2	3	4	5	6	7
○	⦿	○	○	○	○	○

Semantic scale
What was your impression of the store?

Filthy ○ ○ ○ ○ ⦿ ○ ○ Clean

Force rank

Force rank questions give the participant a list of items to sort through and rank against each other. The key difference between the Likert scale and the force rank is the Likert scale evaluates each item in isolation on a numerical scale, whereas force rank compares the items to each other.

An example is to ask respondents to rank a list of product features from most to least valuable. The major drawback with this methodology is that it doesn't give a relative assessment among the rankings. To further explain, if a list of seven items is presented, maybe only the top two actually matter to respondents and the remaining five are just ranked randomly by respondents. By chance, the average rank of some features in that set of eight may end up at a higher or lower placement. This could lead to the false interpretation that those features are more or less valuable than they really are.

Figure 10.2.5 Force rank

Please rank the importance of the following features. (1-most important, 7-least important)

1 ⊡ Comfort
2 ⊕ Sound
3 ⊕ Handling
4 ⊕ Price
5 ⊕ Acceleration
6 ⊕ Towing
7 ⊡ Off-road capability

Max difference

The max difference question type attempts to create polarization among answer options. In a single question there is typically a set of four options to consider. If there is a pool of ten total options to test, the question may be asked repeatedly with a different set of four randomly selected options. Over the course of many responses this polarization will result in an average rating for each of the options that will be assessed against the others.

Figure 10.2.6 Max difference

Please select which of the following features is most important and least important.

Most important	Least important	
⦿	◯	Comfort
◯	◯	Sound
◯	⦿	Handling
◯	◯	Price

Card sort

Card sorting is a type of question in which a participant is asked to take a prompt, such as a product feature, and place it into one of a set of groups. This type of question is particularly useful when you would like to understand how something is perceived but it doesn't fit into a linear scale or on a single dimension. For instance, in product feature testing there may be two dimensions you are interested in learning about. The first dimension may be how necessary is the feature, and the second dimension may be your expectation for whether or not the feature should be included for free or at a price premium.

Figure 10.2.7 Card sort

Please drag each of the features into the group that classifies it best.

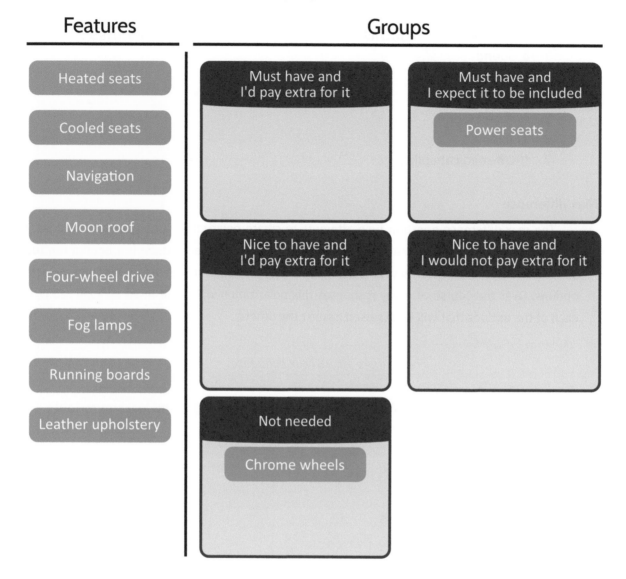

Interviews

Also called IDI (in-depth interview), interviews are the best known and commonly used form of qualitative research. An interview is a real-time open dialogue between a researcher and a participant that affords researchers the opportunity to adjust questioning based on the responses they receive. A benefit of interviews is the depth of knowledge gained from the participant. Conversely, due to the need for real-time dialogue, the amount of time required and the variability in responses prohibit interviews from offering quantitative results.

Focus group

A focus group is like an interview, in that it centers around real-time dialogue. A moderator will ask questions and lead the discussion as an interviewer would, but a focus group is a conversation with multiple participants at the same time in a group setting. A benefit to focus groups is that thoughts may come from multiple sources, which may prompt and further the group discussion in a way that a one-on-one interview may not. Focus groups also allow you to gain more perspectives in less time than an interview.

A benefit but also risk presented by the focus group methodology is the ability of participants to openly converse with each other. This may help provide insights, but if not managed it may derail the session and waste valuable time.

Downsides to focus groups include the likelihood that certain participants dominate the conversation. This may crowd out feedback from other participants as well as lead to the possibility of groupthink. As a moderator you will need to be able to effectively steer and progress the conversation as well as ensure the participation of all respondents.

Heat mapping

This type of research is specific to digital use. Heat maps are most often used on webpages where the scroll, mouse movement, and / or clicks are tracked to show where the most attention on the page is. The heat refers to how the information is displayed. Areas of the pages with more attention are hotter and are shown as red, whereas areas with less attention are considered colder and colored blue.

Eye tracking

Eye tracking is somewhat similar to heat mapping but is more universal in that it may be used for mediums beyond digital. A participant's eye movement is tracked to understand where their focus is in sequence and duration. This type of tracking may range from a magazine article, to a computer screen, to a store shelf.

Data analytics

Data analytics refers to the production of insights through analyzing available data such as customer sales and profiles. Available data may often come from third-party sources such as Google Analytics and advertising platforms. These platforms are particularly useful because they have a broader view of the industry and world than your internal data.

In chapter 11 we will discuss a number of ways that you may garner insights from data. As a marketer, it is expected that you be able to complete many levels of analyses. However, highly complex analyses, such as building predictive models, will likely fall into the realm of data scientists and statisticians. It's likely in your role that you'll need to provide analytics teams guidance regarding the insights and outputs that are useful to you. You may also find yourself in the position of coordinating efforts among the owners of data sources, such as product teams, and the teams that will process the data.

Site design test or user test

Site design testing is a qualitative research methodology to understand how participants interact with and perceive their experience with a digital interface such as a website or application. The participant uses a computer or other device and is given a series of tasks to complete. As participants complete the tasks they are instructed to provide feedback, sharing their perception of the experience. The prompts may be prerecorded, or they may be given live by an administrator.

Pathway and queue observation

In the retail and service industry, understanding how customers navigate and engage with physical locations is vital to delivering a great customer experience. A simple example is to observe customer flow patterns as they navigate their way through a store. To test new experiences, companies with numerous locations will often designate specific stores or markets as test markets. Additionally, it's common for researchers to have simulated store aisles or layouts that are built to mimic the real-life shopping experience.

Pathway and queue observation may be either qualitative or quantitative. An example of qualitative would be to watch video of customers moving throughout the store, noting the patterns that emerge. Quantitative research may manifest itself from gathering data such as average time in queue, average number of customers in queue, and average time in store.

Product use and experience

Product use and experience research will help you better understand the holistic customer journey and the drivers of customer satisfaction. Tracking use and experience over intervals of time can provide valuable insight as product versions are released and consumer perceptions evolve. There are several ways to gain these insights. Here are some of the top methods:

User experience test (UX test)

Tests where you can ask for feedback or observe participants as they use the product or service. As they go through the experience, you will be attempting to understand key milestones, where are their decision, satisfaction, and pain points. The pain points are areas you can target to improve the experience as well as view as an opportunity to innovate.

In-home use test (IHUT)

For various products, particularly in the consumer goods space, you may provide sample products to consumers to try on their own and provide feedback. There is also the potential to request that the study participants allow a researcher to visit their homes to observe use and ask questions.

Beta test

A Beta test is similar to an in-home use test, but fits better within the world of software and technology. A Beta product is developed beyond the minimum point of functionality as it should be a useful product that delivers a positive experience. The Beta version of a product has typically undergone limited testing and may have some less critical features absent. During the Beta test, participants are asked to provide information regarding their experience as well as provide feedback regarding any product bugs.

Product use tracking

Product use tracking is the gathering of data related to use milestones. For example, a company that provides e-commerce software to business owners may track milestones such as how long it takes the business to publish its website, get its first website visit, and make its first sale. Product use tracking may differ from the other types of product use tests in that it does not necessarily require the users' feedback or awareness that the data is being gathered.

Net Promoter Score (NPS)

NPS is a special category of product or service experience research. It specifically asks consumers to rate their experience on a scale of 0 to 10. Zero is the worst score, indicating a poor experience, and 10 is a perfect score, indicating a great experience. The scores are segmented into three groups:

> **Promoters:** 9-10
> **Passive:** 7-8
> **Detractors:** 0-6

NPS is reported as a number from 100 to -100. It is calculated by taking the percentage of promoters, minus the percentage of detractors. The result is then multiplied by 100 to arrive at the NPS.

> NPS = (% of promoters - % of detractors) * 100

NPS scores may be looked at in isolation, but it is best practice to review these scores at a regular cadence and to benchmark against others in the industry. Using a regular cadence allows you to understand how consumers are responding to the product over time as a trend. This will help you identify reasons for concern as well as discern positive effects generated by product developments.

Benchmarking NPS scores is important. While you may strive to have an NPS of 100, it's important to understand how others in your competitive set are doing. Some industries, services, and products are known to be less likely to obtain high NPS ratings. Benchmarking will help you gain perspective relative to others and help you generate realistic goals.

Figure 10.2.8 NPS classifications

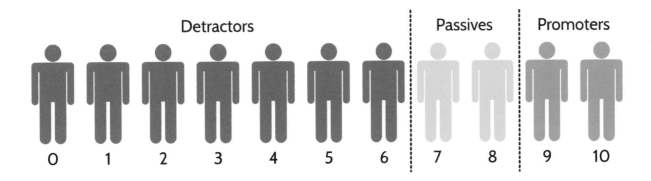

Competitive benchmarking

A basic tenet of any market assessment is to collect information on your competition and substitute products. This information will allow you to benchmark your offerings and determine where points of parity and points of difference exist. Benchmarking may be approached in a variety of ways, each with the potential to deliver a unique set of insights. The method used to gather competitive information will depend on availability, budget, amount of detail, and preference. Here are some of the most common benchmarking methodologies:

Brand health tracking

Brand health tracking may be completed with the goal of understanding varying metrics. The most common health metrics are brand awareness and brand affinity. As discussed in the previous section, awareness is measured in two ways: aided and unaided awareness. Brand affinity refers to the level in which a customer segment feels the brand shares common values. To help understand affinity, a survey may pose the question, "Do you feel that brand "X" is a brand for you?"

The term *tracking* is used to indicate that a brand's health should be measured at regular time intervals. You are tracking the progression of the brand across metrics to view trends. These trends can help you understand the effect of marketing campaigns as well as other factors, such as product innovation or customer service. To gain the most reliable results, questions and the customer segmentation used to select research participants must be consistent.

Promotions, pricing and offers

It's difficult to find a marketing lever that impacts sales and competitive position more than prices and offers. Tracking your brand's and competitive price movements should be a basic, yet important task for any marketer. This tracking over time can provide insights regarding price elasticity. It can reveal your brand's position relative to the competition and potentially unveil opportunities to maximize unit sales, revenue, and / or profit. It may also allow you to find patterns in competitive behaviors, which enable you to anticipate and counter their movements.

Messaging

Similar to the ongoing tracking of competitive pricing and offers, the tracking of how competitors are messaging brands and products may provide strategic insights. You should track messaging across mediums and take note of promotions, core brand messaging, benefit statements, reasons to believe, and product claims.

Market share and financial reporting

You will want to know who is winning and losing in the market. This is done through the use of market share reports, but in cases where these reports are too costly or unavailable, an alternative may be to check your competitors' reports to the SEC (Securities and Exchange Commission). All publicly traded companies are required to file quarterly reports and annual reports. The financials are a good first place to look for insights, but the commentary sections within the text of the reports may provide terrific information. Some companies also hold investor days where they will reveal information regarding their business performance and strategy.

Marketing investment and mediums

Like you, your competitors are looking for ways to effectively market their product or service. And like you, they are likely testing various marketing mediums and investment levels. Monitor channels and take note of how visible your competitors are over time.

For some industries and mediums, vendors exist who can provide competitive levels of spend and share of voice. However, a point of caution: ensure you understand and trust the methodology used by your vendor. Estimating and aggregating spend levels is difficult, so you must use a vendor that you are confident will provide reliable data.

Performance testing

It's highly likely that you will be in competition with similar if not nearly identical competitive products and services. As a diligent marketer acting in partnership with your product or R&D team, you should test your products as well as competitive products. This testing should help you better understand the customer experience and find points of parity as well as points of differentiation. This understanding will help you know exactly where your strengths lie, so that you can tout them. Conversely, you can be prepared to counter any customer objections where your product may fall inferior to the competition. Training sales teams on these strengths and counter points will be vital to their success.

There is no standard way to complete performance testing. For instance, with a product you may test power, comfort, and durability. For services you may check average time in queue. It is your responsibility along with the product teams to build the appropriate tests, considering what matters to your customer segment.

The amount of information readily available on the internet in the form of product reviews is tremendous. These reviews can have a profound effect on your ability to gain consideration. Reviews on third-party sales sites such as amazon.com as well as review sites should be consistently monitored. They will help you understand the perception of your products as well as provide insights into how competitive products are perceived.

Reviews

The amount of information readily available on the internet in the form of product reviews is tremendous. These reviews can have a profound effect on your ability to gain consideration. Reviews on third-party sales sites such as amazon.com as well as review sites should be consistently monitored. They will help you understand the perception of your products as well as provide insights into how competitive products are perceived.

When benchmarking against competitors it's easy to assume they are doing things well. That assumption may tempt you to copy them. If you are considering copying the competition, do so with caution, particularly if you are in a market leadership position. By definition, copying a competitor will at best net you at parity. Additionally, be particularly cautious of reacting to pricing actions. Price wars are often lose / lose situations with the potential to cause problems ranging from irreversible brand damage to low industry profitability.

Concept test

A concept is an idea for a product or service that solves a customer need. Concepts can be generated to introduce ideas for innovation as well as be used as a way to introduce new positioning for a product or service. Expertise in concept creation is a highly desirable skill for marketers tasked with developing innovation.

The format of concepts may differ based on the preference of the writers and testers. Concepts are best kept succinct and simple. They may be just written as a text description or may have a combination of text, imagery, and in some cases be presented with a tangible product. Here is a simple example of a concept that may be used for a new bodywash variant.

Figure 10.2.9 Product concept

New Espresso Martini Bodywash

Customer need:
> I wake up in the morning feeling groggy and dreading the day.

Benefit:
> Uplift your day with New Espresso Martini Bodywash.

Reasons to believe:
> The invigorating espresso martini fragrance wakes you with the thoughts of having fun with friends.
> Infused with menthol to energize your skin and body.

All concepts should be written with the benefit and RTBs directly linking to the customer need. In this example the benefit of uplifting the customer's day solves the problem of grogginess and dread. The RTBs are directly tied to the benefit by explaining how this bodywash can deliver on the promised benefit.

Learning to write good concepts can take time and practice. An extremely common pitfall is to get distracted by appealing features that don't directly link to the need or benefit. For this bodywash example, maybe the bodywash contains an ingredient that moisturizes the customers' skin. While this ingredient is great, it doesn't directly solve the customer need and deviates from the benefit statement. Mixing the benefit and RTBs can confuse customers or cause them to think the product isn't really built to solve their need. Conversely, when testing concepts, the inclusion of several benefits into a single benefit statement or combining multiple RTBs and calling them one may make the product score well. The problem is, it's unknown why the product scored well because messages are mixed and the source of the positive reaction is difficult to discern. When the product combo message is put into marketing channels, the effectiveness becomes diminished because real-life customers don't concentrate on ads or on trying to understand product concepts.

Developing and writing a concept

> **Customer segment and need:** A concept should start with a focus on a specific customer segment. For that segment begin with a problem statement or what is also known as a cus-

tomer need statement. This statement defines the customer need or problem. The statement should be concise and specific. When selecting a target customer segment, consider the opportunity size as well as the appeal of your brand to this segment. Can you expect these customers to purchase your brand?

> **Product name:** State the proposed customer facing name of the product.

> **Benefit statement:** A benefit statement should be single-minded. Each concept needs to center on a single core solution that the product or service will provide. Forcing yourself to focus on only one idea can feel restrictive but is necessary to deliver a consistent and straightforward message to customers. To illustrate the importance of this, think of a highway billboard. If you have someone's attention for one or two seconds as they drive by, ask yourself, "What message should they receive?" Similarly, ads on social feeds need singular focus as they garner only a split second of a user's divided attention.

The benefit needs to be rooted in the consumers' goal and explain how this product or service will accomplish the goal in its differentiated way. As we've discussed, the benefit should be focused and single-minded, but it may contain a couple of elements. The benefit can address the outcome as well as how the outcome is achieved. For example, the benefit statement for a product targeted at small businesses is, "the easiest way to grow." The outcome is growth for the small business, and how they get there with this product or service is the easiest way. Be careful to keep the benefit statement linear and single-minded. Do not allow multiple outcomes or multiple ways of achieving that outcome to enter into your concept.

> **Reasons to believe (RTBs):** RTBs support the benefit by providing evidence of how the product or service can believably deliver the stated benefit. The RTB must directly ladder up to the benefit. For example, for a heart healthy cereal an RTB could be that it contains eight grams of fiber. Each RTB should be written as a simple statement in at most two sentences. Focus on how compelling the statement is to the target customer. When writing each RTB reread it and ask yourself, "Does this statement or claim directly and logically support the benefit?" As discussed in the previous bodywash example, it is easy to mistakenly include RTBs that aren't in direct support of the benefit.

Each concept should contain approximately two to five RTBs. The goal is to strongly support the benefit while not overwhelming the customer with information. To more effectively communicate, it is possible for RTBs to be in the form of an image or short video. The only times imagery or video should be tested as part of a concept is if they can be used in promotional messaging.

Testing concepts

During the process of concepting, it's likely that multiple distinct ideas are generated. It's best practice to test three to five concepts and compare the results. If you are working through a research vendor, it is helpful to get their perspective on how the tested concepts compare to other concepts that have been tested in the same or similar industries.

Testing of the concepts is commonly completed as a monadic study. This is to limit the respondent fatigue that is created by the number of questions and thoughtfulness required for the evaluation of a single concept. The monadic methodology also prevents the bias that is made possible by presenting multiple concepts for comparison.

The benefit statements and RTBs should be tested as part of the full concept but should also be individually tested. This is done for two primary reasons:

> To understand the strength of each individual statement. For instance, you may find that of the three RTBs tested as support for your top concept, one is poorly received, while the other two compensate enough to make the overall concept a winner.

> To learn the strength of statements (benefit, RTBs) regardless of the concept they are associated with. This can lead to insights that may help you to recognize a new customer segment or help you refine the winning concept.

In addition to the concept, it may be beneficial to include pertinent information about the product or service as background information for the study's participants. Pertinent information may include table stake features that consumers require but can't assume is included in the product. If this information is not included as background in the study, the participant may question the inclusion of these items and it may detract from the evaluation of the concept.

It is best practice to complete a qualitative study of the concepts prior to doing a full-scale quantitative study. A qualitative study is less costly and can provide a more in-depth level of feedback that may help reveal common concept pitfalls such as:

> A confusing concept

> A concept that is too abstract or revolutionary, which consumers won't understand

> Missing background information that a consumer needs in order to usefully evaluate the concept

> A concept that is too good to be true that creates skepticism

> Including a concept that is inferior compared to the others or compared to consumer expectations

Concepts, benefit statements, and RTBs should be measured across all or a selection of several different metrics:

> Purchase intent / interest (primary metric)

> Appeal

> Uniqueness

> Believability

> Relevance

> Persuasion

In addition to the metrics listed, it is also beneficial to get open-ended feedback regarding the concepts to understand the rationale behind the concept ratings.

As you develop the study, there are a couple of decisions that must be made that can significantly impact purchase intent:

> Should the price be included with the concept?

> Do the participants have sufficient knowledge regarding the market, alternative solutions, and their prices?

The qualitative step in your research can help to inform the answers to these questions. You can then adjust as needed prior to the quantitative study.

Bringing the concept to life

Following the determination of a winning concept, you'll be eager to get the idea into market. Concepts and customer-facing creative assets are related but substantially different things. The concept is the foundational idea that needs to be portrayed via the creative message. Creative messages are built on the foundation of the concept, but tailored to fit requirements of specific mediums such as paid search ads, television, and print. Each medium may perform best with slightly different imagery or wording that is learned through testing and optimization. Each medium may also differ in how audiences are segmented, allowing for either more or less targeting precision. Despite the differences among mediums, the foundation of the message should be based on the concept and be consistent.

Potential weaknesses of concept tests

There are three substantial issues to be cognizant of when reacting to the insights generated by a concept test:

> In the vast majority of tests, the concept is written and does not give the customer the ability to see or experience the product. To address the issue, product use tests or in-home use tests may be beneficial to field and link to your concept.

> The issue of isolation refers to the lack of competitive alternatives available for consideration during the research study. The concept is favorably presented, it is top of mind, and it is assumed that respondents will adequately weigh the concept against the available substitutes. To objectively weigh the concept is difficult. To help understand this issue's prevalence you may choose to benchmark against competitive concepts.

> As previously mentioned, respondents will be focused on the concept, with a desire to understand it and give feedback. In real-life situations, customers receiving advertisement messages will not have the same level of concentration or interest.

Bear in mind the results of the concept test will give you a directional view of predicted customer behavior. Reality will most likely differ, but can differ in either a negative or positive direction. Your diligence in test setup will drive the accuracy of the test.

Conjoint test

Conjoint tests are done to understand the value of features, bundles of features, and tiering. They are used by marketers when there is a need to set or reset pricing and features for a product or service. Tiering may refer to bundled solutions such as the good, better, best, lineups but may also be used to refer to tiers within features such as the amount of storage a computer hard drive contains.

Conjoint studies are highly sophisticated and are best completed by researchers with expertise in the methodology. Due to the complexity and sophistication of conjoint studies, expect them to be both expensive and long in project duration.

Conjoint studies ask respondents to place a value and price on features otherwise known as willingness to pay. This information is valuable to understand how to price and bundle products. However, a weakness of conjoint studies, and why expertise is so important, is that stated willingness to pay is often overestimated as respondents are hypothetically spending money. In real life their habits are unlikely to match the hypothetical situation.

Multidimensional scaling

Multidimensional scaling is an analysis that allows us to visualize similarities and dissimilarities in response data. This is a methodology that measures each individual case, respondent, or instance along a pair of variables. Multidimensional scaling is the underpinning analysis for a research-based perceptual map.

Figure 10.2.10 Perceptual map

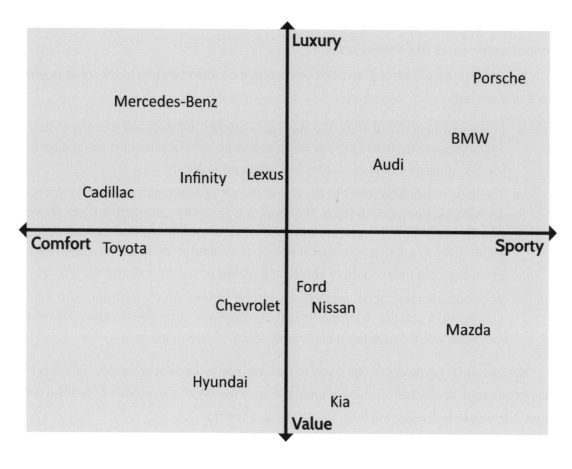

In this hypothetical perceptual map, individual survey responses would have been analyzed to inform the placement of each brand considering the attributes on the X and Y axes. Statistical software is best utilized to run these analyses, and as part of that analysis they can provide regression statistics that inform the strength and validity of the placements.

Sales and customer support feedback

Research is often thought of as going out and getting direct feedback from customers. Sales teams and customer support teams have frequent interaction with customers and can be an invaluable source of information. Within these groups you can practice different methodologies to gather information, from surveys, to interviews, to focus groups. You may also take a pre-planned approach by requesting they ask certain questions of customers, then the teams can report their findings back to you. When building a research plan, don't underestimate their potential to contribute to the project.

10.3 Common secondary research sources

Secondary research is research that is conducted by a third party and made available to marketers such as yourself, typically for a fee. While secondary research may be highly useful and time saving, there are two distinct downsides. First, the research was not built to answer your precise questions. You may be able to glean the insight you hope, but it may prove difficult. The second downside is the lack of exclusivity. Secondary research is conducted by a third party that will sell the information to you as well as to your competition. The insights that you are able to gather may be exactly the same as your competitors, thus rendering you in a position of parity.

General internet research

When conducting research, the first and easiest method is to simply do a search of the internet. As with all information available on the internet, it should be vetted by you for its reliability. Another common pitfall of internet research is the likelihood of hitting paywalls. Sites with research reports and quality information want to charge for that information, so if you aren't willing to pay, you may end up wasting a lot of time scouring the internet.

Industry reports

Industry reports are available for virtually every industry. They offer in-depth analysis of current and past market information, trends, as well as growth projections. These reports can be several hundred pages long and cost thousands of dollars for access.

Blogs and review sites

Typically found through a general internet search, blogs and review sites are particularly interesting to marketers for two reasons. First, the sites are often built for monetary reasons. The blog or review site was built to gain compensation for any sale or lead they provide to companies mentioned on their site. As you research, do you think this is a site that you want to partner with? The second interesting aspect of these sources is the rampant bias due to the pay-to-play nature of the blogs or sites. Companies that pay more per lead will get more favorable placement on the site. As you research these sites recognize the potential for bias, but also understand that these sites do impact customer perception. Some customers may not recognize the bias, and even if they do, they may still be influenced.

10.4 Common marketing research goals

Marketers are responsible for a vast array of strategic business decisions. Marketing research should serve as the foundation to form recommendations and decisions. Due to the wide variety of marketing responsibilities, no list of marketing research goals can be exhaustive. In this section we will discuss a variety of the most common and important marketing research goals.

Customer segmentation / customer personas

Customer segmentation

A customer segment is a group of customers who can be grouped together based on their characteristics. These characteristics can be any combination of demographic, psychographic, or geographic characteristics that may affect their behavior as a customer and consumer. In chapter 3 we introduced customer segmentation and discussed the following characteristics in which segments can be defined:

> **Descriptors ("who")** - Demographic information such as age, income, education, family status, and profession.

> **Bases ("why")** - Psychographic and anthropological information such as needs, preferences, and lifestyle.

> **Behaviors ("what")** - Actions such as product experience, sources of information, loyalty, or offer seeking.

> **External ("where")** - Factors driven by location such as country, community, terrain, or weather.

> **Time ("when")** - Life stages and timeliness such as graduating from college, having a baby, or launching a business.

In that chapter we also discussed the need for segments to meet the following criteria in order to be useful:

> **The segments are distinct** - The customers within the group should be similar, and there should be little overlap with other groups.

> **The segments are operational** - The segment should be identifiable and accessible in marketing channels.

> **The segments are engaging** - Marketing communication to the segment should be able to connect with the customers in an impactful and engaging manner.

> **The segments are substantial** - The segment is large enough to be compelling from a revenue and / or profit perspective.

Customer segments can be created through the use of a number of methodologies. To reliably construct customer segments, you will need quantitative data with a sample size large enough to permit cross-tabulation across several variables. Those variables should align with the characteristics previously discussed. It's advised to complete customer segmentation with the guidance of experienced researchers and statisticians. Advanced statistical software can be used to complete cluster analyses that will process and cross-tabulate data, looking for similarities in the sample to build segments. The use of multidimensional scaling can aid with to completion of analyses that will place the segments onto a perceptual map.

Customer personas

A persona differs from a customer segment in that it doesn't describe a group of customers but rather personifies a customer segment and serves as a way to bring a customer segment to life. A customer persona is manifested by a fictional person who could be someone that you would meet in real life. The persona is given a name and assigned characteristics that depict the customer segment. This fictional person will serve as the representative for a given customer segment. Here is an example of a customer persona for a customer segment that is interested in getting a website to support his business.

Figure 10.4.1 Customer persona

Website customer persona - Novice Nick

Nick Hernandez
Anaheim, California, U.S.A.

Entrepreneur baker who owns a bakery and catering service with four full-time employees. He loves baking and enjoys being his own boss, but he struggles with the business side of being an entrepreneur.

Situation:
Nick knows he needs a website in order to market and expand his business. He is not confident with tech and doesn't know where to begin.

Plans:
- Go online and search how to get a website
- Wants to build the site himself to save money
- Wants to get the website listed on Google and Yelp

Quote from Nick:
"Every customer I talk to tells me how much they love my product but they want to be able to see my menu and order online. I need a website but have no idea where to begin."

Photo by fran hogan on Unsplash

Need: A website

Budget: $50 per month

Price Sensitivity: Medium

Top product needs:
1. Guidance and support
2. Ease of use
3. Marketing tools
4. Maintenance tools

Cross-purchase:
1. Domain name
2. Email

In addition to the research conducted to develop customer segments, persona development should always include interviews as one of the research methodologies. Please note that it is a mistake to use a single customer story to craft a persona. While the persona will tell the story of one customer, the story should be representative of all customers within the segment.

Shopper behavior

Marketers are often stereotyped as the function that drums up demand. While it's not the only function of marketing, generating demand is critical and understanding shopper behavior is needed for success. In chapter 14 we will discuss some ways in which shopper behavior is depicted and communicated, such as a shopper funnel or decision journey map. There is a myriad of ways to gather information about shopper behavior.

Common research methodologies

- Surveys
- Interviews
- Focus groups
- Heat mapping

- Data analytics
- Pathway and queue observation
- Sales and customer support feedback

Customer journey

One of the most critical roles fulfilled by marketers is to understand and capitalize on their expert knowledge of the customer journey. In chapter 8 we introduced journey maps and discussed the customer journey map in detail. In chapter 14 we will delve into the topic of acquiring customers through promotion and advertising and will discuss the decision journey map as well as introduce the customer journey loop.

Common research methodologies

- Surveys
- Interviews
- Focus groups
- Heat mapping

- Data analytics
- Pathway and queue observation
- Sales and customer support feedback
- Product use and experience

Message effectiveness

Prior to investing funds on marketing campaigns, it is useful to research the effectiveness of the messages that will be used. These messages include things such as claims, reasons to believe, benefit statements, value propositions, visuals, videos, as well as specific ads that could be ready to launch. Maximizing the effectiveness of a message will help to reduce cost, limit the risk of lost sales, and help protect against the possibility of negative customer reaction.

Common research methodologies

- Surveys
- Interviews
- Focus groups
- Concept test
- Sales and customer support feedback

Claim substantiation

Claims can be the keystone of a powerful marketing message, but as discussed in chapter 8, claims must be substantiated to reduce the risk of lawsuits and challenges. As a marketing professional your role may range from gathering data to support substantiation, to coordinating efforts with colleagues in research and development or engineers. These colleagues often understand regulatory requirements and are those who can gather test data to support a claim. If a claim is a perception claim such as "9 out of 10 doctors recommend product XYZ," you may lead research such as a survey to substantiate the claim.

Substantiation should adhere to industry requirements and should be approved for use by legal counsel. Documentation should be kept and updated at regular intervals as suggested by the legal counsel or as required by regulations.

Brand and product perception

There is a classic saying in marketing: "Perception is reality." You could have an amazing product, but if the perception of your brand or products is negative, they won't sell. A very simple example is when a brand is boycotted for political reasons. The perception of the brand is tarnished, and sales are negatively impacted without a product-based reason.

Most times the perception and its influence on the success of brands or products isn't as obvious as the boycott example. Differences in perception may exist between customer segments, or maybe it's a seemingly small aspect of a product that may impact perception enough to crater sales due to high competition. Therefore, conducting research to understand perception is vital.

Perception studies will help you understand key aspects of your brand such as its perceived quality, prestige, or its relatability to a customer segment. Brand equity and likewise perception are incredibly difficult to build and change. As a marketer you must understand how your brand and product is perceived, and if a shift is desired, you should be cognizant of the difficulty and the investment required to complete the shift.

Brand awareness

For customers to perceive your brand they must first be aware of your brand. This is called "brand awareness." Within brand awareness there are two types: aided awareness and unaided awareness. Aided awareness is found by giving a research participant a list of brands, and then asking which of them provide a product or service. To find unaided awareness the respondent would be asked the same question, but is not given the list of brands to choose from.

A survey is most commonly used to research brand perception and awareness. It is best practice to build these surveys so that they are repeatable. You may then field the survey at regular intervals, which allows you to understand how perception and awareness evolve over time.

Industry and competitive landscape

To build a sound strategy, marketers need to understand the current state of their industry as well as where it is heading. An important aspect of understanding the industry is to assess competitors, substitutes, and complements. The information gathered through industry research should be fed into any of the various frameworks we discussed in chapter 9, such as the SWOT analysis.

Common research methodologies

- Surveys of consumers
- Surveys of partners (e.g., retailers)
- Focus groups

- Competitive benchmarking
- Sales and customer support feedback
- Industry reports

Create a new product idea

While the development of the next big innovation may be through luck, it's much more likely that it will require a unique understanding of the customer need. Researching the behavior of consumers, mapping their journey, and understanding their pain points will help you create a winning innovation. An additional aspect to the research is to understand the value of the innovation and the various functions or features of the product.

Common research methodologies

- Surveys
- Interviews
- Focus groups
- Data analytics
- Pathway and queue observation
- Product use and experience
- Concept test

- Conjoint test
- Multidimensional scaling
- Sales and customer support feedback
- General internet research
- Industry reports
- Blogs and review sites

Validate a product idea

Once a new product innovation is identified and feasibility is confirmed, customer interest for the idea should be validated. The most common way to gauge interest is by fielding a concept test. The concept test presents the idea to customers and renders you feedback to help you understand how well the innovation resonates. Concept tests ask customers to provide feedback across a number of dimensions, such as uniqueness and purchase intent. In the section 2 of this chapter we reviewed all of the dimensions typically measured. Some research companies have the capability to deliver an estimate of sales potential based on the results of a concept test. One most notable is the BASES test administered by the company Nielsen.

Design tests

The testing of designs can manifest in numerous ways. For instance, with physical goods a design test may consist of package and label tests. This will help you understand how impactful the design is at attracting customer interest and subsequently its effectiveness in converting a sale.

Alternatively, in the digital space, webpages or ads may be tested for visual appeal, persuasiveness, and usability. In the digital realm, designs can be tested as sample research studies, but they may also be done with real customers using A / B tests. Some examples of the desired outcomes are lower bounce rates, higher conversion, and higher average order size.

Finally, in the physical retail and service industries, design can be tested in a number of ways, including the layout of a space, the order in which tasks are performed, décor and ambiance, employee presentation, etc. These providers will want to measure changes in conversion, time in queue, spend, and satisfaction among other metrics.

Common research methodologies

- Surveys
- Focus groups
- Heat mapping
- Eye tracking
- Pathway and queue observation
- Product use and experience

User experience (UX) tests and product use tests

User experience and product use testing is done to understand how consumers interact with a product or service. These tests will reveal positive and negative aspects of the product as well as potentially offer insights that lead to innovation. These tests can culminate in the creation of customer journey maps, which are a useful tool to communicate opportunities for improvement.

Common research methodologies

- Surveys
- Interviews
- Pathway and queue observation
- Product use and experience

Understanding cancelation and lapsed purchase

Sales to loyal customers and recurring subscription sales are highly desired as they are typically the most profitable and create a dependable baseline level of volume and revenue. These profitable sales contribute to your ability to invest in marketing and grow the business. Due to the important nature of these customers, you will need to understand why they cancel subscriptions or lapse from their normal purchase cycle. In addition to learning about why customers have left, you will likely also learn how to improve the experience of current customers.

Common research methodologies

- Surveys
- Interviews
- Product use and experience
- Sales and customer support feedback

Which features to include and how to price and bundle

To maximize product appeal, revenue, profit, and / or sales volume, it's crucial to have the right combination of features and bundled products available at the right price. Most marketers are faced with extreme competition where the differences between their products and competitive products are minute. The failure to include a feature could remove your product from consideration thus plummeting sales and potentially causing detriment to your brand's reputation. However, the inverse may be true if you can create a supremely appealing product offering.

Common research methodologies

- Surveys
- Interviews
- Focus groups
- Data analytics
- Product use and experience
- Competitive benchmarking
- Conjoint test

Predict customer behavior

The ability to anticipate customer behavior can put you at an advantage versus the competition. You'll be able to maximize relevance and budget efficiencies by tailoring promotions and offers. Predictive models may be built using data analytics. A simple example could be the knowledge that people who visit a product page on your website for over two minutes are highly interested shoppers. But models can be extremely complex and require analytical expertise as well as advanced statistical software that can process dozens, if not hundreds of variables.

10.5 Creating a research plan

To efficiently and properly conduct research, you should create a plan that will guide you and other key stakeholders through the process. Completing this plan at the onset of the research project will help drive alignment to the goal and define the process. This can act as a reference point during the research as undoubtedly new questions will arise with the potential to distract from the goal and cause scope creep. The research plan should contain the following elements:

- Goal
- Output
- High-level questions
- Scope
- Involved parties
- Research methodology
- Research subjects
- Steps and timing
- Budget

Now let's dive into each of the elements in greater detail.

Goal

Every research project should have a clearly stated goal. The goal is the highest level of insight you want to achieve. An example could be to understand the shopping journey of the young professional customer segment.

Output

The research output refers to the format of how the results will be presented and summarized. In the example of understanding the shopping journey of the young professionals, the output could be a decision journey map.

High-level questions

To help guide the line of questioning in the research study, a few high-level questions may prove incredibly useful. These questions will help to ensure that as the study's questionnaire is developed, it stays aimed at delivering on the goal. The focus on the goal will also aid with avoiding question proliferation, as discussed earlier excessively long studies will cause respondent fatigue.

In the shopping journey example, a high-level question may be, "Where does this customer segment conduct their research prior to purchase?" To contrast this high-level question with one that may be in a survey, the associated survey question may be, "From the following list, which of the information sources did you utilize prior to making your purchase?" Then a follow-up question may be, "Of the options you selected, which was the most influential and why?"

Scope

Establishing and adhering to a scope for research projects is of vital importance. It will allow you to properly plan and execute the research on time and within budget. Equally important, it will set specific expectations for the research project and help stakeholders to understand the need for subsequent research if further investigation is desired. Some of the items that should be included in the scope include the following:

- Region

- Customer segment
- Test frequency: one-time versus a recurring study

Involved parties

From the onset of the research project, you should ensure that all key stakeholders and decision makers are involved. The level of involvement of each stakeholder will differ by organization and project. You as the leader of the research project must take care to coordinate this up front, otherwise you risk disagreement on the goal and increase the chance of stakeholders questioning the validity of the study.

Research methodology

In a research plan, one methodology may suffice but often research projects will require multiple steps and methodologies. For instance, the validation approach to research will utilize at least two methodologies.

Research subjects

Determine and document who will be the participants in your research study. This should also include an estimate of the number of participants you will require for each research methodology. As you complete this section, consider how the results will be cross-tabulated. For instance, if you anticipate the desire to compare shoppers in your study by age bracket, you will need to have at least a minimum sample size in each bracket to allow for the opportunity to gain statistically significant results.

Steps and timing

Document the steps of the process and the timing. This should include the setup and fielding of each research methodology, time to process the data, and date the results will be ready for review.

Budget

After completing the previously listed aspects of the plan, you will be able to create a budget to complete the project.

10.6 Delivering insights

After fielding your research and gathering the data, the next steps are to analyze the data and translate it into actionable insights. As you go through this process, refer back to your research plan to ensure that you are answering the key questions as well as achieving the research goal.

Use quality data

As you prepare your data for analysis it is vital to ensure only good data is used. There's a well-known saying used by analysts and statisticians when referring to data and results: "Garbage in, garbage out." This saying means that without quality data, there is no way to get valid insights.

There are a few major indicators of bad data that you should check for as you prepare for analysis:

- **Test completion time** - Respondents completed the survey at an unreasonably fast speed. It demonstrates they are not taking care to give quality answers.

- **Answer patterns** - Refers to respondents who simply just answer the same way for every question. For instance, they click the answer in the first position for every question.

- **Incompletions** - These are results that are returned without a full set of data. This may be due to the respondent quitting the study early, which may indicate a lack of quality feedback.

- **Outliers** - Outliers are data points that are oddly incongruent with the rest of the data set and may skew analysis metrics. For example, there may be a question that asks respondents to enter their salary. While nearly all respondents answered in the $40,000-$60,000 range, there is one respondent who answered $5,000,000. That single response may skew the average salary higher, yielding a misleading metric, so the data point should be removed.

Stated action versus real action

The phenomenon that is commonly seen in marketing is the difference between the rational versus the real customer. Rational customers are those who act with perfect information and in alignment with logic. Real customers, however, have incomplete information, biases, urgency, and emotions that impact their purchase decisions.

In research, this phenomenon is relevant when a respondent states a planned action during a research study, but then in real-life circumstances takes a different action. There are some common ways in which this manifests itself.

- **Willingness to pay** - In research studies, respondents are often less price sensitive and will claim that they are willing to pay more for items than is the case in real life. Additionally, if asked how important price or an offer is, respondents will often understate its true influence on their purchase decisions.

- **Resistance to persuasion and bias** - Respondents to research studies are often much more rational than in real-life situations. Respondents take care to emphasize objectivity and resistance to marketing messages while they are being "tested" in a research study. However, in real life, time, biases, emotions, influences, and persuasive marketing messages can alter that previously stated logical behavior.

Knowing that there is a difference between stated and real action should not dissuade you from conducting marketing research. It should, however, be a consideration as you plan studies and review results. When implementing research learnings and going to market, it should factor into your expectations.

Make it actionable

During the planning phase of the research, you defined a goal for the project. Your delivery of the research findings should unequivocally achieve your goal. In your achievement of that goal and as you answer the key research questions, don't just answer the what, but also answer the "so what." The "so what" is your recommendation of what should be done based on the insights that you've gained. These recommendations are an opportunity to demonstrate your ability to think strategically and drive the business. When presenting your results and recommendations, be prepared for people to challenge them. This discussion is healthy and is an opportunity to show colleagues that you can think critically and provide valuable strategic insight to the organization.

Anticipate questions

When you prepare your presentation of the research results, you should anticipate and be ready to answer questions. To help you prepare for a broader presentation, it may be beneficial to present the findings to a smaller group of colleagues who can provide feedback and ask questions.

A very common type of question is for people to ask how a sub-segment of the presented sample answered the question and if it was significantly different from other segments. For instance, in a research study of women's shopping behavior, it may be asked how mothers responded to the question versus women college students without children. If you can anticipate these questions it may be beneficial to provide such information in an appendix to your presentation.

Don't be surprised if questions are asked that fall outside the scope of your research. Remind the group that the goal of the research was to answer a hypothesis and that their question may be best answered in subsequent research. Lastly, don't feel that all research needs to present an amazing a-ha moment where the results deliver an insight that no one has seen before and challenges conventional thinking. In many organizations research has been done prior to yours, and if that research is valid, it should be the case that your conclusions align with what was found in the past. The goal is that you have generated incremental insights building on past results.

Note, in the leadership and business etiquette chapter, we will further discuss how to effectively create and deliver a presentation.

10.7 Statistical analysis

In this section we will review some basic information regarding statistical analyses and how to properly interpret them. We will not go into the details of how to conduct these various analyses as entire semesters of college-level coursework are required to gain proficiency. If you encounter a situation where you are unable to complete a statistical analysis, find a colleague or vendor with expertise to assist. To take these on without training is not only extremely difficult, but also a potential trap for drawing the wrong conclusions.

Null and alternative hypotheses

The word *hypothesis* is often used as a fancy word to refer to a research question. However, in the statistical realm the term *hypothesis* has a specific meaning and usage.

The hypotheses for a research question have two categories: the null hypothesis and the alternative hypothesis. The easiest way to demonstrate the difference between the two is to analogously compare the two outcomes of a criminal trial. The null hypothesis is the assumption that the criminal is assumed to be not guilty or innocent. The alternative hypothesis is similar to the decision of guilty in that it will need to be proven beyond a reasonable doubt. In statistics, the reasonable doubt is judged by the level of statistical significance.

A common marketing application of the null versus an alternative hypothesis is a test of two webpages. The existing webpage is known as the control side of the test and would be referred to as the null hypothesis. The alternative hypothesis would refer to a new test version of the webpage where alterations were made with the intention of producing a better result. To prove that the test page is better than the control page, it will need to produce a result that is better by a statistically significant margin.

Statistical significance

Measuring and understanding statistical significance are extremely important when interpreting data and results. In the absence of statistical analysis, it is easy to draw conclusions on merely directional results, which can lead to bad recommendations and bad strategic decisions. Here are some the of terms you should be familiar with and how they are used:

- **Population** - The entire segment of people that the test sample uses to establish an understanding of.

- **Sample** - A subset of the population that is researched.

- **Variance** - The amount of difference between the individual sample data points and the overall average. A high level of variance is characterized by data points that are scattered widely away from the average. Conversely, low variance is when the data points are closer to the average. Variance impacts the ability of results to reach statistical significance. A wider variation in the data makes it more difficult to reach significance because there's less uniformity and predictability.

- **Confidence interval aka interval estimate** - The range of values that is estimated to contain the result of the total population. For example, if you had a test sample that averaged a 10% higher conversion rate than the control, you may have a confidence interval that ranges from 2% to 20%. The range indicates the expected population outcome within the level of certainty required by the confidence level. These intervals exist because the sample data is a predictor of the population, as it is not perfectly accurate.

- **Margin of error** - This is the number of percentage points above or below the point estimate. It leaves room for error to include the point at which the actual population result would lie. In the confidence interval example, the point estimate is 10% and the margin of error above is 10% (20% to 10%) and the margin of error below is 8% (10% to 2%).

- **Confidence level** - The confidence level is the required level of certainty that the confidence interval range will include the actual result of the total population. Confidence levels usually range from 90-99%, and most often a 95% confidence level is used. In a given analysis, the higher the confidence level, the wider the confidence interval. A lower confidence level has a tighter confidence interval. This is because in order to be more confident you are correct, you need to allow for a broader range of outcomes.

- **P-value** - A p-value is the probability metric used to determine whether or not to reject the null hypothesis. The lower the p-value, the stronger the evidence is to reject the null hypothesis. For a confidence interval of 95%, a p-value of less than 0.05 would indicate statistical significance. For a confidence interval of 99%, a p-value of less than 0.01 would indicate statistical significance. Note that for a two-tailed statistical test, the p-values need to be halved: 0.05 to 0.025 and 0.01 to 0.005. In this text we will not delve into the intricacies of a 1-tail versus a 2-tailed test.

Top box scores

A research result often used with marketing research is top box and top two box score. The box term is used to describe the number or percent of respondents who answered a question in a certain way. For example, a survey question asks respondents to score the appeal of a feature on a scale from 1 to 5, one is least appealing to five is most appealing. The top box score would be the percentage of respondents who rated a feature a five. The top two box score would be the percentage of respondents who rated the feature a four or five.

Causation vs. correlation

When evaluating statistics, a common error is to mistake causation for correlation. Correlation is the relationship between two things happening in tandem consistently. Causation is when two things happen in tandem consistently, but the relationship is due to one of those things impacting the other. Correlation may exist despite no relationship between the two things that happen in tandem, it's merely coincidence.

Here's a real example of where correlation and causation were confused. An email marketer found that when he sent emails to larger contact lists, he achieved higher sales. That seemed to make logical sense, so the email marketer recommended the company purchase contact lists in order to increase the number of emails that were sent out. When these contact lists were utilized, the sales did not materialize. This was despite the fact the lists were vetted, quality leads. The email marketer's conclusion that a larger list produced more sales appeared incorrect.

Upon further review of the original email data, it was discovered that when the larger email lists were used, it was in service of promoting better and more aggressive offers. The larger contact lists were correlated to higher sales, but the higher sales were actually caused by more aggressive offers, not the size of the lists.

CHAPTER 11: INSIGHTS THROUGH ANALYTICS

Data comes in a variety of forms and sizes, and the list of potential data sources is virtually endless. Regardless of the data type or the source, it is your responsibility as a marketing professional to be able to derive insights and use them to guide strategic decisions. In this chapter we will discuss best practices to track and understand data, as well as how to systematically perform a business analysis.

11.1 Data integrity

In the previous chapter we introduced the importance of data integrity or data quality and shared the ever relevant saying, "garbage in, garbage out." The first step in any data analysis is to ensure that the data used is of good quality. If not, don't waste your time and encourage others to do the same. Move on to other projects that will progress the business forward. Unfortunately, it often happens that companies and marketers cling to any available data even if they know a data source is incorrect. They just hope that it will give them some comfort in knowing directionally what is happening. With bad data, that directional understanding could be completely wrong and drive bad decision making on top of wasted time on analyses. Don't be one of the people who shares data and includes a disclaimer that the data is suspect. Be an advocate of finding a source of good data, and until that source is ready, focus on more fruitful tasks.

Another common issue related to data analytics is the availability of multiple data sources that provide similar information. Multiple data sources are unlikely to precisely match, which can cause disagreement. This disagreement can confuse stakeholders and create a multitude of unnecessary questions and follow-up analyses. To alleviate this issue, a single good data source must be proclaimed as the "source of truth".

11.2 Key performance indicators (KPIs)

Key performance indicators are metrics that help measure the health of a business. These measures may be across both financial and non-financial goals. KPIs are often communicated via dashboards that are updated and reviewed at consistent intervals. The dashboards are used as a simple resource to help managers quickly understand how the business is performing.

Figure 11.2.1 KPI dashboard

	Week 21			May			Year to date	
	Total	Vs. prior week	Vs. prior year	Total	Vs. prior week	Vs. prior year	Total	Vs. prior year
Revenue	$620K	-4%	5%	$12.4M	10%	3%	$55.8M	9%
Units	1,813	-1%	13%	35.2K	9%	9%	165.5K	19%
Avg. order size	$342	-3%	-7%	$352	1%	-5%	$337	-8%
New subscribers	547	-10%	3%	11.3K	3%	-19%	55.2K	5%

Examples of common marketing KPIs:

- Revenue
- Units sold
- Market share
- Average order size
- Profit
- Number of active subscribers
- Number of new subscribers
- Points of distribution
- Net promoter score
- Customer retention rate

Guidelines for creating a KPI dashboard:

- Provide an effective measure of business health.
- KPI dashboards may be created for various organizational levels where goals differ.
- Limit metrics to those directly related to goal achievement and top performance drivers.

- Avoid lower-level driver metrics. Focus on the outcome. Separate business driver reports should be created to explain the cause of KPI shifts.

- Group KPIs that are related to each other such as new revenue and new unit sales.

- Avoid redundant or overlapping measures.

- Metrics must be quantifiable.

- KPI data should be attainable with reasonable effort matching to the importance and frequency of KPI reporting.

- Use meaningful time periods, day, week, month, year, trend versus point-in-time.

- Metrics should be consistently measurable over time.

11.3 Market sizing and forecasting

The role of a marketer is not to just drive demand, but to also determine total market demand as well as forecast the size and growth of the business. There are numerous methods to arrive at these estimates, and we will discuss some approaches in this section. Marketers don't have a crystal ball to know the future, so forecasting involves elements of both science and art, or data and assumptions. The assumptions should be based on analysis, research and experience, and the rationale for each assumption should be clearly documented for stakeholders to understand.

Market sizing & forecasting - terminology

Term	Explanation
Market share	The proportion of a defined market that a firm, brand, or product has captured over a set period of time. A market may be defined in a number of ways. For example, the global shoe market, or it could be more limited to a more precise market, e.g., U.S. men's casual shoes. To determine the best market share definition, consider your target customer and determine where the brand or product can reasonably gain consideration.
Total addressable market (TAM)	The total sales that a firm may generate by capturing 100% of the market share. When determining the TAM, it is the responsibility of the firm to determine what are appropriate market size limitations such as country restrictions.

Term	Explanation
Bottoms-up forecast	A forecast that is built using more granular driver metrics to arrive at a forecast of the goal metric. For instance, if the goal metric is revenue, the forecast may be as a function of units sold and the revenue per unit. These two metrics multiplied will supply the revenue forecast.
Tops-down forecast	A forecast that has a stated top-level goal such as deliver $600 million of revenue or deliver 15% revenue growth. From that goal, the forecast for driver metrics will be adjusted and determined as needed to deliver a forecast that satisfies the goal.

Market sizing & forecasting - inputs & considerations

Industry reports

Nearly every industry has published reports that provide information on the market size, key players, market trends, growth projections, plus other valuable information. The quality of these reports may differ drastically, and prior to purchase it is wise to both contact the research provider for a sample report as well as an explanation of the methodologies used to gather and analyze data.

Substitutes and complements

Entry into any market will have a set of substitutes and complements. Referencing these as benchmarks can help provide estimations for market size and potential.

The review of similar product launches is a great way to understand expectations for a new launch. This is particularly true in situations where the new launch is an improvement or new variant to an existing product line.

Location

> **Geographic** - Geographic boundaries such as limiting sales to certain countries or regions will have significant market size implications and should be an early consideration when determining market potential.

> **Retail and channel distribution** - The availability of a product in various sales and retail channels is a critical driver of sales potential. Large brick and mortar retail chains can drastically increase or decrease forecast expectations based on their decision to sell your product or brand. In e-commerce, selling through company websites, along with other third-party marketplaces such as Amazon and social channels, will significantly impact forecasts.

Surveys

Surveys can be used to gauge consumer interest and market potential. Specifically, product concept tests may be used to provide an indication of consumer interest. A long-time standard in the consumer goods industry is to test concepts using a Nielsen BASES test. These tests provide information regarding the sales expectations, including sales expectations based on varying levels of marketing investment.

Marketing investment

The amount of awareness for a product or brand is critical to its success. A product may be amazing, but without awareness, it will not sell. Marketing investment forecasts should account for the spend and the anticipated results for all forms of promotions and offers that are used, from public relations to coupons.

Generating the forecast

When creating the format and model for a forecast, it is best practice to build it with flexibility. Wherever possible, avoid hardcoding values in the model. Instead use formulas that are linked to inputs that may be toggled to adjust assumptions and outcomes. Building in flexibility will save numerous hours as forecasts get reviewed and critiqued. An additional benefit to building a model in this manner is the ease in which you will be able to see the model's sensitivity to the adjustment of assumptions.

As you build a forecast specifically for a new launch, consider the need for demand, supply, and distribution to ramp up. It's unlikely that a new launch will immediately reach its full market potential overnight.

Forecasts are built utilizing a set of dimensions and measures that will help guide goals, strategies and tactics. To create a suitable forecast, it should be built at a level of detail that will provide cross-functional stakeholders such as demand planners and finance team members the information needed to build their coordinating plans.

Examples of forecast dimensions:

> Brands including sub-brands

> Product and product lines including tiers, categories or variants

> Sales channels

> Geography, countries or regions

> Time periods such as daily, weekly, monthly, quarterly, yearly

> Time horizons, how far out must the model extend

Examples of forecast measures:

> Revenue

> Market share

> COGS (Cost of Goods Sold)

> Profit

> Unit sales

> Volume sales

> Subscribers

> Marketing investment

Figure 11.3.1 is an example of a forecast for a set of two new product variants. These new variants will be launched as additions to an existing product line. This forecast shows the aggregate (total) results of the two variants, each variant individually, and the forecasted incremental contribution of two variants. The difference between the aggregate and incremental forecast is attributed to cannibalization. Cannibalization is present because there is the expectation that the new variants will steal some sales from the existing variants in the product line. The incremental amount is what the two new variants will add to the business minus the cannibalized amount.

Figure 11.3.1 Forecast

Assumptions

Retail distribution	90%
Cannibalization (Units)	60%
Marketing Spend (Annual)	$3,000,000

Notes

Based on initial buyer commitments
Using prior year launch cannibalization rate
Committed spend via GM approval

Market Size

Dollars	$600,000,000
Units	4,000,000

20XX Launch is U.S. only		Jan	Feb	Mar	Apr	May	Jun	Jul	Aug	Sep	Oct	Nov	Dec	Total / End
Total	Dollar Mkt Share	0.34%	0.54%	1.05%	1.14%	1.23%	1.33%	1.43%	1.55%	1.67%	1.81%	1.95%	2.11%	2.11%
Total	Revenue (Millions)	$2.01	$3.26	$6.33	$6.83	$7.38	$7.97	$8.61	$9.29	$10.04	$10.84	$11.71	$12.64	$96.89
Total	Unit Mkt Share	0.35%	0.46%	0.88%	0.95%	1.03%	1.11%	1.20%	1.29%	1.40%	1.51%	1.63%	1.76%	1.76%
Total	Units Sales	14,000	23,000	44,000	47,520	51,322	55,427	59,862	64,650	69,822	75,408	81,441	87,956	674,409
Total	Avg. Price Per Unit	$144	$142	$144	$144	$144	$144	$144	$144	$144	$144	$144	$144	$144
Variant 1	Dollar Mkt Share	0.18%	0.26%	0.55%	0.60%	0.65%	0.70%	0.75%	0.81%	0.88%	0.95%	1.03%	1.11%	1.11%
Variant 1	Revenue (Millions)	$1.05	$1.58	$3.33	$3.59	$3.88	$4.19	$4.52	$4.89	$5.28	$5.70	$6.15	$6.65	$50.79
Variant 1	Unit Mkt Share	0.15%	0.23%	0.48%	0.51%	0.55%	0.60%	0.65%	0.70%	0.75%	0.81%	0.88%	0.95%	0.95%
Variant 1	Units Sales	6,000	9,000	19,000	20,520	22,162	23,935	25,849	27,917	30,151	32,563	35,168	37,981	290,245
Variant 1	Avg. Price Per Unit	$175	$175	$175	$175	$175	$175	$175	$175	$175	$175	$175	$175	$175
Variant 2	Dollar Mkt Share	0.16%	0.28%	0.50%	0.54%	0.58%	0.63%	0.68%	0.73%	0.79%	0.86%	0.93%	1.00%	1.00%
Variant 2	Revenue (Millions)	$0.96	$1.68	$3.00	$3.24	$3.50	$3.78	$4.08	$4.41	$4.76	$5.14	$5.55	$6.00	$46.10
Variant 2	Unit Mkt Share	0.20%	0.35%	0.63%	0.68%	0.73%	0.79%	0.85%	0.92%	0.99%	1.07%	1.16%	1.25%	1.25%
Variant 2	Units Sales	8,000	14,000	25,000	27,000	29,160	31,493	34,012	36,733	39,672	42,846	46,273	49,975	384,164
Variant 2	Avg. Price Per Unit	$120	$120	$120	$120	$120	$120	$120	$120	$120	$120	$120	$120	$120
Incremental	Dollar Mkt Share	0.13%	0.22%	0.42%	0.46%	0.49%	0.53%	0.57%	0.62%	0.67%	0.72%	0.78%	0.84%	0.84%
Incremental	Revenue (Millions)	$0.80	$1.30	$2.53	$2.73	$2.95	$3.19	$3.44	$3.72	$4.01	$4.34	$4.68	$5.06	$38.76
Incremental	Unit Mkt Share	0.14%	0.23%	0.44%	0.48%	0.51%	0.55%	0.60%	0.65%	0.70%	0.75%	0.81%	0.88%	0.88%
Incremental	Units Sales	5,600	9,200	17,600	19,008	20,529	22,171	23,945	25,860	27,929	30,163	32,576	35,182	269,763
Incremental	Avg. Price Per Unit	$144	$142	$144	$144	$144	$144	$144	$144	$144	$144	$144	$144	$144

11.4 How to conduct a business performance analysis

The first and most important step to a business analysis is to have a stated question you are attempting to answer. As you progress through the steps of an analysis it is easy to become distracted by tangential insights. A lack of focus on the stated question increases the likelihood of "analysis paralysis". This phrase refers to the state of disarray people encounter when they try to look at too many pieces of information and get stuck. The stated question will help you maintain focus on the insight you have set out to gain. As you move through the analysis, you may want to take note of additional insights or analyses, but don't pursue them until after you've answered the stated question.

Often business analyses are initiated due to a change in a KPI. For instance, a KPI is revenue, and on the KPI dashboard it is noticed that revenue, which had been typically at 2% year over year growth, is now all of a sudden 11%. From this change in business performance the stated question is, "Why did revenue increase from 2% to 11% year over year?"

With the stated question in place you should then establish a scope for the analysis. Like the purpose of the stated question, establishing a scope is critical to avoid getting lost in the data. KPI dashboards will most likely provide high-level information that will help establish the scope, information such as the time period that the change was noticed, or perhaps the country the change occurred in. The scope should be built to ensure that all relevant data are considered.

KPIs are typically higher-level metrics that are the aggregate of driver metrics. For example, revenue may be a function of units sold multiplied by average unit price. Units sold and average unit price would be driver metrics. There may be multiple levels of driver metrics. Average unit price may be driven by product mix among other dimensions. Your analysis should review the various drivers to determine which are causing the change to the KPI. You may find that more than one driver is causing the KPI change. It should be quantified to what extent each driver has affected the KPI. For instance, one may account for 75% of the effect, whereas the other is 25%. As you move through your analysis be sure to validate your learnings and be pragmatic. Focus on the drivers that made a significant impact to the business.

The method of starting with the high-level KPI and then moving step-by-step through various drivers is the funnel method. This approach is a simple methodology that will help you maintain focus and move through a business analysis in an efficient linear manner.

Example of the funnel method:

Here is a hypothetical situation to demonstrate how to utilize the funnel method. On a KPI dashboard it is found that July revenue grew 11% year over year for product line "A." This is a surprising contrast to the prior few months where growth was only 2%.

Stated question:

Why did July revenue increase 11% year over year when the growth trend for the last four months was only 2% year over year?

Scope:

> Product line: "A"

> KPI metric: Revenue

> Time frame: March 2021 - July 2021, March 2020 - July 2020

Funnel steps:

These are the items that are expected to help explain the answer to your stated question.

> Time periods – both trends and year over year

> Region

> Unit sales

> Sales channel

> Product mix

> Price / order size / offer change

> Inventory level

> External factors

The structure of your analysis funnel should begin with the broadest or most encompassing dimensions or metrics, then as you progress down, the steps should become narrower. To illustrate how a step may be broader than another, let's compare region and pricing. The prices of the products in product line "A" vary by region; therefore, region is a broader driver because there are multiple prices that are coordinated or dependent on the region.

As you progress down the funnel the difference between steps may lessen to the point where the order becomes interchangeable. At this point, consider placing steps with simpler or more easily accessible data higher in the funnel. Figure 11.4.1 depicts the funnel with the steps we will use to answer the question about the change in revenue growth.

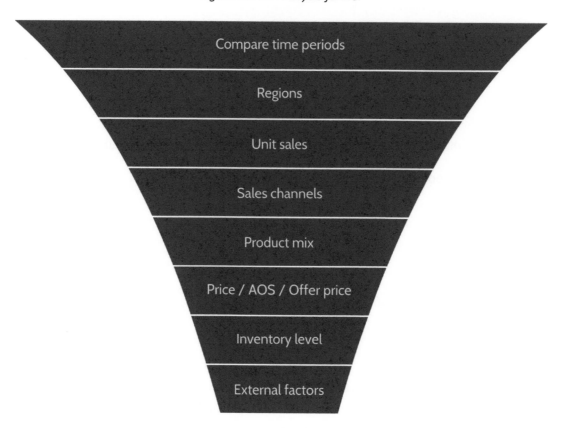

Figure 11.4.1 Analysis funnel

Compare time periods

Regions

Unit sales

Sales channels

Product mix

Price / AOS / Offer price

Inventory level

External factors

Step 1: Compare time periods

When comparing time periods, review both year over year and trend data. Year over year data refers to the comparison of a month such as July this year to July last year. Trend data refers to monthly data such as a comparison among April, May, June, and July. A simple snapshot of year over year (Y/Y) data may not tell the full business performance story and vice versa. You may analyze trend and Y/Y together where you first get the result of April this year versus April last year, May this year versus May last year, June this year versus June last year, and so forth. With this data you may compare the monthly trend of the Y/Y results.

Here's an example of the importance of seeing Y/Y data combined with trend data. In the following chart (figure 11.4.2), Y/Y monthly revenue has been positive throughout the year; however, in July the Y/Y revenue surprisingly increased by 11%. Looking at the July Y/Y comparison in a silo without a review of the 2020 and 2021 trends, you may conclude that something amazing happened to the business in July 2021. However, the trends reveal that revenue has been steady in 2021, therefore, something happened in July 2020 that generated a favorable comparison.

In a situation such as this where the trend shifted in the prior period (year), it's worth noting whether that prior period shift continues as a trend or returns back to normal. As shown in figure 11.4.2, the drop is isolated to July and the 2020 trend reverts in August.

Figure 11.4.2 Time period comparison

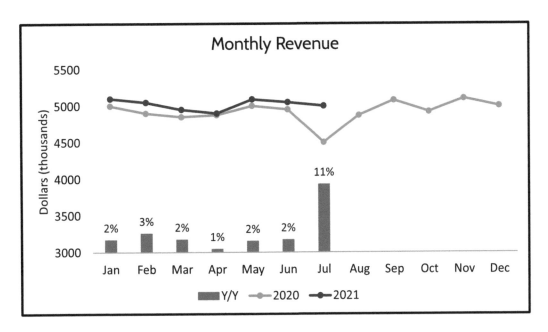

Step 2: Regions

You've identified that the change occurred in 2020. Now it's time to understand what caused the drop. Step 2 is regions. In this example you have three regions: East, Central, and West. Following are three charts (figure 11.4.3) showing the same metric that we reviewed in step 1, but broken down into the three regions.

Figure 11.4.3 Regional comparisons

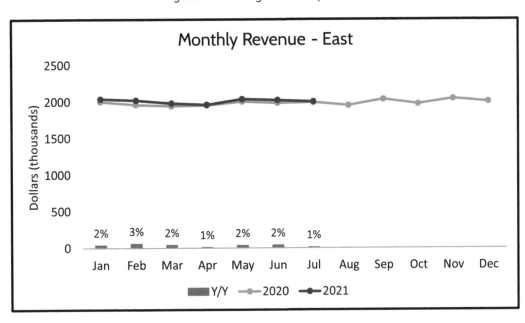

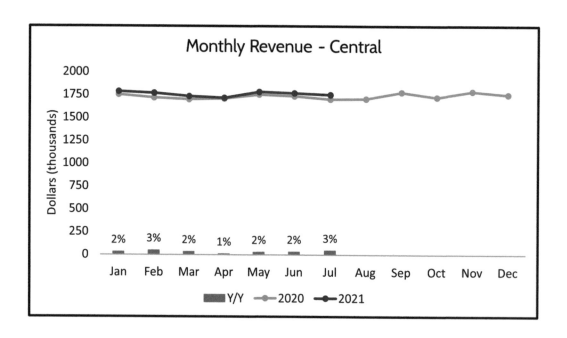

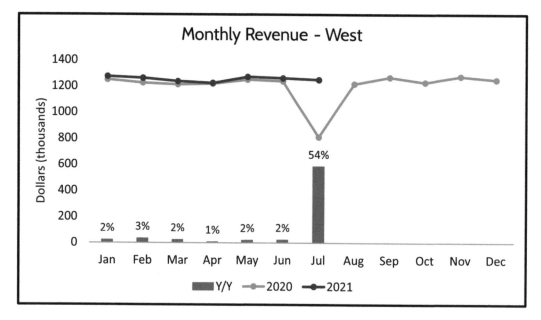

Here you will see that the business change occurred in the West region where revenue increased 54% Y/Y, while the revenue in the East and Central regions remained consistent.

Notice that we used three charts, all with similar formatting, to help visualize and compare the data. We also ensured that we again reviewed the Y/Y numbers by month as well as the trend. Continuing to review Y/Y and trend is important to avoid missing key facts. For instance, you may encounter a situation where the West performed badly in July 2021 and 2020. But, in 2021 another region performed strongly so the aggregate revenue of the regions looks normal, which would be a missed insight.

Be pragmatic. Let's say there were a dozen regions to review, yet 90% of your revenue is explained by the three regions listed previously. It is not a prudent use of time to start your analysis with an investigation of the other nine regions that contribute only 10% of the revenue. Based on the magnitude of the change observed in the three primary regions, you can feel confident you've captured the significant change to the business.

Step 3: Unit sales

Based on the regional data we know the West region is where the change occurred. The first two steps evaluated revenue. We need to understand what drove the revenue drop in July 2020, and units is the most likely driver of shifts in revenue.

Figure 11.4.4 Unit sales analysis

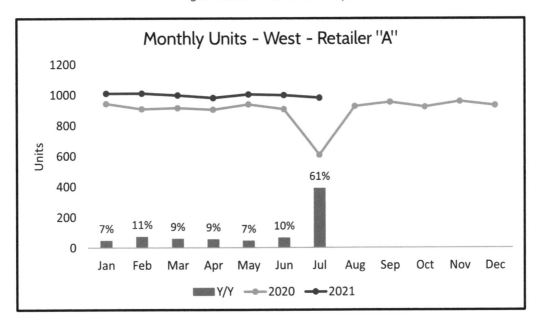

A review of the data in this chart (figure 14.4.4) makes it clear that units are a key driver of the revenue change. To judge its impact on the revenue change, you may compare the percent decline in units to the percent decline in revenue. In this case it's 51% and 54%, respectively. If the unit decline were only 3%, then it would be apparent there is another driver to examine.

Step 4: Sales channels

It is now apparent that a decline in units sold is the reason for the revenue drop. The next step in the analysis is to answer, "Did the drop occur because of a certain sales channel?" For this example, there are two channels: Retailer "A" and Retailer "B."

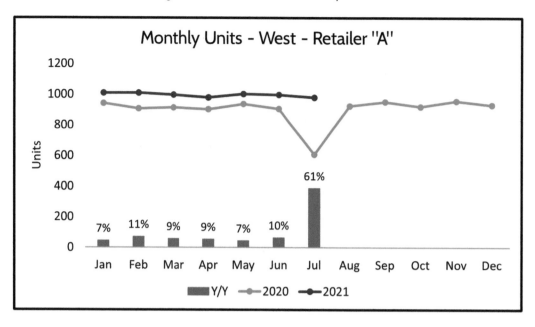

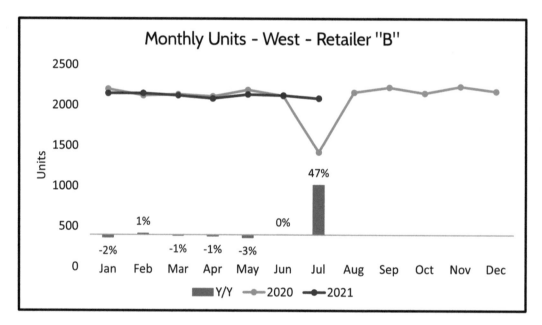

Both retailers are showing the same trend as the step 3 unit chart, so you may conclude that it's not an individual retailer that is driving the change.

Stay in scope. While it may be interesting or alarming that retailer "A" is growing around 10% prior to July while retailer "B" is about flat, don't get distracted. Remember the stated question you have been tasked to answer. A comparison of the retailers' performance would be a different analysis outside of the current scope.

Step 5: Product mix

Step 4 showed that the retailers did not drive the change in performance. The product line has two unique versions, "X" and "Y."

Figure 11.4.6 Product mix comparison

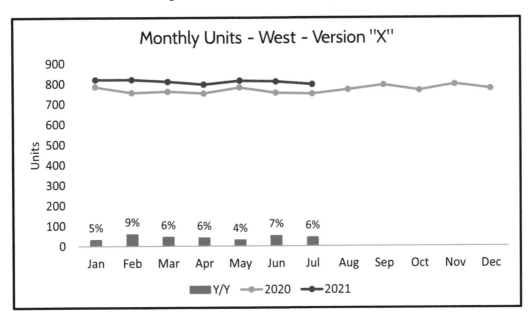

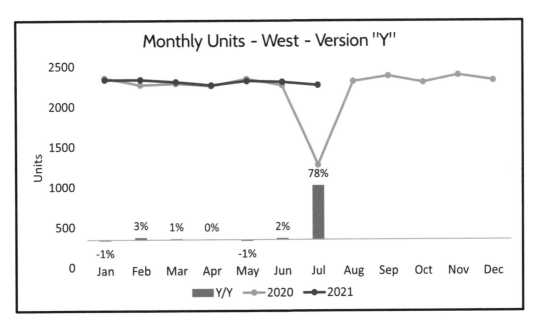

A review of the two product versions shows that version "X" was consistent throughout the last few months, including July. Version "Y" shows that it faced a major decline in July 2020, having broken away from a fairly consistent trend prior.

Step 6: Price

Product "Y" was identified as the driver of the performance change. Let's next assess whether or not a price change drove the change in performance.

Figure 11.4.7 Average price analysis

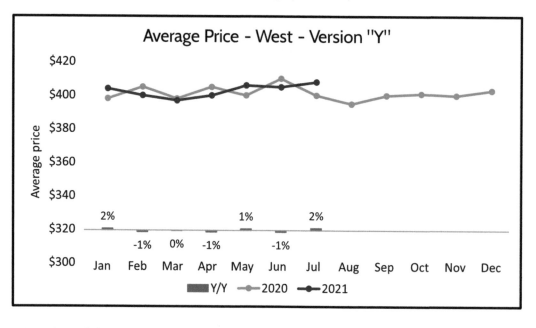

A review of the average price by month shows that the average price of product version "Y" in the West has been consistent throughout all of the time periods in the scope of this analysis.

Step 7: Inventory level

Price didn't cause the change in unit sales, so next let's review inventory levels. A disruption in inventory availability can have a major impact on unit sales.

Figure 11.4.8 Average inventory analysis

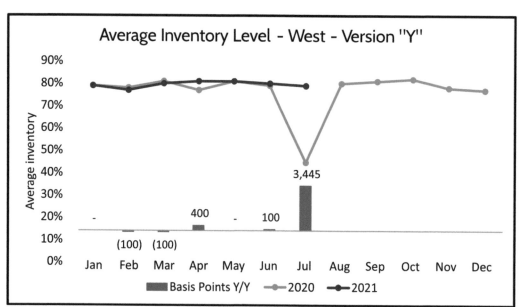

Until July, 2020 inventory levels were on average 79%. In July, the inventory level dropped to only 45%, this results in a Y/Y delta of 3,445 basis points. A conversation with the supply chain team confirmed that in July 2020 there was an inventory outage of product version "Y" in the West region. In this straightforward analysis we can conclude that virtually 100% of the July Y/Y revenue variance was due to an inventory shortage that occurred in July 2020. In real-life situations you may have multiple drivers, and you should attempt to quantify the significance of each.

11.5 Common drivers of business performance

In the example analysis we went through seven steps to arrive at the cause of the KPI change. Here is a list of common analysis metrics and dimensions as well as events that are useful to consider as you take on a business performance analysis.

Events

- Seasonality (holidays)
- Act of God (e.g., blizzard, hurricane)
- Offer change
- Outlier large order size
- Exceptional competitive offer
- Number of business days in a given period
- Product launch
- Promotion or event
- Inventory shift
- Industry shift (e.g., regulatory change)

Metrics and dimensions

- Compare time periods (e.g., trend, Y/Y)
- Unit or volume sales
- Sales channels (retailers)
- Order size
- Staffing level
- Retailer display support
- Competitive price change
- Region or geography
- Product mix
- Price
- Inventory level
- Call hold time, queue time
- Returns

Track milestones

When completing business analyses, the tracking of dates or milestones that had significant business impacts can save you and the organization a tremendous amount of time and headache. In the example of the monthly revenue growth KPI that we analyzed in section 11.4, we could have saved a tremendous amount of time by consulting a milestone tracker. The step 1 analysis showed us that the driver shift occurred in July 2020. A simple review of a milestone tracker would reveal that an inventory constraint occurred at that time, which explains the KPI shift. You may then immediately focus on calculating the extent to which the inventory problem explains the KPI shift.

11.6 Common analysis types and outputs

Sensitivity analysis

A sensitivity analysis is a way to evaluate the impact created by altering a variable input to a mathematical model. They can be used to help business managers understand the trade-offs created by adjusting a single or multiple inputs to find an expected outcome.

To illustrate, figure 11.6.1 is an example depicting the scenario of a marketing manager who currently has $400,000 to advertise for an upcoming month. There is an opportunity to increase the budget by approximately $50,000. The manager must decide whether or not to request the $50,000 to boost advertising spend or to keep the $50,000 as profit. The advertising dollars are used to purchase media impressions. The impressions drive customer store visits that lead to product sales. In the following analysis, the marketing manager gathered a number of inputs for the model. A constraint to the model is that impressions must be purchased in increments of 1 million.

Figure 11.6.1 Sensitivity analysis

Inputs	
$15.00	Cost per thousand impressions if total buy <30,000,000
$14.00	Cost per thousand impressions if total buy >=30,000,000
155	Store visits generated per million impressions
23	Units sold per 100 store visits
$1,450	Average product cost if <1000 units are sold
$1,350	Average product cost if >=1000 units are sold
$2,000	Revenue per product sold

Analysis						
Advertising spend	Impressions purchased	Store visits	Units sold	Product cost	Revenue	Profit
$375,000	25,000,000	3,875	891	$1,292,313	$1,782,500	$115,188
$390,000	26,000,000	4,030	927	$1,344,005	$1,853,800	$119,795
$405,000	27,000,000	4,185	963	$1,395,698	$1,925,100	$124,403
$420,000	28,000,000	4,340	998	$1,447,390	$1,996,400	$129,010
$435,000	29,000,000	4,495	1,034	$1,395,698	$2,067,700	$237,003
$420,000	30,000,000	4,650	1,070	$1,443,825	$2,139,000	$275,175
$434,000	31,000,000	4,805	1,105	$1,491,953	$2,210,300	$284,348
$448,000	32,000,000	4,960	1,141	$1,540,080	$2,281,600	$293,520
$462,000	33,000,000	5,115	1,176	$1,588,208	$2,352,900	$302,693
$476,000	34,000,000	5,270	1,212	$1,636,335	$2,424,200	$311,865
$490,000	35,000,000	5,425	1,248	$1,684,463	$2,495,500	$321,038

The result of the analysis is that the $50,000 increase in budget could yield about a $300,000 increase in profit, which seems like an easy decision. The analysis also reveals a couple points at which there are step change increases in the profit. The first is at the point of spending $435,000 for 29 million impressions. At this point product costs are reduced due to achieve a break point in the manufacturing costs. An additional step change occurs at the point of spending $420,000 for 30 million impressions. The advertising vendor offers a price break if 30 million or more impressions are purchased.

Tree diagrams aka driver tree

A tree diagram is a useful method to display hierarchical or sequential data. The tree begins with the highest level of data and then branches out to additional levels that reveal the underlying data that is aggregated in the level above.

A tree diagram may be used in a variety of scenarios. A few examples: breaking down the drivers of high-level results, geographical or regional performance, and the example in figure 11.6.2 depicting performance by sales channel. In the example, note that the top level (total revenue) is the aggregate of the level below (online and phone). Then both online and phone are the aggregate of the level that sits below them. As the data is reviewed top to bottom it becomes known what contributed to the higher-level results. In this example the OurCompany.com website drove $350,000 of the total $400,000 growth versus the prior period.

Figure 11.6.2 Tree diagram

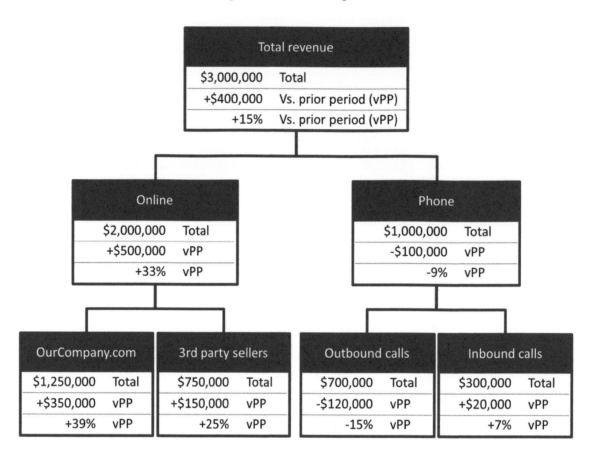

Leakage Trees

A leakage tree is a methodology used to understand and quantify the opportunity created by capturing a greater "share of wallet", which is a term used to describe the share of what consumers spend in a particular category. The leakage tree depicts a series of decisions that shoppers make during the purchase journey. These trees are very common for businesses that sell through retailers. The tree analysis will help you understand the dynamics of the category size, how effective a retailer is at converting shoppers for a category, and how effective you and the retailer are at selling your brand or product. By comparing time periods, you will be able to see if the category, the retailer, and your product are performing well compared to the alternatives. As stated, this methodology is well established in the retail space but is equally useful to many industries, including e-commerce. Figure 11.6.3 is an example of a leakage tree for a retailer "A" who sells coffee brand "A."

Figure 11.6.3 Leakage tree

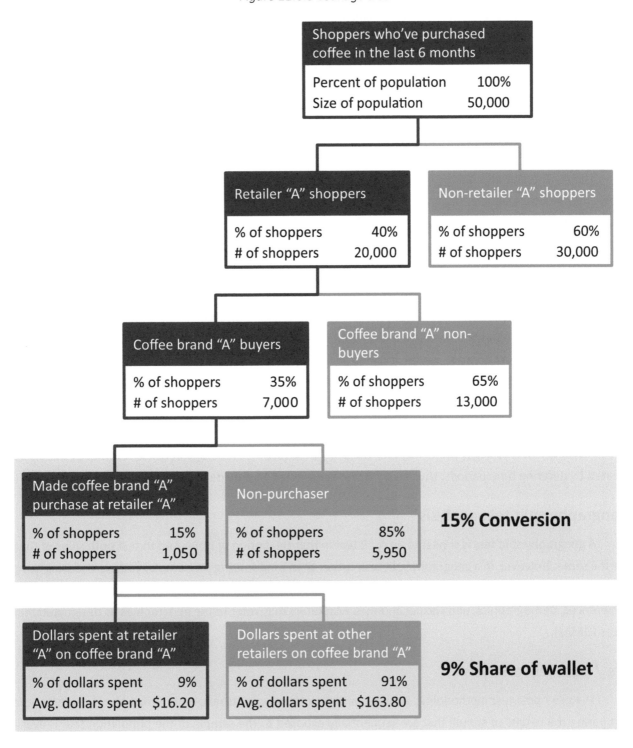

Similar to the tree diagrams, a leakage tree is hierarchal where the higher levels are the aggregate of the levels below. Toward the bottom of the diagram are two key data points. The first is conversion; of the coffee brand "A" purchasers who shop at retailer "A," only 15% of them made a purchase of coffee brand "A" at the retailer during this time period. The second is share of wallet, for the 15% of shoppers who purchased coffee brand "A" at retailer "A," only 9% of their total dollars spent on coffee brand "A" occurred at retailer "A." This would indicate that there is a large opportunity to get these buyers to buy coffee brand "A" more often when they are at retailer "A." The quantification of the opportunity could be stated as such: by increasing the share of wallet by 100 basis points (a movement from 9% of dollars to 10% of dollars), the dollars spent by coffee brand "A" buyers at retailer "A" would increase by $1.80.

In addition to the information that is available in this example, leakage trees may also contain information about where the leaked shoppers and purchases are going. For instance, in a broader leakage tree analysis the non-retailer "A" shoppers may be expanded to reveal the share of retailers "B," "C," "D," and "E."

A / B test analysis

The A / B test methodology is particularly common in digital marketing testing in areas such as ads, websites, and marketing emails. This methodology is characterized by randomly splitting the sample and exposing one part of the sample to an "A" (control) version of the test stimuli and exposing the other part of the sample to the "B" (test) version of the stimuli. Once enough sample data has been collected, the results from the two versions of the stimuli are compared.

The comparison of the results should be completed using statistical analyses. The test should have a null and an alternative hypothesis that are accepted or rejected based on the statistical outcome. Tests should be scheduled to run for enough time that it allows for a sample size that can deliver a statistically significant result. Bear in mind that in many cases statistical significance may never be achieved. This is due to the inability of the test version to significantly outperform or underperform the control version. In situations such as this, other methods of decision making or analysis may be used to determine an outcome, such as the Bayesian probability method, which we will not delve into for the purpose of this text.

An A / B test is typically preferred over the pre / post test methodology because it removes the variables created by differing time periods, thus an A / B test is expected to provide greater accuracy.

Geography split test analysis

A geography split test is similar to an A / B test in that the period of time used to test both sides of the test are the same. However, in a geography split test, rather than randomizing the sample, you are choosing samples based on location. In choosing the locations, you must do your best to control for variations in areas such as preferences, demographics, and socioeconomics. Marketers may refer to the geographies as designated market areas (DMAs).

Pre / post test analysis

The pre / post test methodology is simple and wide-ranging in its use. A pre / post test is characterized by comparing the results of stimuli that are sequentially exposed to the sample of the population that is available during their respective pre and post time periods. For example, a comparison of a new webpage. Webpage "A" was live for the time period June 1-15, and all visitors to the website saw that version of the page. Then webpage "B" was live from June 15-30, where all visitors to the website saw that page. The analysis will compare the metrics for the two pages for the time periods in which they were live on the website.

The pre / post methodology is less accurate than an A / B split test but is often easier to implement and is sometimes the only viable option. Its accuracy is diminished due to the inability to control external factors that may arise during separate time periods. You must do your best to minimize the impact that different time periods cause. Here are best practices to minimize time-based factors.

Guidelines to selecting the time periods

> **Business volatility:** Based on the type of business you work on, volatility may be a small factor or it may create substantial swings in key metrics on an hourly, daily, weekly, or monthly basis. Think through the tradeoffs of shorter or longer periods and how to reduce noise and outliers.

> **Balance the test length:**

>> **Too long:** The longer the time frame, the more opportunity there is for external factors to affect the tested change.

>> **Too short:** A test may have an initial dramatic impact that will normalize over a period of time. For instance, a price drop may spur an initial rush of sales that may dissipate over time. Conversely, changes to the layout of a webpage or product package may cause an initial drop in conversion as customers become acclimated to the change.

> **Avoid holidays and seasonality:** These predictable occurrences should be thought through and avoided.

> **Check the weather:** Whenever possible take note of the potential impact that upcoming major weather events may have, such as an approaching tropical storm.

> **Balance weekends and weekdays:** In many businesses the metrics between weekdays and weekends differ significantly. Ensure you are balancing the number of each.

> **Avoid promotions and offers:** Some competitive promotions are predictable. Avoid these as well as internal promotions that may influence the results.

> **Check for outliers:** Before completing any analysis you should review the data and remove outliers.

> **Analyze multiple time periods:** When the test data are available, analyze multiple time periods to assess how much variation there is in the data. Let's say you have a test setup for 20 days pre and 20 days post. It would be of interest to analyze the data at 10 days, 15 days, and 20 days pre / post. Based on the time periods, you may see that the results are changing or trending in a certain direction.

11.7 Communicating the data

The presentation of an analysis should be thought of as the telling of a concise story. The stakeholders that you communicate to are balancing many priorities, so it's imperative your presentation of the information is efficient and effective. As you develop your insights, consider their implications on the future direction of the business. In your communication, be clear about the following points that may be better remembered by using the acronym "DESC":

- **Define** - Why you set out to learn this information and the scope

- **Explain** - What your methodology was

- **Solve** - What the output of the analysis was

- **Conclude** - What to do about it... your conclusion and recommendation

When presenting the analysis, consider the audience, including their level of background knowledge, and the amount of granularity desired. Try to anticipate questions so that you may answer them upfront, which may demonstrate a high level of critical thinking.

Visuals such as charts are powerful tools to communicate the analyses. However, if not used properly they may detract from your message and confuse stakeholders. Here is a list of best practices for building analytics visuals:

Best practices for visuals

Visuals such as charts are powerful tools to communicate the analyses. However, if not used properly they may detract from your message and confuse stakeholders. Here is a list of best practices for building analytics visuals:

- **Keep visuals and charts simple** - Your audience should be focused on the content and insights, not how to interpret the format of your chart.

- **Make it interesting but not overdone** - Highlight, circle, point to key data but don't overdo it and create a mess with too many items competing for the viewer's attention.

- **Use high contrast** - Be cognizant of color usage and contrast. Colors often look more vibrant and easier to discern on your computer screen than they do on televisions or projection screens.

- **Don't overload slides** - Often people are asked to keep a presentation to a certain number of slides. This causes them to cram an enormous amount of information onto each slide. Don't focus on the number of slides; focus on the amount of time to present. Use more slides to keep them useful and visually appealing. If there is a strict limit on slide count, focus on the most important point(s) of the slide. Supporting or additional information may be placed in the appendix or on a hidden slide.

- **Make it quickly discernible** - In presentations, don't ever present a slide that you feel compelled to introduce as an "eye-chart." This means your slide is worthless as part of the presentation. The text is too small, and it's too busy. If you want the presentation to contain a more comprehensive supporting set of data that requires time to review, it is better located in the appendix.

- **Make it transferable** - You won't always be available to explain the slide and the data. Ensure the information is complete enough for people to understand the insights without your personal explanation. It is possible to utilize the slide notes feature to add context, but know your audience, as often slide notes are overlooked.

  If it's a slide that uses animation, it's likely the slide will be viewed outside of presentation mode. This means all of the animated elements on the slide will flatten and will be shown stacked on top of each other. Ensure the slide remains readable in that situation.

- **State your source** - Use sources with adequate detail to allow others to verify the data if needed.

- **Don't be captain obvious** - In a presentation, don't use bullets to state the obvious information contained in a chart or table. The bullets should be insights supported by the visual. Use the slide headline or bottom-line to communicate the main takeaway. If there is not a takeaway, ask yourself if the slide needs to be presented.

- **Optimize** - Test out different styles of tables and charts to ensure the data is presented in the best manner.

Chart and table usage

Charts and tables can be highly effective tools to communicate data and facilitate telling the story. However, if used incorrectly, charts and tables may cause confusion and hinder your ability to convey the intended message. To illustrate this, we will compare three options to communicate the same data. The data is a comparison of the tier mix of product units in the U.S. and Canada. The stated question is, "How does the tier mix of product units differ between the U.S. and Canada?"

Option 1: Pie chart

Figure 11.7.1 Pie charts

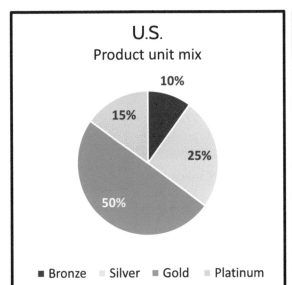

Pie charts effectively show the percent tier mix of product units within the U.S. and within Canada. However, some may find it difficult to compare the results between the two countries. To compare, you are required to visually jump between charts and compute the difference.

Option 2: Bar chart

Figure 11.7.2 Bar chart

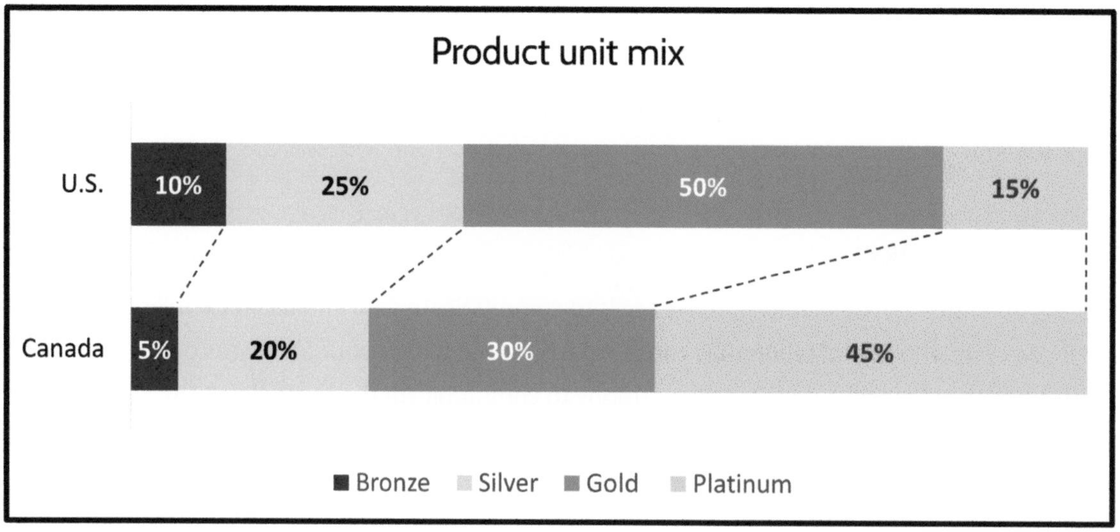

Product unit mix

U.S.	10%	25%	50%	15%
Canada	5%	20%	30%	45%

■ Bronze ■ Silver ■ Gold ■ Platinum

The bar chart is a more effective way to visualize the difference in mix between the U.S. and Canada. A downside to this visual is (with the exception of the bronze units) the starting points for each of the comparable segments are misaligned.

Option 3: Table

Figure 11.7.3 Table

		Region		Delta (bps)
		U.S.	Canada	
Tier	Bronze	10%	5%	500
	Silver	25%	20%	500
	Gold	50%	30%	2,000
	Platinum	15%	45%	-3,000

In this example, a table succinctly shows the results of both countries and the difference between the two.

Two chart types you should know and use

Histograms

A histogram is a chart that depicts the count (frequency) of data values that fall within various ranges. For example, a histogram can be used to effectively show the number of customers who spent different ranges of dollars during their shopping trip. You can see in figure 11.7.4 that the most common amount spent in a shopping trip is between $11-$21. Fourteen shoppers fell into that range.

Figure 11.7.4 Histogram

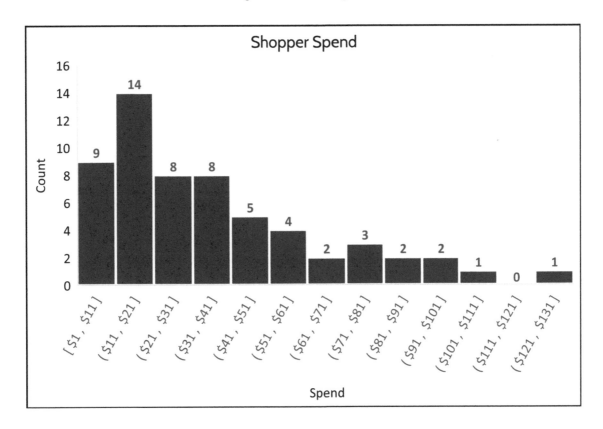

Waterfall charts

A waterfall chart is a preferred way to show a starting point, an end point, and the quantification of the factors that yield the end point. Figure 11.7.5 is an example of a sales goal set at the beginning of 2020, the amount each region over- or under-delivered on their individual goal, and the final (actual) result as an outcome of the regional performance.

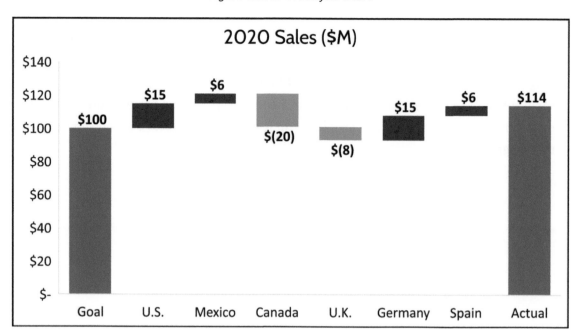

Figure 11.7.5 Waterfall chart

—————————

CHAPTER 12: PRICING

The implementation of a strong pricing strategy is vitally important to the success of any product or service. Simplistically, if your price is too high you are at risk of limiting the demand for your product, and if you're priced too low you may leave money on the table and hurt profitability. A price strategy may be extremely complex with various offer tactics, subscription options, bundles, channel discounts, volume discounts, and more. In this chapter we will discuss how to understand price sensitivity, its effect on demand, various price strategies, and how to set price targets.

12.1 Price sensitivity

Price sensitivity is a measure of the customer reaction or sensitivity to a change in price. Price sensitivity is also known as the price elasticity of demand. Products are considered to have either elastic or inelastic demand. Price sensitivity is measured as a ratio using the following calculation:

- Price sensitivity = (Percent change in quantity purchased / Percent change in price)

- For example, the price of a widget increased 15%, causing the number of units sold to decline by 50%. Logically this indicates that the product has high price sensitivity, the percent units drop outpaced the percent increase in price. The net effect of this change would be a loss in revenue. Putting the formula into practice:

- Price sensitivity is (-50% / 15%) = -3.3

- For every percentage point of change in price, the units sold will be inversely affected by a factor of 3.3 times that number.

While this formula can help understand expectations from a specific price change, drastic movements in price may invalidate modeling. Small upward price changes for a product may provide great revenue potential; however, large changes may fail due to price thresholds. A threshold is a price point that changes the decision of customers to either buy or not buy. A threshold for a bottle of water may be $1.00. Any price above a dollar will cause many customers to balk at the idea of purchasing. If you were selling bottles of water for $0.50 and decided to test $2.00, a drastic jump, you may see a loss in revenue because so many customers walked away. This could erroneously cause you to think that $0.50 is a good price. However, if you were to test a smaller price increase from $0.50 to $0.75 or $1.00, you may have seen a different customer reaction to the price change and achieved a better revenue result.

12.2 Price sensitivity and the elasticity of demand classifications

Price elasticity of demand (PED)

The price elasticity of demand refers to the responsiveness of the quantity of customer demand relative to a change in price. The more elastic the demand, the larger the reaction. The less elastic, the smaller the reaction. Price elasticity is a useful tool for marketers to maximize revenue and profit. It helps to project the number of units that would be sold at a given price, thus delivering an expected revenue outcome.

Drivers of price elasticity

Driver	Example
Available substitutes	At a grocery store you may find eight brands of ketchup available. With so many substitutes, a small increase in the price of one brand can easily cause its sales to significantly decline. If only one brand of ketchup were available, an increase in price would likely have a much lower effect on its sales as there are no alternatives.
Necessity	A drug that helps control a critical health ailment such as cancer can sustain equal demand at higher or lower prices. A drug with purely cosmetic purposes such as one that helps eyelashes grow fuller would see demand decline as the price goes up.
Timeliness	As storms and hurricanes approach, it is not uncommon to hear stories of price gouging for plywood. With the storm imminent, sales of plywood remain strong despite high prices.
Habit	Consumers who make their daily purchase of coffee may not react to small price increases over time. Coffee is part of their routine, and it will take something disruptive to break it.

Price elasticity classifications

There is a set of guidelines to help classify whether a product should be considered price elastic or inelastic. First you must calculate the price sensitivity using the formula discussed in the prior section.

- Price sensitivity = (Percent change in quantity purchased / Percent change in price)

Figure 12.2.1 is a table that defines the classifications of price sensitivity.

Figure 12.2.1 Price sensitivity classifications

Ratio	Classification
> 1 (greater than 1)	Elastic (high price sensitivity)
= 1 (equal to 1)	Unitary elastic (price sensitive)
< 1 (less than 1)	Inelastic (low price sensitivity)
= 0 (equal to 0)	Perfectly inelastic (no sensitivity)

In nearly all cases the calculated price sensitivity is negative. This is due to the downward slope of the demand curve—price goes up, units go down, and vice versa. On a rare occasion a product may be priced so low that people assume it's inferior, so less is purchased at a lower price. A higher price would raise consumer confidence, and more would be purchased.

When assessing your calculated price sensitivity, the value should be evaluated as an absolute number. Therefore, both a calculated value of -0.6 or a value of 0.6 would both constitute inelastic demand. Values of -3.3 or 3.3 would both constitute elastic demand.

12.3 Price strategies

Utilizing the correct price strategy will maximize product revenue and profitability. There are numerous approaches to pricing, and in this section, we will review several of the most common.

Common price strategies

Strategy	Explanation
High-low	This pricing strategy is exemplified by drug stores in the U.S. Items are set to a high standard price, but then are discounted significantly to draw customer action and impulse. The high prices capture added margin for sales made while there are no deep discounts.
EDLP (everyday low price)	This pricing strategy has become keystone for several national chain stores. Rather than constantly shift prices up and down, EDLP offers value to customers by providing consistent overall low and competitive prices. This assures customers that while a particular product may not be the cheapest price available, the total basket of goods purchased will be less expensive there than at a competitor.
Off-sale pricing	Off-sale pricing is a common strategy where products are discounted at an amount such as 25% off. This is a type of offer, but is also a price strategy as often it is evergreen or indefinite in duration.
Loss-leader	The loss-leader strategy lures people in with an offer so low that the primary purchase is near or below cost. For example, video game consoles are sold at little to no profit. However, once a consumer is hooked into the console's ecosystem, the games that are subsequently sold provide high-profit margins. For retailers, doorbusters are a term that litter Black Friday ads. A set of amazingly low-priced products is meant to lure customers into the store with the goal of selling the one item for a loss, but the profit is recouped on the sale of additional items.
Tiered pricing	For business to business sales, the concept of tiered pricing is highly relevant. For example, a contractor may purchase 100 sheets of drywall from a store on a weekly basis. The store values this contractor's business so much that they will place him into a pro tier and discount his purchases in an effort to maintain his loyalty.

Strategy	Explanation
Bulk discounting	A bulk discount refers to a reduction in price based on the quantity purchased. Bulk discounting may also reward the purchase of higher quantities of time. For example, a subscription service may utilize this and offer a discount price for annual terms versus monthly terms.
Subscription pricing	The subscription price strategy has become increasingly popular due to its continued flow of revenue. A subscription model is where a customer signs up for a service or a cadence for product delivery that extends into recurring purchases. It's common to use a discounted initial price to attract customers and then at a later date switch to a higher renewal price.
Free trial	A free trial allows consumers to try a product or service before they make a purchase. This is commonly done via a couple of different methods. One method is to limit the amount of time a customer has to use a product for free, such as a 7-day free trial. The second method is to limit the functionality of a product, such as a free version of a game that only allows a player to access the first level.
Freemium	The freemium strategy is similar in ways to free trial and is very common in SAAS and digital products. A freemium product allows a consumer to use a version of a product for free; however, the product is monetized through the use of upgrades and paid features.
Utility pricing	Utility pricing charges consumers based on their usage. For instance, for the utility electricity, there is a set price per kilowatt used. Your bill will be a function of the amount of electricity used and your rate.
Cost-based	The cost-based approach starts with a product's cost and then applies a specified markup percentage or dollar amount in order to arrive at a price. Cost-based pricing is usually not a recommended approach because prices should be determined by the customers' willingness to pay rather than the cost of a product or service.
Psychological (odd pricing)	This pricing strategy is simple, but utilizes a powerful psychological insight. Rather than show the price of a product as $200, odd pricing is the practice of reducing the price to the next lowest odd number which is $199 and thus changing the price from being immediately perceived as in the 200s, to being in the 100s.

Strategy	Explanation
Price creaming (skimming)	Price creaming is a practice commonly used in industries such as technology where significant R&D efforts are invested prior to a launch. Price creaming is the practice of launching a new innovation at a high price with the product targeted to less price sensitive early adopters. This is done to increase profitability and recoup the money that was invested into R&D.
Decoy pricing	Most often used in situations where a product line is available. In a product line, a product variant may be purposefully built to offer less value so that another variant in the product line appears highly appealing. A typical scenario is a product line with three options. The first option will be priced lower, while the other two options will be priced higher and about the same. This pricing strategy will draw attention to the two higher plans. Of the two higher plans one will have more desirable features, the goal is to have it gain the majority of sales while the other is just a decoy.
Price anchoring	Price anchoring plays on the psychology of customers. By showing customers a high-priced option first, it makes the lower priced item seem inexpensive. This is a common practice for restaurant menus, the highlighted items may be the big-ticket specials, so then when the customers review the regular entrées, they appear more reasonable.
Penetration pricing	This price strategy is commonly used by new industry entrants who seek to quickly gain market share. It involves pricing the product significantly lower than competitors and where they expect to price the product long-term. This may be done to gain needed share, but may be harmful to the product category. If competitors respond by lowering their prices, the result is a price war that harms all parties.
Dynamic pricing	This is a price strategy that involves the practice of constant price adjustments that are based on supply, demand, and competitive benchmarks. Hotels and airlines have become adept in this price strategy. Their prices can update by the second as availability and demand change.

Offers / discounts

Offers and discounts are ways to deliver additional value to shoppers. They should be factored into your price strategy whether they are evergreen or time-bound. Many of the strategies just discussed use an offer as a core component of the pricing. The use of offers should be strategic and implemented to accomplish a goal. We discussed the strategy of using a loss-leader or penetration pricing, which are great examples of how offers are used to achieve a goal.

The use of offers may come with a few potential risks. When determining the need for a discount and the amount to offer, here are a few things to consider:

- **Depth** - Offer depth should be decided as a combination of considerations including price sensitivity, profitability, and industry norms. While it's obvious the coordination of prices with competitors is illegal in the U.S., it is advisable to benchmark against the competition and understand the risk that an offer can spark a price war.

- **Clarity** - Offers should be easy for customers to understand. If an offer is too complex, its usefulness is diminished, defeating the purpose of implementing the offer.

- **Scale** - Shoppers have become very savvy. Offers can immediately go viral and be taken advantage of. Think through the availability and limits that need to be placed on any offer.

- **Consistency** - Shoppers quickly become trained to expect offers of a certain depth or at a certain cadence. A simple and extreme example is Black Friday. Customers will hold off purchases for things such as TVs in order to pay less during the anticipated sale. Is developing a cadence such as this something that is desirable for your business?

- **Layering** - Offer layering is when customers utilize multiple offers or discounts in a transaction. You must be privy to all of the ways in which your product is getting discounted. Profitability can quickly erode along with marketing budgets if layering isn't fully understood. Some examples:

  > In retail, a shopper may have a paper coupon, a digital coupon, an on-shelf price reduction, as well as the redemption of a gift card for buying the specified quantity of items. Oh, and don't forget the loyalty app vendor that you pay to reward the customers for scanning their receipt.
  > Web discounts are often layered through promo codes, partner website commissions, and discount companies such as Honey or Rakuten who offer additional savings.

To help avoid these pitfalls, marketing teams should track not only marketing activities, but other activities such as retailer promotions that may affect the product pricing. Bounds should be set to avoid discounting too deeply and creating a situation in which shoppers come to expect a discount level lower than what is desired.

Humans gravitate towards the middle

A well-known psychological factor of shopper behavior is that customers gravitate toward the middle. With uncertainty or limited information, shoppers will tend to avoid extremes such as the cheap option or the expensive option. This is the reason why you often see three tiers in a product lineup; it helps give shoppers a sense of comfort in their decision. This also mitigates the likelihood that in a two-product lineup customers gravitate toward the less expensive option.

Bundling

A bundle offer is a discount to shoppers where if they purchase an additional item or items with their primary item, they receive additional savings or incentives. Product bundling is an important tool that in many instances increases cross-selling and order size. It is also a great way to gain trial for complimentary products. Bundling may be set up to work within a company and brand, or it may extend across companies as part of a partnership. An example of a partnership bundle could be encountered during barbeque season, in which a hot dog brand and hot dog roll brand partner to offer a discount when the two are purchased together.

12.4 Establishing price targets

As your price strategy is shaped, it is necessary to consider various price metrics and targets. These will help you determine and manage to the target price for the product. As you evaluate the various metrics to determine the price, you should also take into consideration the prices of substitutes and complements to your product. The need to benchmark against substitutes should be known without saying, but compliments may be equally important. Take, for example, the price of tires for a luxury roadster automobile. The ability to sell the tires at a low price may exist, but doing so would be a missed opportunity to capture additional profit. The affluent customer segment that is driving these cars has a willingness to pay above the typical low tire price. There are many considerations as you shape your price and strategy. Here are some common metrics and target bounds to help you effectively manage the price of your product or service.

Common price target metrics

Driver	Example
High price	Determine what is the highest price a consumer should encounter when shopping for the product.
Low price	Determine what is the lowest price a consumer should encounter when shopping for the product.
Average price per unit	Set a target for the average price each unit is sold for.
Average price per amount of volume or contents	Set a target for the average price of each unit of measurement such as gallons, ounces, uses, pounds, or grams.
Average order size / Average cart size	Set a target for the average size of a single purchase transaction.
Manufacturer suggested retail price (MSRP)	Set a price that may be generally accepted by sellers of your product. However, sellers always have the ability to alter the price as they see fit, so it is very common to encounter prices that aren't aligned with the MSRP.

Driver	Example
Breakeven price	The breakeven price is the price at which it equals the cost of the unit sold. We will discuss how to calculate breakeven price and how to build a product profit and loss (P&L) statement in the understanding financials chapter. When evaluating breakeven price, it may be relevant to consider the subsequent or cross-purchase of other products, particularly in the case of a loss-leader strategy.
Bulk discount tiers	Set the thresholds and discount levels for bulk purchases. Develop an easy to understand price scheme that rewards larger purchases.
Introductory or sale price	Common in subscription services, the product has a lower initial price to gain more users when they are deciding which service to use and are most sensitive to price.
Renewal price	Common in subscription services, the product has a different, usually higher renewal price to maximize customer lifetime value and profit. This is possible because once in the subscription service, a customer's price sensitivity is likely to be lower.
Lowest offered price	Considering offer layering, determine the absolute lowest price that shoppers may purchase the product for.
Percent sold on offer	Determine what percent of the product's sales should be sold as part of an offer. This may be measured in terms of percent of dollars, units, or volume.

Part 3: Executing the plan

Part 3 chapters:

CHAPTER 13: DESIGN, ARTWORK & PACKAGING

Marketing sometimes has the stigma as the job function where people just play with designs and colors. The ability to brief and lead the creation of winning designs are capabilities of great marketers. There is much more that goes into design than what is seen at the surface. In this chapter we will discuss some of the science and details of how design, artwork, and packaging come to life.

13.1 Color

Importance of color

Colors or the intentional removal of color can drastically alter the emotion evoked by a design. Colors can drive liking; 60% of people decide they are attracted to a message based on color alone. Furthermore, the use of color can reinforce brand recognition by up to 80% (Hooker, 2016). When creating designs and evaluating artwork, consider color and the psychology behind it. Here is a list of the emotions evoked by color.

Color associations

Color	Association
Red	Energy, aggressiveness, power, danger, high-visibility
Black	Elegance, power, formality, mystery
Brown	Nature, simplicity, warmth, neutrality, honesty
Orange	Joy, creativity, friendliness, youthfulness, energy, affordability

Color	Association
Yellow	Happy, positive, warm feelings, high-visibility
Green	Fresh, health, natural, balance, peacefulness
Blue	Trust, loyalty, comfort, confidence, reliability
Purple	Royalty, luxury, sophistication, mystery, wisdom, creativity
White	Calming, purity, simplicity, minimalism, cleanliness

Color standardization

Color standardization is the practice in which colors are matched across media. We learned that brands are reinforced by color, and that color should be consistent everywhere, whether it be on a bottle, a t-shirt, or a menu.

PANTONE® is a company that is the gold standard for color matching and standardization. PANTONE colors came into existence to ensure consistency among designers, marketers, and printers as they worked across various geographies (Budds, 2015). PANTONE created a book of standard colors that is printed with precise colors so that a book in New York will exactly match a book in Tokyo. To communicate the exact color, a designer can simply use the descriptor such as Classic Blue number 19-4052.

While PANTONE has done wonders for the standardization of print color, the digital world struggles. If you were to look at a webpage on your computer monitor side-by-side with the same page on your cell phone, you will most likely see a drastic difference. This difference is not one that can be overcome. Display screens vary in settings, age, and quality. As a best practice, ensure that adequate contrast exists between colors. Designers often work on high-resolution monitors that offer amazing color vibrancy; conversely, an average customer may have a monitor that lacks vibrancy and the ability to display differences between similar colors. Be cognizant of this as you review and approve artwork.

Types of color coding

Along with the standard developed by PANTONE to match print colors, there are a few additional ways in which precise colors are communicated. There are four commonly used color codes for artwork:

Color code	Use and description
PMS	Used in printing, PMS (PANTONE MATCHING SYSTEM®) is the patented color palette and printing inks developed by PANTONE. PANTONE colors are communicated using an alphanumerical code (e.g., 401C).
CMYK	Used in printing, CMYK (cyan, magenta, yellow and black) is commonly used for digital and offset printing. At-home printers will commonly have ink cartridges for each of these colors. CMYK colors are communicated by a percentage for each color (e.g., C 59%, M 71%, Y 0%, K 35%).
HEX	Used on monitors and most typically used in web design, each color is specified as a 6-digit code (e.g., #0000FF).
RGB	Used on monitors, RGB (red, green, blue) is commonly used for TVs, phones, applications, etc. Each color is coded as the combination of the three colors red, green, and blue (e.g., 0, 0, 255).

13.2 Image and graphic types

Vector vs. raster images

Vector images

Vector images are graphics that are constructed with hard lines that cannot be blended or blurred. They are built with graphic elements that are foundationally mathematical, and due to the mathematical construct of these designs, it is possible to zoom in or expand the image infinitely without pixilation. Vector images are also commonly referred to as source files because text and design elements may be easily manipulated.

> The most common software used to create vector designs and artwork is Adobe Illustrator.
> Common file types are .ai, .eps, .pdf, and .svg.

Raster images

Raster images are created with pixels, which are points of color that may be set to a certain level of precision called pixels per inch (PPI). The higher the PPI, the better the image quality. Because the images are created with individual pixels of color that are tiny squares, they may be blended together to form smoother lines and color transitions.

As the PPI increases, the file size of an image also increases. When raster images are used for digital applications such as an image on a website, it is common to use a PPI of 72. This contrasts with designing for print in which it is desired to use a PPI of 300 or greater. Note: PPI is not to be confused with DPI (Dots Per Inch), which is a term used to define print quality.

> The most common software used to create and edit raster images is Adobe Photoshop.

> Common file types are .jpg, .jpeg, .gif, .png, and .tif.

Most common image file types

File type	Use and description	Image type
JPG (or JPEG)	Great for use on webpages, this format can be optimized to balance file size and quality. A similar image in JPG format may be a smaller file size than a PNG. JPG files must have a visible background, whereas the background of PNG files may be transparent.	Raster
PNG	Great for use on webpages, this format can be optimized to balance file size and quality. The key differentiator of PNG files is that they can have a transparent background, whereas JPG files must have a visible background.	Raster
GIF	GIF images utilize the RGB color code and has up to 256 colors to choose from. Due to the high number of colors supported, GIF photograph file sizes may be enormous. GIFs are best for use on simple graphics like icons and website buttons. They are commonly used by web developers because they may be animated.	Raster
TIF (or TIFF)	TIFF images are large files that are best used for high-quality printing. Due to the large file size they are not suitable for web use.	Raster
EPS	As a vector image, EPS file can be built with a combination of illustrations, graphics, and text. These files offer the ability to edit without size restrictions or pixilation. EPS files are best suited for graphics, print designs, or logo files.	Vector
AI	AI files are similar to EPS but are proprietary to and can be only edited and saved using Adobe Illustrator, the industry leading vector design software. Other applications may be able to open AI formatted files, but to edit and save the file format must then be changed.	Vector

Artwork layers

Designs are created and altered utilizing layers. The noticeability or visibility of layers to the customer seeing the artwork differs based on the design intent. Layers operate similarly to the way people use PowerPoint on a daily basis. For instance, a layer on your slide may be a chart. Then an additional layer on top of the chart may be an arrow that points to a specific bar (figure 13.2.1).

Figure 13.2.1 Layers

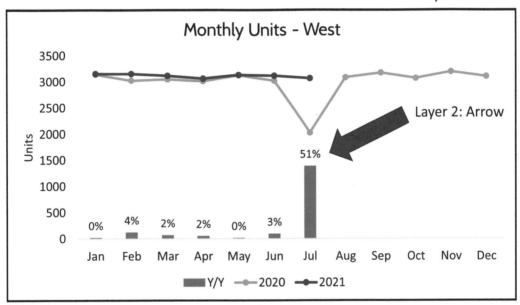

Another example of layer in everyday use is on your phone. If you take a picture and apply a filter to make the image become "cool" or "warm," you are actually adding a partially transparent layer of blue or red respectively. In the printing section, we will discuss why layers and the number of layers is so important in artwork.

13.3 Packaging types and design

From toothpaste tubes, to corrugated boxes, to plastic bottles, to wooden crates, the number of packaging solutions available today are virtually limitless. Rather than attempt to cover each of the available options, we will focus on some of the key things to consider when determining what type of packaging to use. Prior to moving into the next section, it should be noted that packaging extends beyond just what you see on the shelf at your local store. Packaging also includes the movement of the product from the manufacturing location to its final destination. The packaging that we are familiar with and see on the store shelves is known as primary packaging. Here are common packaging types and terms you should know.

Package type	Use and description
Primary packaging	The packaging that is closest to the manufactured product.
Secondary packaging	Packaging that houses and is possibly used to protect a primary package. For example, taco meal kits that contain taco shells, taco seasoning mix, and taco sauce. The secondary package is the box that you would see on the store shelf that contains those three primary packages. Primary packaging and secondary packaging may be in a 1-to-1 ratio. For example, medicine that is sold in a box that contains the bottle of medicine. The box is secondary, while the bottle is primary.
Case pack	These are the packages that contain multiple saleable product units. There is a wide range of how these may look. Some may simply be a plain brown box that a consumer is never intended to see, or it may have color graphics and is intended to be used as an easy to setup display.

Figure 13.3.1 Case pack

Package type	Use and description

Inner packs and padding — Within a case pack, inner packs may be used to help fill empty space or help protect the product from damage during transport.

Figure 13.3.2 Inner pack padding

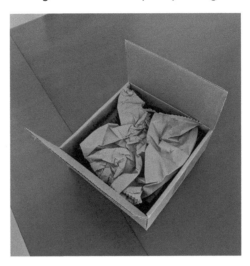

Pallet — Pallets are the large wooden square or rectangular bases that forklifts use to safely move items. Pallets are used in all types of shipping and logistics, so when planning the package types listed above, it is critical to consider the ability of those packages to fit and stack on a pallet.

Figure 13.3.3 Pallet

Package type	Use and description
Display	Some products are expected to be merchandised without the use of a store fixture such as a peg hook or a shelf. Display packaging allows for great merchandising flexibility such as a standalone cardboard tower. Displays can benefit manufacturers by offering additional space to communicate its marketing message. This type of packaging may also serve as a shipping box.

Figure 13.3.4 Display

Packaging considerations

As mentioned, there is a virtually endless number of packaging solutions available today. Rather than attempt to discuss the pros and cons of each solution, the following is a set of considerations to take when selecting and designing a product package.

Stock vs. custom

Custom, proprietary packaging offers the ability to make something unique and ideal to the marketer's vision. However, custom packaging will likely come at a much higher start-up cost and potentially higher ongoing production costs. These costs don't just apply to the production of the packaging, but also the process to place the product and the packaging together. The custom design may just be unfeasible. With high-volume or high-profit products, the ability to use custom packaging increases.

Stock packaging is manufactured for and available to any potential buyer. It is an option that can help to alleviate the high costs associated with custom packaging. However, the use of stock packaging will force you to sacrifice the use of a proprietary design. This packaging type should save you start-up costs as well as ongoing manufacturing costs because the quantities produced are in excess of just your demand. If stock isn't desired and custom is cost prohibitive, it is also possible to take a hybrid approach where certain parts of the package are custom while others are stock.

Intuitive to shoppers

It's important to ensure that the package design effectively communicates what the product is. A strange package can cause confusion and hinder the ability of the product to gain adoption. An example of incongruent packaging is milk packaging in Canada versus the U.S. Both solve the same need, but for those who travel between the two countries, it may be confusing to encounter. In the U.S. milk is packaged in rigid plastic gallon jugs. In Canada, milk is packaged and sold in soft plastic bags that usually contain three roughly one-liter pouches.

Figure 13.3.5 Canadian milk pouch

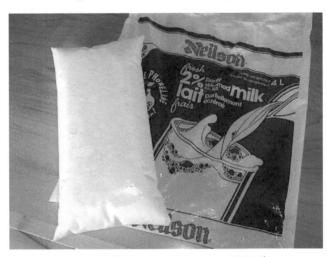

Source: (UX User Experience, 2014)

Supports the brand

Ensure the package supports and if possible amplifies the correct brand message. A premium brand should have packaging that conveys as such. A brand known for its stance on sustainability should use a sustainable package.

Presence

The package should command attention. Be mindful of the colors and how they may look versus the surrounding products and clutter. Consider the opportunity to create a discernible, consistent section of color that makes your products prominent on a shelf, commonly referred to as a "brand block."

Ensure the packaging fits within the merchandisers' guidelines. Anticipate all of the possible ways the product may be merchandised: hanging up, laying down, sideways, front-faced, side-faced, top-shelf, bottom-shelf, or eye-level. Also consider the need for a way to dispense the product, such as the drop-down dispensers commonly used in canned soup aisles.

Shopper evaluation

Anticipate the need of customers to experience the product prior to purchase. How can the packaging facilitate that evaluation to prevent the destruction of the packaging or product? A few methods to do so include scratch and sniff stickers, tamper resistant seals, or clear windows in the packaging that reveal critical components.

Cost

Packaging cost, particularly in the high-volume fast-moving consumer goods industry, is critical to business health. Even a penny or two of excess cost may dramatically change profitability.

Price targets

Product usage and price point, understand the need of retailers and customers to shop for certain price points, such as one dollar. Make the product an appropriate size, volume, or quantity to match their needs. Product usage refers to the amount of utilization the product gets and how frequently customers are expected to repeat purchase. It also refers to usage needs, such as single use, travel friendly, or family size.

Source and availability

The location of where parts originate from can have drastic implications on lead time and flexibility. Vendor reliability should be considered and backup manufacturers should be in place to minimize the length of supply disruptions.

Durability and protection

The ability of the package to protect the product from damage or leaking. There is also potentially the need to protect the product from light, air, heat, or another contaminant that could ruin the product. Lastly, there is the possibility that the product may interact with the packaging, such as causing a metal can to rust.

Deters theft

Retailers will not want to sell your product or merchandise it in a customer accessible area if theft is easy and costly. In the example of the medicine bottles packaged within a box, the box not only provides better shelf presence, but also helps deter theft. The boxes make the product larger and bulkier, and they often also include an RFID tag that will sound exit alarms if not deactivated during the checkout process.

Fill and settling

For products to run through manufacturing lines at high-speeds, packaging cannot typically be filled completely. They are underfilled. Additionally, many products are loosely placed into packages with the likelihood of settling to occur. In both of these scenarios, transparent packaging may give the impression to customers that they are getting cheated because the packaging is oversized compared to the actual amount of product. In instances such as these, consider the opacity of the package and what the impression customers get if the package doesn't look full.

Sustainability

Consider the importance of sustainability to your brand and target customers. Including the potential need to make trade-offs between cost and aesthetics.

13.4 Printing processes

For production-level printing, there are a few dominant methods used today. Here is a quick review of the most popular methods.

Most common printing methods

Offset lithography

The most widely used production printing method today. It utilizes printing plates most commonly constructed from aluminum. Ink is applied to the plates and from the plate placed or "offset" onto a rubber blanket. This rubber blanket is applied to the substrate. The substrate is the final material that is desired such as a label, poster, cardboard box, etc. In a prior section we discussed artwork layers and their importance. Each plate represents a layer and each layer is restricted to a single color or function. If the production line is restricted to 4 layers, your artwork must be built accordingly.

Flexography "Flexo"

Utilizes printing plates typically constructed of rubber, which is then transferred to the printing surface. Its applications are most commonly packaging and labels.

Gravure

Rather than utilizing print plates, this method utilizes cylinders to apply ink to the substrate.

Digital printing

Digital printing is useful across a variety of applications too numerous to list but can range from phone cases, product labels, to ceramic tile patterns. This method does not use print plates, which creates a couple of advantages. Setup is faster and cheaper, so smaller quantity production runs are feasible. The initial costs to print digital are lower because print plates do not need to be created.

Two common types of digital printing dominate:

> **Inkjet:** Utilizes nozzles that place drops or "dots" of color onto the substrate. In a previous section we discussed PPI (pixels per inch); for inkjet printing the precision of the print is measured by dots per inch (DPI). The higher the DPI, the better the print quality.

> **Xerography (laser):** Most typically used for printing on paper and similar substrates. These printers utilize a drum that creates an electrical charge that pulls toner in a selected pattern that will be then be melted onto the substrate.

Screen printing

Well known for t-shirt production, screen printing can also be applied to various other materials such as wood or tile. Screen printing is done by placing a screen on top of the substrate. Areas of the screen will be blocked by an unprintable surface that are not intended to receive the layer of color that is applied through the screen. This process can be repeated to apply multiple layers or colors.

Figure 13.4.1 Screen printing

Source: (emarts, 2021)

Print setup

Number of layers or colors

Printing is completed utilizing a certain number of layers that act independently or may overlap if desired. The number of layers used can impact the cost, speed, and quality of printing dramatically. More colors typically offer marketers and designers more flexibility. The standard range of layers used in any print process is between one to eight. Layers may be commonly thought of as colors, but they may add other types of design detail such as foil, embossing, or a protective gloss.

Dye lines

During the package and printing process, packaging elements such as boxes or labels will need to be cut to a specified size. The cuts will likely be performed by cutting dyes where the cutting occurs using a metal template pressing down onto the uncut material. The building of custom dyes can be expensive and easily add thousands of dollars to the fixed cost of creating the packaging.

Color and print standards

A quality product and brand must have consistent colors regardless of when and where a production run occurs. To maintain consistency, standards are created and stored to serve as the target for every subsequent production run. Standards can be single color swatches as well as the final fully printed and dye cut substrate. Often, designers or marketers will attend first production runs to review and sign off on the standards that will be used as the production target for years to come.

13.5 Writing a design brief

A design brief is a document that marketers provide to designers, which contain critical information about the project you would like them to complete. There is a wide breadth of information that you must provide to designers to facilitate the creation of great artwork. While it may seem like a daunting task to gather this information, level-setting and building this foundation with the design team will ultimately save time and money through the reduction in clarifying questions, revisions, and more. In the following list of the elements of a design brief, you will notice that many of the items are found within a brand book. If you have an existing brand book or style guide, it should be included with your design brief. Here are the elements of a complete design brief:

Elements of a design brief

- **Company background** - Provide information about your company such as history, recent success, size, brands, as well as any other pertinent information. This information helps the designers to better understand the originator and the motivation for the request.

- **Project goal** - Define the project goal.

- **Brand and product information** - Share information across the 4P and 3Cs for your brand and product(s). As part of the customer section of this deliverable, include specific detailed information about the target audience intended to experience the design.

- **Project overview and scope** - Provide project details and deliverables including information such as:

  > Projects KPIs

  > What the purpose of the designs are. For example, to raise awareness, close a sale, etc.

  > Where the designs will be seen and used

  > Variations of the designs such as size, format, and substrate

  > The number of designs needed

  > Deadlines

  > Expectations of further projects that will be related to this original project

- **Mood boards** - A mood board is a collage of imagery, colors, and other visual prompts that provide designers a vision for the design. As the common phrase says, "A picture is worth a thousand words." A mood board is a powerful tool to communicate design intent. The caveat to the use of a mood board is to ensure you are not leading the designer too closely and unintentionally limiting creative freedom.

- **Requirements** - If possible, list exactly which types of designs and formats you would like delivered. Providing these upfront will increase the efficiency of the project and reduce the chance for cost overages:

  > Product views (e.g., two-dimensional front view, side-view, three-dimensional corner view)

  > Package size

  > Package types

  > Print requirements and restrictions

  > Variations including translations

  > Image size

  > File type

  > How and where files will be transferred

- **Provide brand style guide** - Give the designers the standards they need to follow.

- **Provide files** - Give designers the elements they may need such as logos, UPCs, photography.

- **Project schedule** - Share your key dates and timeline requirements.

- **Budget** - Depending on your negotiation methodology, you may or may not want to include budget information. Some follow the rule of thought that you should provide a number first to anchor the vendor to a lower price. Others may suggest you allow the agency to provide a price first. If you provide the agency a budget, it may be likely they find a way to match it or exceed it regardless of the amount of work.

- **Points of contact and roles** - Provide information for the various project roles such as the driver, contributor, and approver. Also provide contacts for relevant partners such as the printer or web developer.

CHAPTER 14: PROMOTION & ADVERTISING

Promotional activities are what people most commonly associate with the marketing profession. Marketers are tasked with generating demand through activities such as advertising, events, and public relations. The successful use of these methods will depend on a number of factors, including the understanding of where the target customer segment may not only be reached, but also consciously or unconsciously open to influence.

14.1 Understanding customer acquisition

A core function of the marketing profession is to generate demand and sales. In order to do this effectively, you must understand the process consumers take as they navigate and ultimately purchase a product or service. Multiple frameworks have been developed to help marketers structure their approach to driving sales. In this section we will review a few of the most popular.

The purchase funnel

The purchase funnel is a simple and widely used tool to map the customer acquisition process. The funnel is characterized by a linear step-by-step process whereby the number of potential purchasers reduces at each stage of the funnel as different purchase considerations are made.

Some marketers are critical of the purchase funnel because of its simplicity. Criticism of the model is often related to its linear and ending process. This understates the importance of the customers' ongoing experience with the product and brand. Repeat purchases and advocacy are often the source for the majority of established brands sales. Therefore, the purchase funnel doesn't adequately depict the most important source of sales and profit. Despite the criticism, the purchase funnel is widely used and remains a useful tool if its shortcomings are accounted for.

Figure 14.1.1 Purchase funnel

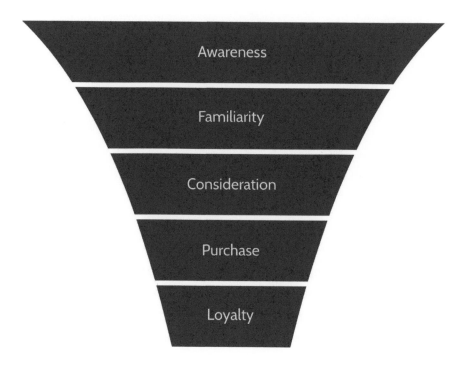

Purchase funnel steps

- **Step 1: Awareness** - Shoppers gain visibility and awareness of the potential brands and products available to meet their needs.

- **Step 2: Familiarity** - The shopper forms knowledge and opinions beyond just awareness for a subset of the possible brands or products.

- **Step 3: Consideration** - Based on their knowledge and opinions, the shopper will only seriously consider purchasing a certain set of the available solutions. This is known as being in the shopper's "consideration set".

- **Step 4: Purchase** - The shopper makes the final purchase decision, which could be based on a number of factors such as immediate availability or price.

- **Step 5: Loyalty** - The consumer of the product will gain experience with the product that may create loyalty or the opposite, a brand rejector.

Later in this section we will discuss the path to purchase. In that discussion you will encounter what some of the common marketing tactics are to reach people at various stages of the funnel.

Decision journey map and the path to purchase

The decision journey map and the path to purchase (P2P) are similar frameworks. Both frameworks detail the step-by-step process that customers follow to make a purchase. The core difference between the two is the focus of the process. The decision journey focuses on the experience and thoughts that customers encounter during the process. The P2P focuses on the channels and touchpoints that customers encounter during the purchase process. Both frameworks help indicate where and when customers are available to influence.

Decision journey map

The decision journey map follows a similar approach and structure as the customer journey map. It is a portrayal of the average experience of the specific customer segment. The decision journey map differs from the customer journey map in that it focuses on the steps taken prior to purchase, whereas the customer journey map focuses on the journey during and following the purchase.

Similar to the customer journey map, there are various sections in the decision journey map:

> **Columns:** Represent stages in the journey. Notice that the stages are levels in the purchase funnel.

> **Linear steps:** The steps are represented as circles with a brief description of the step. In some customer journey maps, the diameter of the circle may differ to indicate varying levels of impact to the overall journey; larger circles indicate higher impact.

> **Departments:** At the bottom of the decision journey map is a list of the company departments that may directly impact the steps with each stage.

Figure 14.1.2 is a simple example of a decision journey map that depicts the process of a customer deciding on and purchasing a new television.

Figure 14.1.2 Decision journey map

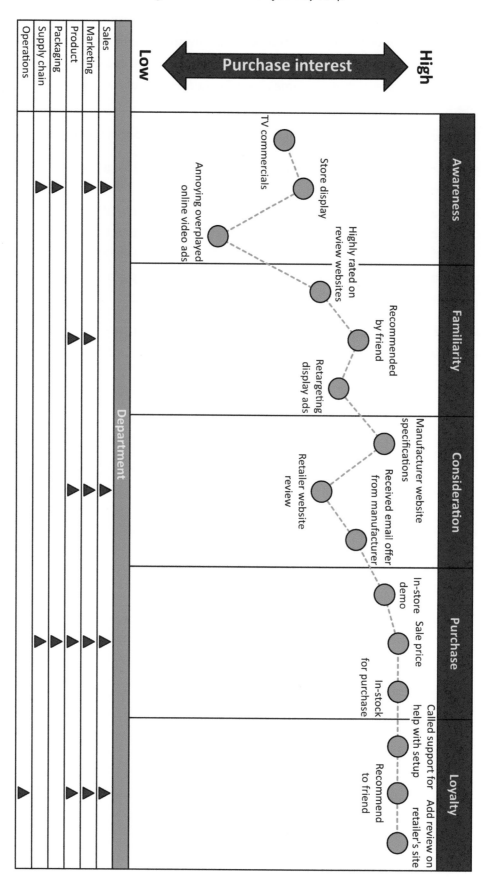

Path to purchase (P2P)

The path to purchase is a similar exercise to the decision journey map in that it maps the steps in the customer's journey. As previously mentioned, the path to purchase is more focused on the channels and the possible touchpoints that you can utilize to increase customer purchase intent.

Figure 14.1.3 Path to purchase

Awareness	Familiarity	Consideration	Purchase	Loyalty
› TV commercials	› Word of mouth	› Company website	› Company website	› Product registration
› Public relations	› Review websites	› Company blog	› Sales representative	› Support representative
› Sponsorships	› Trade magazines	› Social media pages	› Store associates	› Encourage reviews
› Social media ads	› 3rd party blogs	› Online reviews	› Displays	› Referral bonus
	› Retargeting ads	› Email marketing	› Coupon (affiliate) websites	› Newsletters
	› Online video	› Retargeting ads	› Demos	
		› Online video		
		› Landing pages		

From the path to purchase framework, you can understand the combination of the marketing tactics and the message type best suited to influence customers during the stages of their path to purchase. Message type refers to the difference between an informational message better suited for someone toward the beginning of their path versus an offer message with the intent to close a sale.

Creating a path to purchase or a decision journey map can be a complex task, requiring substantial research. This is particularly true for high-involvement purchases where customers do extensive research prior to making their purchase decision. For both frameworks, it should be expected that marketers and firms have their own variations of stages and layouts. These will be due to preference, so if tasked with building one of these be sure to understand what preferences exist.

Customer journey loop

As with many frameworks in marketing, there is an evolution in how researchers depict processes and customer behavior. The decision journey map and the purchase funnel both depict the purchase process as being linear. The customer journey loop, developed by McKinsey & Company, depicts the purchase journey as a circular motion (Court, Elzinga, Mulder, & Vetvik, 2020). The framework is built on touchpoints that repeat as the purchase process repeats. There are, however, areas of the process that may be skipped or deprioritized depending on a shopper's level of loyalty.

Figure 14.1.4 Customer journey loop

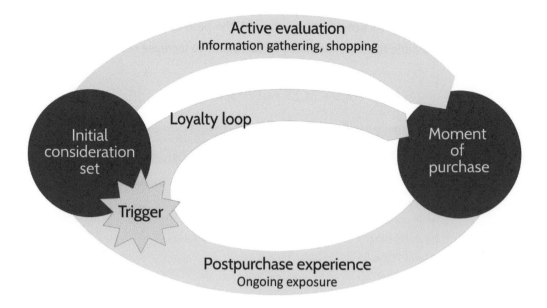

Customer journey loop steps

- **Trigger** - This is the moment in which a catalyst occurs that initiates the purchase process.

- **Step 1: Initial consideration** - In the first step, customers form an initial consideration set of brands and solutions from existing knowledge.

- **Step 2: Information gathering** - The second step is the information-gathering step where brands and solutions are evaluated, added and subtracted from consideration based on the shopper's perception.

- **Step 3: Moment of purchase** - The third step is the moment of purchase. The final product selection occurs, and there is the potential for decision changes at this moment based on influences such as price, wait time, or availability.

- **Step 4: Experience and evaluation** - During this step the customer will use or experience the solution and thus form opinions. These opinions will impact subsequent purchase decisions with a potential outcome being the formation of loyalty.

- **Loyalty loop** - The loyalty loop is a shortcut in the purchase process. If a customer has developed loyalty to a brand and solution, they may forego the process of information gathering and evaluation.

Moments of truth (MOT)

The moment of truth is a phrase that was originally created by A. G. Lafley, the Chairman, President and CEO of Procter & Gamble (P&G) in 2005 denoting the most important moments that a shopper interacts with a brand or solution. These moments derive their importance due to their profound effect on the purchase decision.

- **First moment of truth (FMOT)** - The time at which a customer is first exposed to a product and is relevant to both browsing offline or online. It is the first several seconds when a person encounters a product and marketing efforts have the ability to convert a browser to a buyer. P&G describes the FMOT as the "moment a consumer chooses a product over the other competitors' offerings."

- **Second moment of truth (SMOT)** - This is the moment or moments when a consumer experiences the solution and formulates a perception of it and its delivery of the brand promise.

- **Third moment of truth (TMOT)** - The moment at which the consumer outwardly shares information regarding their experience with the solution. This may be in several forms including online reviews, word-of-mouth, or social media posts.

- **Zero moment of truth (ZMOT)** - This term, created by Google in 2011, references the pre-purchase research that consumers conduct in preparation to making the final purchase decision. The ZMOT has become a critical step in the purchase journey and is evidenced by Google research indicating that 88% of U.S. customers conduct online research prior to making a purchase (Google LLC, 2011).

Purchase influencers

As you learn about customer segments and the steps that precede purchase, purchase influencers may come into the picture. They are a source of information or bias that influences a customer's purchase journey. Influencers can have a profound impact on the purchase decision. An example is a child who demands that a parent buy a specific type of cereal. In the assessment of the purchase process, the presence of influencers should be understood and where you may effectively influence them.

14.2 Experiential marketing

Why experiential marketing?

As much as humans insist that they make well-thought-out purchase decisions that are free of influence or bias, the truth is that purchase decisions are mostly based on emotion (Chierotti, 2019). Earlier in the discussion around brands and their importance, we reviewed how brands can deliver an emotional connection that leads to loyalty. A product with a strong unique selling proposition based on a set of features can in most cases be replicated or surpassed by a competitor. The power of branding and emotional connections is the difficulty competitors face when attempting to convince customers to abandon and switch their loyalty. Experiential marketing focuses on the intangible experiences that surround the brand that can foster the emotional connection between the brand and consumer.

The realms of experiential marketing

When you think of experience marketing, an amusement park may come to mind as an obvious example. This is true, but experiential marketing is relevant to all types of businesses and all types of interactions. A grocery store delivers an experience, a website delivers an experience, as does a phone call with a customer service representative.

To help marketers envision the best type of experience to support their brand, the framework of the "realms of experiential marketing" was developed (Pine II & Gilmore, 1998).

Figure 14.2.1 Realms of experiential marketing

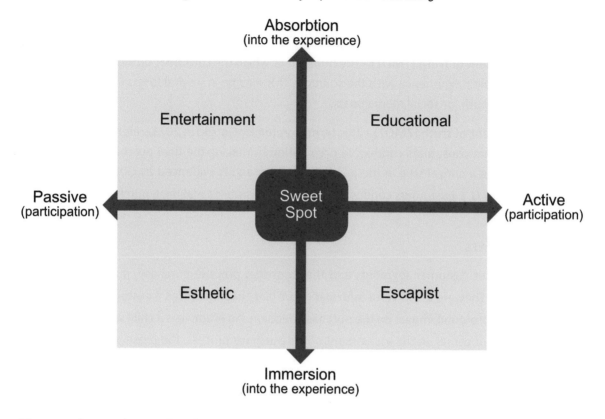

There are four realms or classifications of experiences. These are simply referred to as the "four Es."

- **Entertainment** - A passive form of experience where guests observe with no expectation or need for participation. There is, however, the possibility of responses such as laughter or applause.

- **Esthetic** - A passive form of experience that makes the experience seem welcoming from a sensory standpoint, such as the presentation of clean and updated décor.

- **Educational** - An active form of experience where guests are expected to actively learn and consciously engage to understand what is being taught.

- **Escapist** - An engaging form of experience where guests are encouraged to actively participate and become a part of the experience.

14.3 The promotion playbook

This section is designed to offer a view to the breadth of promotional marketing opportunities. As you build marketing plans, this may act as a playbook to source ideas of possible tactics.

Events

Gain in-person interaction with potential customers or influencers. Events allow for high-impact conversations and sales opportunities, but may be limited in reach.

- **Convention** - An event where people are gathered to learn and discuss a certain interest, such as the latest technology. If desired, a company may participate or even organize its own convention to bring people together that share an interest that is relevant to the product or service it provides.

- **Trade show** - Similar to a convention but differing slightly in the intent. A trade show is held for companies to attend and showcase their solutions to industry members.

- **Road show** - A series of events meant to engage with audiences across different markets in an effort to increase reach.

- **Demo (demonstration)** - A demo is when a product is used in front of an audience to highlight its benefits and features. May occur in a variety of venues including concerts, markets, in-stores, and even street vendors in highly trafficked areas. Similar to events, demos may have a high impact but limited reach.

The types of available events to participate in are wide ranging, such as festivals, flea markets, and farmers markets. They offer the opportunity for high-impact, live, or in-person interactions.

Advertising

Definitionally, advertising is the paid announcement of a product or service to the public.

Digital advertising

- **Display ads** - Also known as banner ads, display ads are the common advertisements that are typically square or rectangle blocks on webpages. Display ads can be static or contain animation. There are two types of customer targeting.

  - > **Prospecting:** These are ads served to a target customer segment that has not visited a website under your control. A third party such as Google may serve ads to target customers based on their profiles.

  - > **Retargeting:** These are ads that are targeted to customers who have visited a webpage you control or have taken an action that allows you to follow the customer's future actions and serve ads.

- **Paid search advertising** - Also known as PPC (pay-per-click) or SEM (search engine marketing). This form of advertising is where money is paid to place an ad listing on the results page of a search engine query. The phrase "pay-per-click" refers to how the ads are monetized. Each time an ad is clicked, there is a fee charged by the search engine.

- **Affiliates** - Affiliate marketing is the use of third-party websites or apps to provide sales and leads. There are two common ways affiliate websites work.

  - > As a coupon or offer aggregators such as Honey, RetailMeNot, or Coupons.com.

> An informational site that speaks about certain products and may offer links to facilitate the purchase of those products. Many of the websites list the "best of" for various solutions, such as best credit cards or best televisions.

- **Review sites** - These types of sites have grown tremendously in the last several years. They are websites that are often at the top of search results when people search for "best product 'X'" or "best service 'Y.'" These sites typically operate as affiliate websites using a pay-to-play model where if you want your product listed and listed favorably the site curators demand a bounty for your presence and every lead sent to your company. Other examples are websites and apps that offer to help you find a sports bar nearby or a good roofer.

- **Social media** - Advertising through social media channels via their websites or apps such as Facebook, Instagram, Snapchat, Twitter, LinkedIn, and others. Social influencers are another tactic used via social marketing where certain entities with large followings are paid to promote a brand or product. This form of advertising has exploded in importance over the last decade as 79% of all online adults in the U.S. have a Facebook account and 71% of Americans use Instagram (Smith, 2019).

- **Blog placement** - A commonly used source of information for many shoppers. A blog is an article available on the internet where any number of topics can be covered such as recommendations of places to visit on a trip or which natural cat food is the best. Within these blogs, ads may be placed both overtly or discreetly. A discreet ad may be a subtle recommendation for a bar to check out while you are at the must-see beach.

- **In-app** - A rapidly growing form of advertising, in-app ads offer another touchpoint similar to and may complement display and social media ads.

- **Online video (OLV)** - Video advertisements through video-based content hubs such as YouTube or websites that serve video content such as news channel websites.

- **Short message service (SMS)** - More simply known as text marketing, using this form of marketing can be quite disruptive. Due to its disruptive nature, this form of marketing is closely scrutinized and falls under the regulation of the FCC (Federal Communications Commission).

- **Sponsored content** - On news and article sites a tactic often used is sponsored content. This type of content is designed to look like an article that provides information, but is intended to present information that paints a positive picture or need for a product.

- **Native advertisement** - Similar to sponsored content, native ads are commonly located on news and article sites. These ads follow the format of the newsfeed so they appear "native" to the experience.

Television advertising

- **Traditional ad** - This refers to the standard 15-second, 30-second, or 1-minute advertisement that dominates ad formats during most broadcasts, particularly primetime TV and sporting events.

- **Over the top (OTT)** - Television advertising that is delivered via streaming services rather than traditional providers.

- **Direct response television (DRTV)** - This is a type of advertising in which the goal of the ad is to spur immediate action by providing a clear call to action such as to call a phone number or to visit a web address.

- **Infomercials** - These TV ads are typically seen in either short or long formats with the length most commonly being 2 or 4 minutes, or 30 or 60 minutes, respectively. They provide detailed information about the product and often include demonstrations. This format is most often used as a DRTV ad in which they attempt to gain an immediate sale.

Physical Mail

- **Direct mail** - Ad-hoc or recurring form of advertisement that can be highly targeted down to the personal address level. This granularity of targeting can come at a high price per piece of mail sent.

- **Circulars / flyers** - Mailings that are commonly sent by vendors on a recurring basis, such as weekly or monthly. Marketers may purchase space in the mailings. Target areas can be selected with precision, such as zip codes, making it a particularly useful form of advertising for local businesses.

- **Free standing insert (FSI)** - A printed piece of marketing collateral such as a booklet or card that is loosely inserted into a magazine, newspaper, or other medium. Most commonly this refers to the coupon booklets found in U.S. Sunday newspapers.

- **Door-to-door flyers** - In certain areas groups are available for hire that will go door-to-door throughout neighborhoods to distribute flyers. Based on instruction they will place the marketing collateral on doors or at another conspicuous location.

- **Samples** - Due to the nature of physical mail, there is the opportunity to advertise with the inclusion of product samples.

- **Mail lists** - List of names and addresses are available through vendors for purchase. Often these lists can be segmented by certain demographic and household characteristics.

- **Designated market area (DMA)** - Areas such as a city, metro area, zip codes, county, etc. that a mailing distributor clusters together. This allows marketers to specify areas that they'd like to receive their advertisements.

- **Farm** - A term commonly used in sales and in particular real estate marketing. A farm is when a selected area is targeted for mailings. The intent is to build and maintain awareness so when the need for the service arises, the company is in a customer's consideration set. This is done through consistent messaging over time, like watering the crops so they will be eventually ready to harvest.

Out of home (OOH)

- **Billboards** - A classic form of advertising most commonly found along roadways. The message must be both quick to understand and disruptive.

- **Public areas** - Advertising in public areas can offer both high reach as well as the potential for high impact. An example of high impact is an advertisement located at a bus stop where people waiting have an extended time to review and absorb the message. Public areas may also offer free advertising space, such as pinboards.

- **Public transit** - Examples: Metro, buses, and school buses. Advertising on both the inside and outside of these forms of transportation can offer different types of messaging opportunities. Inside, there is a captive audience that is likely to have significant time to view and absorb the message as they wait to arrive at their destination. Outside, there is the opportunity for higher reach as the mode of transportation moves by various audiences.

- **Vehicle advertising** - Car wraps, decals, and advertising trucks are some of the ways in which vehicle advertising is manifested. This tactic is best suited for awareness and reach, but may also be very useful for businesses that operate locally such as home service providers.

Sponsorships

- **Charity or cause** - A common tactic in which a brand attaches itself to a cause. This is with the belief that the association will increase goodwill with its target customer segment. For example: Breast cancer awareness is a cause largely targeted by female-centric brands where for a period of time a product may adopt pink packaging and send a portion of its profit to an associated charity.

- **Events** - As an event host or sponsor, a brand may attain greater relevance and goodwill with a customer segment by showing support of a shared interest. At events there is also the opportunity to make direct contact with attendees and have high-impact interactions.

- **Teams** - A sponsorship of a team may aid with building awareness and goodwill. This may be particularly fruitful at a local level where the sponsorship of a high school team or even a professional team increases relatability with the community.

- **Spokesperson** - The person or entity who speaks or acts as a representative of a brand. Often athletes, entertainers, characters, and celebrities may be effective spokespeople who provide a brand with personality, credibility, and potentially favorability with a loyal fan base. However, a brand may also designate an unknown person or entity as their spokesperson and realize success, such as the Progressive brand's Flo, or the Geico Gecko.

- **Movie** - A sponsorship of a movie can build favorable associations, thus helping a brand connect with a target segment.

- **Co-op / co-branding** - Agreements to work with another company and brand offer the chance to cross-pollinate the strengths of multiple brands. It can offer awareness and credibility to brands plus an entry point to a new customer base.

Product placement

This is a tactic where a fee is paid to have a product present in a medium such as a movie. Most commonly the intent is for the product to feel like it's a part of life and used by the subjects of the medium. An example is a branded beverage that is highly visible on the table in front of the game show judge who is seated behind that table. A second example is the branded semi-trailer truck that sits in the background of a movie scene.

Print

- **Newspaper** - A written publication that focuses on current events. Usually printed in black ink on grey or off-white paper, but some do offer color printing. Advertising space is available on the publication as well as the opportunity to place loose inserts or FSIs.

- **Magazines** - A written publication that may have one of many focal points. Usually printed in color on gloss or sometimes matte paper. Advertising space is available on the publication as well as the opportunity to place loose inserts or FSIs.

- **Trade magazine** - A form of magazine that is highly focused on information related to a trade or product. These will often provide reviews and product recommendations. Like affiliate review websites, some may be 100% objective while others may use a pay-to-play model.

Radio

- **Standard radio** - An audio communication medium that is free for listeners to access. Radio stations are typically funded through ad revenue. Ads may take the form of commercials or as endorsements by radio personalities.

- **Satellite radio** - An audio communication medium that requires a subscription for listeners to access. Ads may take the form of commercials or as endorsements by radio personalities.

- **Streaming radio / podcast** - An audio communication medium that is offered over the internet. It can offer some advantages over standard radio, such as the ability for better targeting and the potential for a better call to action responses since the user is directly connected to the internet.

Non-paid promotional tactics

Public relations

- **Press release** - A prepared statement that is written to officially announce news related to the brand or company with the goal of it getting picked up by various media outlets. Often, marketers will work with a public relations agency to share the release with their network of influencers and media teams. Examples of the news found in press releases are the announcement of events, sponsorships, and product launches.

- **Boilerplate** - A boilerplate refers to a statement that is listed at the end of a press release. It's a consistent statement that succinctly describes the company in the form of a short paragraph.

- **Press brief** - A group meeting set up to inform various media outlets of news in which they may editorialize. Public relations agencies may also set up a series of individual press briefs referred to as "desksides."

- **Event** - An event may be hosted to gather people, often influencers, to discuss the latest news regarding a product or brand. These events are designed to create goodwill with the influencers so that they will say positive things about the subject of your event to their audience.

- **Seminar / webinar** - A presentation either in person or via video conference. The presentation can allow for audience interaction and participation, often in the form of Q&A sessions. These may be open to any who would like to attend or may have a limited audience with the potential to charge an admission fee.

Organic content

- **Email** - An efficient way to spread messages to a list of recipients. Can be used as ad-hoc communication or be sequenced as part of a "nurture" email campaign that is intended to maintain communication. Marketing via email in the U.S. is regulated by the FTC by the CAN-SPAM Act. Before using this tactic, ensure compliance with the regulations.

- **Blog** - A blog is a website that acts as a repository for various content posts curated by the website owner. To raise awareness and consideration, marketers may advertise or write for third-party blogs. They may also create their own blogs to post content with the intent to gain organic search traffic.

- **Social media / discussion boards** - Includes an ever increasing number of options such as Facebook, Instagram, Reddit, Twitter, and more. These communication channels may be used to disseminate information and contribute to conversations regarding relevant topics.

- **Wiki** - A website that openly allows third-party contributors to edit its content. Marketers may use wikis in one of two ways. The first could be to post or edit information on an existing wiki that may help raise awareness or consideration for their product. The other may be to launch a wiki as a way to demonstrate expertise and stewardship on a topic that supports the brand.

- **White paper** - A published report that is meant to provide an authoritative view on a specific issue. Marketers may publish a white paper to explain how a new product or service delivers a new and better solution to a need.

Influencers / advocates

- **Social media influencer** - A form of digital advertising, social entities with large followings may or may not be compensated to use or associate with a brand or product in order to promote it.

- **Endorsement** - More than simply using or associating with a brand or product, an endorsement is a stronger message where the entity with influence actually states approval or support. Like social media influencers, endorsers may or may not be compensated.

- **Family / friends** - A source of referral and word of mouth influence. Marketers can incentivize these influencers to advocate for their solution. Marketers often extend the incentive to both the referrer and the referent.

- **Experts** - Influencers with expert knowledge can be compelling. For example, a salon worker may be told by her supervisor with 25 years of experience that a certain brand of scissors is the best.

- **Multi-level marketing (MLM) / network marketing** - A business model in which a company has a commission-based sales force of non-employees. These individuals are compensated for selling products as well as for referring additional salespeople to the network. On an ongoing basis, the referrer receives compensation for the revenue generated by the salespeople they had referred in. This compensation strategy is used with the intent to exponentially grow the network of salespeople.

Sweepstakes

A form of contest where a prize or prizes is awarded to the winner(s). This is a method used with the intent to raise awareness and encourage engagement. Sweepstakes are a useful tactic to gather leads. For instance, to enter a sweepstakes, contact information may be required such as name, email address, and phone number.

Referrals

Word of mouth is an extremely powerful form of influence. Referrals may be encouraged and come organically, however incentivizing referrals can drastically boost advocacy and result in a powerful sales force. Research completed by Nielsen showed that 92% of people trust recommendations from friends and family (Nielsen, 2012). Additionally, 75% of business to business sales leaders have found that referral leads have a higher conversion rate (Williams, 2015).

Samples

May be provided to consumers in a variety of ways including direct mail and events. An important consideration must be made before investing in the production and distribution of samples. The sample must be good enough to increase purchase interest.

14.4 Advertising checklist

We have discussed several of the ways in which you can promote your brand and solutions. In this section we will list some of the considerations along with best practices you should employ as you prepare ad messaging and creative assets.

Brand fit

Your brand and products have a target customer. During the creation of an ad campaign, start with the customers, their need, and how you will deliver a solution to that need. Also consider the higher-level need and think back to Maslow's hierarchy of needs. Your brand should have a position, and every advertisement should consistently reinforce that position. Use and follow the brand book.

Relatability

As you work to build a brand, a key measure is relatability. Relatability is commonly measured by asking target customers if they agree with the statement: "Brand 'X' is a brand for me." Your advertising needs to foster brand relatability.

Campaign-ability

Prior to embarking on the creation of an advertisement or the purchase of ad space, have a strategy in place including the expectation of the ad intent, considering if the ad is planned to be a one-off or as part of a campaign. A campaign may span several mediums, so imagery and message need to be developed so that it is compatible across the mediums. Campaigns may also span long periods of time yet need to remain fresh. Evaluate the campaign story for its ability to deliver longevity and evolve.

Breakthrough

Advertisements that go unnoticed are obviously ineffective. To garner attention, the ad needs to break through the noise and stand out versus all of the stimuli competing for the customer's attention. This can be accomplished in many ways. The saying "sex sells" is a classic way in which marketers have attempted to break through. Also consider where and how the audience is consuming the advertisement. Think of television commercials during football games where people are packed in bars watching the TV. During the ads bars commonly switch the audio to music, so then the sound of the ads shown becomes obsolete.

Hook'em

Advertising, particularly digital ads, needs to go beyond just breaking through and gaining attention. The message needs to contain a hook that spurs interest so that the ads are not skipped or plainly ignored. These hooks should be immediate in order to capitalize on the viewers' initial attention. An example of a hook would be an intriguing statement such as "What if I told you, you could never need to fold laundry again?" This statement is said with the intention of immediately arousing interest and wonder.

Focused and simple

Concept tests are designed to reveal the most compelling single-minded benefit. Advertising is where that single-minded benefit is put to use. Advertisements need to effectively deliver a message while typically gaining only a small fraction of a viewer's attention. The advertising message needs to be straightforward so that it has a chance to be understood. In addition, the layout and fonts of the creative must also be simple for customers to quickly comprehend. Also, as you evaluate creative assets bear in mind that you are reviewing the asset with a perfect understanding of context. A real customer would not be served the ad with the same context.

Legible

Creative assets must be legible. Fonts, colors, and contrast need to be used intelligently. Screens and monitors greatly differ in quality and color. Don't assume people have great vision, including those who use corrective lenses. Only 75% of people in the U.S. are seeing with good vision (Dr. Johnson, 2018).

Call to action (CTA)

Every ad should have a goal of producing a result, delivering a customer action. The action may be overt such as "call now" or may be subtle where the goal is to increase consideration. As you plan your creative brief, clearly define the call to action best suited to achieve your business goal. For omni-channel campaigns, expect the call to action to differ based on the medium and its placement on the path-to-purchase.

Avoid trouble

Here are a few items to consider that will help mitigate the chance that your advertising will get your brand and company into legal trouble.

- **Quality assurance (QA)** - This is a critical step in the creative development process. Errors can be costly and may carry a multitude of risks including bad customer experience, poor creative effectiveness, legal challenges, and costly liabilities. Despite the ever-constant push to move quickly, demand that adequate quality assurance is done.

- **Making claims** - Ensure any claims or demonstrations contained in the advertising are accurate and factual. They should be researched for validity and documented prior to placing in an ad. Some mediums such as TV networks may ask to review your claim substantiation prior to agreeing to air your ad.

- **Calling out competitors** - As a marketer it is your job to differentiate your brand and solution against competitors. Direct comparisons and speaking about competitors can produce positive results, but can also open up a Pandora's box of legal challenges and increased competition. This isn't a recommendation to avoid competitive comparisons, but a call to understand the potential ramifications. Think back to the discussion of game theory.

- **Using trademarks and protected content** - All too often creative development teams and marketers make the mistake of using protected images and words that they do not have permission to use. This can be a costly mistake in that you may need to pull down an ad at a critical time and pay for it to be altered. Some trademarks are repeatedly used erroneously such as March Madness® and the Super Bowl®, using these marks may get you a cease and desist letter or worse yet, legal action against your company.

- **Legal review** - In many but not all cases, customer-facing messaging should be reviewed and approved by legal counsel. Sometimes to marketers their recommendations may seem overly conservative, but their feedback is valuable as their primary goal is to protect the company from lawsuits and legal challenges.

14.5 Purchasing media

How to purchase media

Given the vast number of media types, media buys can take several forms. For non-digital media, purchasing directly from a media outlet is an option, but many companies prefer to go through advertising agencies. In general, agencies may provide a simpler way to purchase and manage media placement. They can leverage relationships to develop creative assets, can provide expertise in strategy, budgets, and placement, and can use their size to receive preferential advertising rates. Many agencies aren't equally qualified across various marketing mediums. They often specialize. They may be great with DRTV, but may be weak in out of home.

When purchasing media, budget is extremely important. Some mediums may require high investments in the form of building creative assets, printing, and the minimum costs required to gain adequate reach and frequency.

Prior to moving forward with a media buy, it is advised to understand the data and KPIs that will be used to determine success. For instance, cost per impression. Not all impressions are created equal. The precision of targeting for each of those impressions may differ. Digital advertising has grown tremendously over the past decade due to its efficiency and ability to accurately attribute the source of online purchases.

Frequency and reach

Frequency and reach are two primary metrics to consider when building a promotional campaign. Reach is the number of target customers who will be exposed to the message, and frequency is the number of times each target customer sees the message. A balance between the two must be reached to maximize campaign effectiveness. Too much reach with little frequency will yield customers who can't recall an ad campaign. Too much frequency with too little reach will limit the number of target customers exposed to the message, as well as for those exposed it may come to the point of over-exposure, where they begin to detract because the message becomes repetitive and annoying.

Research has shown that in digital awareness campaigns the optimal number of frequency exposures is between 5 and 9 (Okadar, 2017). For campaigns attempting to drive purchase intent, 10 or more is optimal (Burton, Gollins, McNeely, & Walls, 2019). These, however, are guidelines for digital and based on the ability of the message to break through the noise and drive action. The necessary frequency may differ in individual cases.

In addition to the total number of exposures, research completed by Facebook found that customers should see the message at least twice a week to capture 95% of potential purchase intent lift. Figure 14.5.1 illustrates the data from Facebook and also indicates that more than two exposures per week yield little to no additional benefit (Facebook IQ, 2016).

Figure 14.5.1 Frequency curve

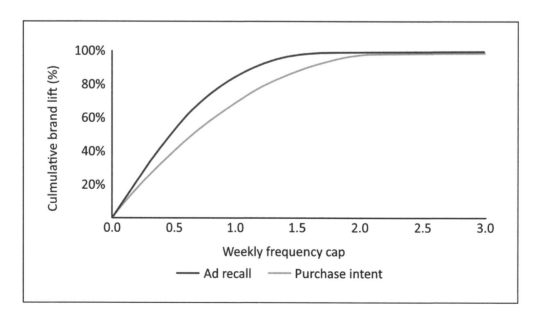

Purchasing ad space in different mediums

In this section, basic information for the most common advertising mediums—also known as channels—will be discussed. This section will not discuss specific customer targeting capabilities. Each medium offers varying degrees of targeting by geography, demographics, and psychographics, and these variances may further differ by vendor.

Digital

Digital advertising comes in many forms as reviewed in the promotion playbook. There are, however, a handful of dominant types.

> Display ads

> Social media

> Paid search

> Online video

> Affiliates

In the digital space, three advertisers—Google, Facebook, and Amazon—account for almost 70% of digital ad spend (Sterling, 2019). For digital advertising, cost is associated with performance metrics such as the number of impressions, the number of clicks, the number of conversions (sales), the number of leads, or the number of video views.

In digital, rather than having a predetermined quoted price or an insertion order, advertisers typically use a utility pricing model. There is a set price per unit of a metric, and as the quantity of units go up, the cost goes up. To protect against overspending, marketers can specify a spending limit or "cap." Pricing in digital marketing is also typically dynamic; it constantly fluctuates based on supply and demand. Constraints on how much you are willing to spend on a per unit basis may also be set.

Most vendors have online accounts with an interface where you can set budget information. In these dashboards you are able to directly upload creative assets as well as gather performance metrics.

Television

Traditional television advertising almost always utilizes one of three standard lengths of time.

> 15 seconds

> 30 seconds

> 60 seconds

Often, the longer duration ads are used to launch a campaign and introduce a new solution. Then once awareness and familiarity are established, marketers may shift to shorter and less expensive 15 second ads that are intended to act as reminders.

Television ads are commonly purchased considering time, channels, markets, as well as frequency and reach. Cost is typically calculated in one of two ways.

> Cost per thousand impressions (CPM)

> Cost per point, which is in reference to the number of gross rating points (we will define gross rating points in the advertising terminology & measurement chapter)

Broadcast companies may be more cautious than other mediums about ads that make claims. It is not uncommon for them to require that clients provide the claim substantiation prior to scheduling the ad.

Infomercials

This form of television advertising is specific in that it contains a strong immediate call to action such as to call now or visit a specific website. These differ from traditional television ads in that the lengths are typically longer. Short-form infomercials are typically two or four minutes in length, while long-form infomercials are either 30 or 60 minutes. Due to the length of these ads, they are often shown during off peak hours and / or on cable networks. This is done to maximize return on ad spend by taking advantage of the lower advertising rates.

Print

Print advertising is available in many sources such as newspapers and magazines. Print ads are purchased with various cost considerations.

> Distribution quantity

> Designated market area (we will define designated market area in the advertising terminology & measurement chapter)

> Size and layout of the advertisement

> Location of the advertisement such as back cover versus a page in the middle of the publication

> Number of colors used to print the advertisement

It's common for publications to request a minimum commitment from their clients. For example, they may require a six-month minimum for a monthly publication equaling six total ads.

CHAPTER 15: ADVERTISING TERMINOLOGY & MEASUREMENTS

In this chapter we will define many of the various terms and metrics used across the most popular marketing mediums.

15.1 General terminology

Term	Definition
Integrated marketing campaign	Also known as multi-channel marketing or omni-channel campaign. This refers to marketing campaigns that are present across multiple mediums or channels. The advertising across the various channels is usually coordinated to be simultaneously run so that the campaign message is reinforced and consistent.
Call to action (CTA)	A practice in marketing messages where the target of the message is prescribed an action to take. For example, visit us online at xyz.com, call now, or click here to learn more.
Creative or Creative asset	The advertisement, such as an image, video, or written ad.
Ad spend	The total number of dollars spent on a given ad campaign.
Working budget or Working spend	The number of dollars budgeted or spent to purchase media inventory.

Term	Definition
Non-working budget or Non-working spend	The number of dollars budgeted or spent to build the advertisement creative.
Above the line (ATL)	Refers to mass media advertising channels that are used to reach broad groups of people. • Goal: To build awareness and familiarity • Channel examples: TV, radio, magazines, and OOH • KPI examples: Reach, frequency, impressions, and GRP
Below the line (BTL)	Refers to media advertising channels that are more personalized and targeted. • Goal: To create consideration and drive purchases • Channel examples: Social media, display ads, and direct mail • KPI examples: Site visits, CTR, CR, CPA, followers, and likes
Payment terms	Contracts and invoices should include payment terms that define when the invoice needs to be paid. Common coding for payment terms may look like: • Net 30: this means the invoice total is due within the next 30 days • 1%/10, net 30: this means the invoice total is due within the next 30 days, but if the invoice is paid within 10 days there is a 1% discount
Insertion order (IO)	A formal written authorization to launch an advertisement. It acts as a purchase order and commonly includes details of what the advertiser is committed to deliver.

15.2 Digital marketing terminology

Term	Definition
Uniform resource locator (URL) or Domain name	The web address of a website.
Landing page	A webpage created to be the first page visited by external traffic. These are often pages built to align with specific ad CTAs.

Term	Definition
Microsite	A website that is a subsegment of a broader website intended to have a discrete purpose. For instance, a content blog that is set up as a microsite because it does not contain core information about the company and products.
Search engine rank position (SERP)	The average organic rank position of a webpage. The lower the rank number, the better.
Prospecting	Advertising that utilizes an advertiser's user database to deliver ads. Advertisers most often have criteria available to target users.
Retargeting	Advertising that utilizes first-hand knowledge of the target's history, such as a visit to a specific webpage.
Programmatic advertising	Refers to automated buying and selling of online advertisements. It is designed to increase marketing efficiency and optimize the use of media inventory by using an algorithmic bidding system.
Organic	Refers to the unpaid ranking of a webpage or may refer to a webpage that was created with the intent to achieve a high unpaid search engine rank.
Keywords or Search terms	Words or sets of words that are searched by customer targets when they use search engines to seek information.
Branded search term	A term or phrase that is entered into a search engine that contains a brand name.
Unbranded search term	A term or phrase that is entered into a search engine that does not contain a brand name.
Attribution	Refers to the origin of customers, when and where contact was made with the customer. Marketers may split attribution among various touchpoints, such as a paid search ad and a social media ad if a customer experiences both. Attribution is used to help determine how effective various channels are at producing a desired customer outcome.

Term	Definition
Cookie	A method to track a user's online behavior. For instance, a person browsing the web may click on an ad. This can activate a cookie that will track their future browsing behavior. Cookies help marketers target ads and assign attribution.
Deduplication (De-dup)	Digital marketing activities commonly overlap. For instance, a single person who places an order may have clicked on a paid search ad as well as a retargeting ad. This can result in both channels receiving credit or attribution for the sale. Deduplication is the removal of those double counts by only keeping the primary contact point.
Urchin traffic monitor code (UTM code)	UTM codes are set up as a way to track the information of website visitors. For instance, a click on a display ad will direct a viewer to a webpage. The display ad will have a UTM code that is assigned to it so that when it passes a viewer through to the webpage, it will add the UTM to the webpage URL. This code serves as a tracking mechanism so you may learn where traffic to the page originated from. There are five pieces of information available to track through the use on a UTM code. 1. Traffic source - Where the traffic is from. Examples: Facebook, Google, Bing, or the name of an email list 2. Medium - The channel. Examples: Cost per click (CPC), email, social, referral, or display 3. Campaign name - The name of a specific campaign. Examples: Fall saving event, spring cleaning, or family & friends event 4. Content - The call to action button that was clicked from the originating source. Some sources may contain multiple CTA buttons on the same interface, such as an email or a webpage with CTA buttons located at the top and bottom of the page. 5. Keyword term - Used specifically for paid search ads, this will help you track the exact combination of words searched by a visitor.
Online video (OLV)	Video advertisements through video-based content hubs such as YouTube, Rumble or websites that serve video content such as news channel websites.
Display advertising	Used synonymously with "banner advertising," this is a form of advertising in which content blocks are placed on webpages.
Responsive display advertisement	A display ad that will reconfigure to optimize the ad layout based on the viewers' screen size, such as desktop, tablet, or phone.

Term	Definition
Dynamic display advertising	A display ad that will update based on a viewer's information, such as browsing history or demographic.
Search engine marketing (SEM) or Paid search	An advertising channel where advertisers pay to be placed at the top of search results lists.
Pay-per-click (PPC)	Refers to digital advertising where an advertiser pays for each time an advertisement is clicked. This includes tactics such as display advertising and paid search.
Search engine optimization (SEO)	The optimization of webpage content and information tags to yield the best search engine rank possible.
Social media advertising	Advertising through social media channels via their websites or apps such as Facebook, Instagram, Snapchat, Twitter, LinkedIn, and others. Social influencers are another tactic used via social marketing where certain entities with large followings are paid to promote a brand or product.
Social influencer	A form of advertising where owners of popular social accounts on platforms such as Instagram and YouTube may be compensated to show and endorse the use of a brand or product.
Short message service (SMS) or Text message	Used synonymously with text messaging, SMS may be used as a marketing channel. SMS marketing is subject to FCC regulation via the Telephone Consumer Protection Act (TCPA). Before using this medium, ensure compliance with the regulations.
Affiliate marketing	Is the use of third-party websites or apps to provide sales and leads. Common forms of affiliate websites are coupon aggregators and product review websites.
Remnant inventory	Refers to ad placements that advertisers have not been able to sell in a desired time-frame. These slots may be purchased at a reduced cost as they fill gaps in the advertiser's schedule.
Impressions or Views	The number of times an ad was viewed.
Completed views	The number of times an online video ad was viewed from start to finish.

Term	Definition
Unique impressions or Unique views	The number of people who have viewed the ad.
Cost per thousand impressions (CPM)	The cost of a thousand impressions. • CPM = Working ad spend / Number of impressions * 1,000
Page views	The number of times a webpage is viewed.
Clicks	The number of clicks generated by an ad.
Cost per click (CPC)	The ratio of dollars spent to clicks. Most often this ratio is shown as a percentage. • CPC = Dollars spent / Number of clicks
Lead	A potential buyer. In digital marketing you may have campaigns that intend to get prospects to submit information such as their name, email address, and phone number into a lead capture form.
Cost per lead (CPL)	The ratio of ad spend to leads. Most often this ratio is shown as a dollar amount. • CPL = Ad spend / Number of leads
Calls	The number of calls generated by an ad or campaign with a call to action that instructs viewers to call.
Orders	The number of orders placed. Orders may differ from units due to the possibility that a single order may contain multiple units.
Units	The number of product units that are sold.
Cost per order (CPO)	The ratio of ad spend to orders. Most often this ratio is shown as a dollar amount. • CPO = Ad spend / Number of orders

Term	Definition
Cost per acquisition (CPA)	Use of this term may vary. Commonly refers to the ratio of ad spend to orders or the ratio of ad spend to new customers. Most often this ratio is shown as a dollar amount. • CPA = Ad spend / Number of orders • CPA = Ad spend / Number of new customers
Conversion rate (CR or CVR)	The ratio of orders to page views. Most often this ratio is shown as a percentage. • CR = Number of orders / Number of page views
Monthly active users (MAU)	The number of unique logged-in website or application users in a given month.
Revenue or Sales	The amount of revenue or sales generated by an ad. Often these are used interchangeably, however we will discuss the difference in the understanding financials chapter.
Return on ad spend (ROAS)	The ratio of revenue to ad spend. Most often this is shown as a ratio. • ROAS = Dollars sold / Ad spend
Average order value (AOV) or Average order size (AOS)	The average dollar value of the orders. • AOV = Dollars sold / Number of orders
Average unit size (AUS) or Price per unit	The average dollar value of each unit sold. • AUS = Dollars sold / Number of units sold
Average order discount	The average percent of discount given applied per order. • Average order discount = Dollars discounted / Orders
Coupon use rate or Promo code use rate	The ratio of orders where a coupon or promo code is used to total orders. Most often this ratio is shown as a percentage. • Coupon use rate = Orders using a coupon / Orders

Additional digital marketing terminology specific to websites

Term	Definition
Responsive website	Describes the ability of a website or webpage to reconfigure its layout based on screen size in order to optimize the viewer's experience on desktop, tablet, or mobile.
Page load time	The amount of time it takes for a webpage to fully load.
New visitors	The number of people who have entered the website for the first time.
Return visitors	The number of people who have reentered the website.
Sessions or Visits	The number of times people have entered the website. This differs from visitors because a single visitor may have multiple sessions over the course of a given time period, such as a week. In some situations, a visit and page view may also be used interchangeably.
Page views	The number of times a webpage is viewed.
Unique views	The number of times a webpage is viewed for the first time by a visitor.
Attribution	Refers to the assignment of a visitor's origin. When and where the contact was made with the customer.
Ordering visits	A visit where an order is completed.
Revenue per visitor	The average number of dollars to the website's visitors. • Revenue per visitor = Dollars sold / Number of website visitors
Bounce rate	The percent of website sessions in which only one page is seen. • Bounce rate = Number of single-page sessions / Total sessions
Cart abandon rate	The percent of sessions in which a cart is created but fails to end in a sale. • Cart abandon rate = Number of sessions in which a cart is created and does not result in a sale / Number of total sessions in which a cart is created

Term	Definition
Cart create rate	The percentage of sessions that results in customers placing an item in their cart. • Cart create rate = Number of total sessions in which a cart is created / Number of total sessions
Time on site, session, page	The amount of time a visitor spends on the website or on a given webpage.
No follow or No index page	Webpages may be designated as no follow or no index to prevent it from being found and ranked by search engines. This may be desired to avoid competition between pages with similar content.
General Data Protection Regulation (GDPR)	A 2018 European Union law that requires organizations to safeguard personal data and privacy rights (GDPR, 2020).
California Consumer Privacy Act (CCPA)	A law made effective in 2020 that was enacted to provide Californians with greater control over their personal information. Including: • The right to know about the personal information a business collects about them and how it is used and shared; • The right to delete personal information collected from them (with some exceptions); • The right to opt-out of the sale of their personal information; and • The right to non-discrimination for exercising their CCPA rights. (State of California Department of Justice, 2020)

15.3 Email marketing terminology

Term	Definition
Nurture campaign or Drip campaign	A series of emails that are sequentially sent to customers in an effort to create continuity and maintain relevance.
Sends	The number of emails that were sent.

Term	Definition
Opens	The number of times an email was opened. For instance, an email campaign may have 100 sends and 115 opens. Opens can exceed sends if emails are opened more than once.
Unique opens	The number of recipients who opened the email.
Open rate	The ratio of opens to sends. Most often this ratio is shown as a percentage. • Open rate = Number of opens / Number of sends
Clicks	The number of times an email has been clicked on.
Unique clicks	The number of recipients who have clicked on an email.
Click through rate (CTR)	The ratio of clicks to opens. Most often this ratio is shown as a percentage. • CTR = Number of clicks / Number of opens
Orders	The number of orders placed. Orders may differ from units due to the possibility that a single order may contain multiple units.
Orders per send, open, click or Conversion rate (CR)	The number of orders generated by each email sent, opened, or clicked. Depending on the context, conversion rate may be used to refer to any of these definitions. • Orders per send = Number of orders / Number of sends • Orders per open = Number of orders / Number of opens • Orders per click = Number of orders / Number of clicks
Units	The number of product units that are sold.
Revenue or Sales	The amount of revenue or sales generated by an ad. Often these are used interchangeably, however we will discuss the difference in the understanding financials chapter.
Revenue per send, open, click	The average number of dollars generated by each email sent, opened, or clicked. • Revenue per send = Dollars sold / Number of sends • Revenue per open = Dollars sold / Number of opens • Revenue per click = Dollars sold / Number of clicks

Term	Definition
Average order value (AOV) or Average order size (AOS)	The average dollar value of the orders. • AOV = Dollars sold / Number of orders
Average unit size (AUS) or Price per unit	The average dollar value of each unit sold. • AUS = Dollars sold / Number of units sold
Unsubscribes	The number of emails sent that recipients respond to by unsubscribing from the mailing list.
Unsubscribe rate	The ratio of unsubscribes to sends. Most often this ratio is shown as a percentage. • Unsubscribe rate = Number of unsubscribes / Number of sends
Invalid addresses	The number of email addresses on a mailing list that are known to be false. It is common for people to give false information in contact forms in order to avoid being placed on a mailing list.
SPAM or Junk email	Refers to emails that are viewed by the recipients as unwanted or unsolicited. Many email solutions have SPAM blocking algorithms that shield its users from these emails by quarantining them in a SPAM folder.
SPAM rate	Certain email marketing software solutions contain a tool that will provide an estimate of the likelihood that an email will be flagged as SPAM by the recipients' email solution.
CAN-SPAM Act	Marketing via email in the U.S. is regulated by the FTC via the CAN-SPAM Act. It establishes requirements for commercial messages and gives recipients the right to stop companies from emailing them (Federal Trade Commission, 2020).

15.4 Telemarketing and chat terminology

Term	Definition
Inbound call	A call received by the organization.
Outbound call	A call initiated by the organization.
Toll free number or Telephone number (TFN)	A commonly used acronym that refers to a telephone number and may more specifically be used to refer to toll free numbers such as telephone numbers beginning with 800.
Unique toll free number or Telephone number (Unique TFN)	May be used in different media channels or within a channel as a way to track the source that drove the inbound call. For example, a television ad that runs on four different networks may have four versions of the ad, each with a unique TFN, one for each network.
Interactive voice response (IVR)	An automated system that gathers information from customers prior to connecting calls to live representatives.
Call count	Depending on the context, may be used to describe the number of inbound, outbound, or total calls.
Contact	A call in which contact is made with the client.
Contact rate	The ratio of calls where contact is made to the total number of calls. Most often this ratio is shown as a percentage. • Contact rate = Number of contacts / Number of calls
Availability rate	The ratio of inbound calls that are answered within a specified time criteria to the total number of calls received. Most often this ratio is shown as a percentage. • Availability rate = Number of inbound calls answered in less than "X" time / Number of inbound calls
Average wait time or Average hold time	The average amount of time a caller waits to speak with a live representative. • Average wait time = Amount of time waited / Number of callers

Term	Definition
Abandonment rate (AR)	The ratio of times a caller hangs up waiting for a contact to the number of calls received. Most often this ratio is shown as a percentage. • AR = Number of abandoned calls / Number of inbound calls
Idle time	The amount of time representatives spent without a caller to speak to.
Average handle time (AHT)	The average amount of time a phone representative spends speaking to a caller. • AHT = Time on calls / Number of contacts
Chats	The number of chat conversations.
Message count	The number of messages that are exchanged between the customer and the chat representative.
Call after chat rate	The ratio of chats followed by a customer call within a specified period of time to the total number of chats. Most often this ratio is shown as a percentage. • Call after chat rate = Number of calls answered in less than "X" time after a chat / Number of chats
Ghost chat	A chat started by a customer but then abandoned prior to a resolution.
Ghost chat rate	The ratio of ghost chats to the total number of chats. Most often this ratio is shown as a percentage. • Ghost chat rate = Number of ghost chats / Number of chats
First contact resolution (FCR)	The number of contacts in which the caller's issue is completely solved in the first contact. This can be measured as a ratio against the number of calls received. Most often this ratio is shown as a percentage. • FCR = Number of contacts resolved on the first contact / Number of contacts
Customer service score (CSS)	Many call centers request that customers complete a survey rating following a call. These ratings result in a customer service score.

Term	Definition
Escalations	Depending on the context, may be a call that is passed from a representative to a higher-level representative or manager. It may also refer to a chat in which a customer chooses to end the chat in order to speak to a representative via telephone.
Escalation rate	The ratio of escalated calls or chats to the total number of calls or chats. Most often this ratio is shown as a percentage. • Escalation rate = Number of escalated calls / Number of contacts • Escalation rate = Number of escalated calls / Number of chats
Leads	Potential buyers with available contact information.
Qualified leads	Leads that are contacted by representatives and confirmed to be potential customers.
Unqualified leads	Leads with low to no sales potential. It could be due to them not answering the phone, answering and stating that they are no longer interested, or due to incorrect contact information.
Converted leads	Leads that are contacted and ultimately make a purchase.
Conversion rate (CR or CVR)	Depending on the context, may refer to the ratio of calls with a completed order or it may refer to the ratio of contacts with a completed order. Most often this ratio is shown as a percentage. • CR = Number of orders / Number of calls • CR = Number of orders / Number of contacts
Orders	The number of orders placed. Orders may differ from units due to the possibility that a single order may contain multiple units.
Units	The number of product units that are sold.
Revenue or Sales	The amount of revenue or sales generated by an ad. Often these are used interchangeably, however we will discuss the difference in the understanding financials chapter.
Revenue per contact	The average number of dollars generated by each contact. • Revenue per contact = Dollars sold / Number of contacts

Term	Definition
Average order value (AOV) or Average order size (AOS)	The average dollar value of the orders. • AOV = Dollars sold / Number of orders
Average unit size (AUS) or Price per unit	The average dollar value of each unit sold. • AUS = Dollars sold / Number of units sold
Offer use rate	The ratio of orders that have an offer applied to the number of total orders. Most often this ratio is shown as a percentage. • Offer use rate = Number of orders with an offer applied / Number of orders
Discount rate	The percent number of savings customers get on average when purchasing through the call center. • Discount rate = Dollars discounted / Dollars sold
Refunds	The number of refunds or the amount of dollars refunded.
Refund rate	Depending on the context, may refer to the ratio of contacts that result in a refund to total contacts or it may refer to the number of units sold and refunded to the total number of units sold. • Refund rate = Number of contact with a refund / Number of contacts • Refund rate = Number of refunded units / Number of units sold
Telephone Consumer Protection Act (TCPA)	Telemarketing in the U.S. is regulated by the FCC via the TCPA. Before using this tactic, ensure compliance with the regulations.

15.5 Television advertising terminology

Term	Definition
Television commercial (TVC)	TVC is a commonly used acronym that refers to television advertisement.
Spot	A term used to refer to a television commercial.
Impressions or Exposures	The total number of times an advertisement is viewed. A single person may view an advertisement multiple times, and each view is considered an impression.
Daypart	Refers to different segments of time that are separated based on audience types and number of viewers. Dayparts have different values attributed to them, such as premium primetime dayparts versus overnight hours.
Remnant inventory	Refers to ad placements that advertisers have not been able to sell in a desired time-frame. These time slots may be purchased at a reduced cost as they fill gaps in the advertiser's schedule.
Voice over (VO)	The narration that occurs as the audio in a commercial when the narrator is not visually shown.
Overlay text or Super text	Text that is shown on screen that overlaps other visual parts. These are intended to be read and act as a core part of the message.
Designated market area (DMA)	Advertising areas available for targeting, such as a city, metro area, zip code, or county.
Cost per thousand impressions (CPM)	The cost of a thousand impressions. • CPM = Working ad spend / Number of impressions * 1,000
Frequency	The average number of times an advertisement is viewed by the reached population. • Frequency = Number of impressions / Reach
Reach	The number of different people who will be exposed to the advertisement at least once.

Term	Definition
Gross rating point (GRP)	A measure used to quantify the proliferation of the advertising. • GRP = Percent of the target market population reached * Average frequency For example: A campaign that reaches 25% of the target population with a frequency of 5 will yield a GRP of 125.
Cost per point (CPP)	Refers to the cost per GRP. • CPP = Ad spend / GRP

Additional television terminology specific to DRTV

DRTV ads contain a call to action, usually either to call-in or to visit a webpage. Based on the CTA, the metrics associated with telemarketing or websites will be relevant.

Term	Definition
Toll free number or Telephone number (TFN)	A commonly used acronym that refers to a telephone number and may more specifically be used to refer to toll free numbers such as telephone numbers beginning with 800.
Unique toll free number or Telephone number (Unique TFN)	If the advertisement has a CTA directing viewers to call-in, marketers may use a unique TFN as a method to track which ad was viewed leading to the call. This will be done in an effort to track the effectiveness (attribution) of a specific advertisement. An ad on show or channel "A" may use a certain TFN, while the same ad with the exception of a unique TFN may be used on show or channel "B."
Landing page	A webpage created to be the first page visited by external traffic. These are often pages built to align with specific ad CTAs.
Unique URL or Landing page	If the advertisement has a CTA directing viewers to visit a webpage, marketers may use a unique URL as a method to track which ad was viewed leading to the webpage visit. This will be done in an effort to track the effectiveness (attribution) of a specific advertisement. An ad on show or channel "A" may use a certain URL, while the same ad with the exception of a unique URL may be used on show or channel "B."

Term	Definition
Landing page traffic or Landing page visits	The number of times the webpage contained in the CTA is viewed.
Leads	The number of leads generated by the advertisement.
Calls	The number of calls generated by the advertisement.
Orders	The number of orders generated by the advertisement.

CHAPTER 16: ENGAGING WITH AGENCIES

In a marketing role you will undoubtedly either work with or for an agency at some point in your career. Agencies can serve several functions, including:

- Develop brand or campaign strategy
- Offer additional bandwidth and project support
- Offer design services, including websites
- Buy and manage media
- Lead public relations and events
- Provide expertise in any number of marketing needs

In this chapter we will review general guidelines to building a successful relationship with any type of agency or project.

16.1 Hiring an agency

Hiring an agency is a multi-step process. Here is an overview of some of the key steps in the process as well as best practices for maintaining a successful relationship.

1) Initial research

Prior to engaging with an agency, do research and ask around for recommendations. There are thousands of agencies of all shapes and forms that may be experts in certain fields, all fields, or possibly nothing. You may find it necessary to work with multiple agencies in order to get the expertise desired across different fields.

As you conduct your research, note how well the agency is marketed and how easy it is to find. If you are looking for help to market your business, it should be from those who have proven to market their own business well.

Once your research is complete, plan to engage with at least three agencies and limit yourself to at most five. Speaking to at least three will give you the ability to triangulate relative quality, creativeness, and pricing. Capping to at most five will ensure that you don't spend an inordinate amount of time on the process. Consider speaking with agencies of different sizes and locations, as this can give you a broader perspective of the services available.

2) Create a request for proposal (RFP)

To officially engage with an agency in an effort to understand what they can offer you, a request for proposal (RFP) should be created and presented to the agency. An RFP is a formal document given to potential vendors that provides details regarding the desired services. In many ways an agency RFP resembles a design brief. Often, these RFPs are referred to as an agency brief. Here are informational elements to include in an RFP:

Elements of an agency RFP

- **Company background** - Provide information about your company, such as history, recent success, size, brands, as well as any other pertinent information. This information helps the designers to better understand the originator and the motivation for the request.

- **Brand and product information** - Share information regarding the 4 Ps and 3 Cs for your brand and solutions.

- **The goal** - Define the goal or need that is the impetus for the requested work.

- **Situation analysis** - Give them a summary of the current situation and what your goals are, including the strategy and tactics planned to achieve the goal. It's common for agencies to help with crafting the strategy and tactics, so if these are not defined for the RFP and part of the request, make it known in the project scope.

- **Project overview and scope** - Provide project details and deliverables, including the KPIs used to define success or failure.

- **Requirements** - If known, list exactly what you would like delivered, such as certain creative assets in various sizes.

- **Provide files** - Give the agency any files or data that will help them create a proposal that utilizes existing assets. This will help you gain the most accurate portrayal of their capabilities.

- **Project schedule** - Share your key dates and timeline requirements.

- **Budget** - Depending on your negotiation methodology, you may or may not want to include budget information. Some follow the rule of thought that you should provide a number first to anchor the vendor to a lower price. Others may suggest you allow the agency to provide a price first. If you provide the agency a budget, it may be likely they find a way to match it or exceed it regardless of the amount of work.

- **Points of contact and roles** - Provide information for the various project roles such as the driver, contributor, and approver.

- **Service level agreement (SLA)** - Include service level agreement (SLA) expectations such as turnaround time for revisions.

- **Non-disclosure agreement (NDA)** - The information in your brief is likely confidential and may be highly sensitive. It's advisable to enter into a non-disclosure agreement (NDA) with the agency to avoid the possibility of the information getting leaked.

You will need to pick a methodology for the RFP. In some cases the request may be simple and straightforward, such as to schedule and conduct a photoshoot. Other RFPs may be much larger in scale where the expectation is to launch an ongoing relationship where the type of work extends across projects.

Depending on the need and your methodology, the RFP can be written to reflect a high level of precision where you have existing knowledge of the exact work that needs to be done. Conversely, you may choose to leave the RFP ambiguous and allow the agencies to utilize their expertise to create a proposal for how they feel they can best assist you with achieving your goal.

3) Evaluate the agency proposal

Once the agency receives your RFP, it's likely they will want to meet to understand you and the proposal better. When the agency completes work on their proposal, they will present it to you by either simply submitting the paperwork or by actually doing a presentation. Many agencies prefer to present and to do the presentation in-person.

The proposal should take into consideration and answer the needs scoped in the RFP. Beyond those basics, here are some underlying questions to ask yourself as you evaluate their proposal:

- Did they take the time to understand the company, situation, goal, or did they just use a canned pitch with your logo and tag line?

- Is the work innovative and thought provoking, and are they genuinely adding expert value?

- Did they do additional homework such as reach out to your customer base to get a sense of reaction to their ideas?

- Ensure you meet and are impressed by the account manager who will potentially be your day-to-day contact. Do you feel this person is someone who will help you thrive? The same applies for other critical roles, such as strategy, design, copywriting, ad placement. Is this a team that will accelerate your business?

- Will these folks be working on multiple accounts or dedicated to you?

- Will a relationship with this group make you look good? You are effectively hiring this team of people to complete work that will represent not just your brand and solution but it will also reflect on you personally as a marketer. A good or bad agency will make an impression on others in and outside the company regarding the work you've completed with them. These will be the people you will be dealing with on a daily basis, so ensure they are a team you want to work with.

- What are the hidden fees? Depending on the type of work, such as the creation of artwork, understand what potential added fees may apply subsequent to the initial proposal. Agencies may include two or three artwork revisions, but then charge per additional revision, which can cause fees to increase dramatically. Another common fee is the preparation and release of artwork files in different formats. Ask questions and know what to expect at this stage in the process.

4) Create the statement of work (SOW)

Following the proposal stage, negotiations should take place as part of the creation of the statement of work. During this negotiation period, you may also still be deciding which agency is best to hire. The SOW will describe the deliverables the agency is required to produce and their respective costs. The SOW is a critical document that is your contract with the agency. It needs to be detailed and unambiguous. The elements in a SOW may vary significantly based on the type and scope of work. The following is not a fully comprehensive list but a strong foundation for the type of information that needs to be contained in the SOW:

Elements of a SOW

- **Detailed task list** - Details about the various tasks the agency is required to complete, such as design and printing of brochures in color on a specified paper grade. For work that requires the use of additional parties such as a photographer or models, detail who and how they will be found, negotiated with, and paid. For analytics and reporting of campaign results, specify the desired metrics, the granularity, how often the reporting needs to occur.

- **Cost schedule** - Include specific costs for the various work (e.g., per artwork revision, per ad placement, per page of edited copy, etc.).

- **Team information** - The team members, titles, and labor rates for the various contributing members.

- **Service level agreement (SLA)** - State the SLA to establish expectations for working hours, response times, and completion times for various types of work needed.

- **Budget guidelines** - Travel expectations, budget, and reimbursement.

- **Payment terms** - Payment terms and frequency of billing and payment.

- **Cancellation policy** - Cancellation policy, including the amount of notice required and the possible associated fees.

- **Transfer of files and user access** - Include details (timing and cost) regarding the release of account ownership, delegated access, and file transfers. This is critical to include in the event that an agency relationship ends on bad terms.

16.2 Managing the agency relationship

In many cases, despite the desire to meet the entire agency team during the hiring process, it doesn't happen. The agency representatives will likely be higher level personnel, not the people involved in handling the day-to-day work. At the beginning of the relationship, it is crucial to introduce the teams. Establishing good rapport between the client and the agency can go a long way, and in-person introductions are best to help the teams establish a sense of one collective team.

It is best practice to extensively onboard the agency on the 4 Ps and 3 Cs. The time invested upfront should pay large dividends by saving time, increasing the quality of work, and making the collective team look good.

Successfully managing a client–agency relationship can make the team and its leaders look fantastic in the eyes of their leadership. Conversely, failure by either party can make both sides seem incompetent.

Get organized as a team. Establish key points of contact. Map processes and establish decision makers, contributors, and final approvers. Set expectations between the teams, including a cadence of when meetings should occur, review SLAs, and discuss known deliverable deadlines. Establish communication standards, such as the use of phone, email, messaging applications, or texting. Just as important is to establish the system for project tracking and file delivery. Lastly, get on the same page about work hours. This will be influenced by the SLA, but the team needs to be completely clear about availability and the expectation for a fast response.

If a rift does occur in the relationship, do not let it fester. Be transparent about the issues and attempt to resolve them. If there is no progress after a discussion, escalate the concerns to your leadership. As stated previously, sub-par work on either side of the relationship will negatively affect the perception of both sides, regardless of fault. Get issues resolved as soon as possible or end the relationship. These scenarios are why establishing the cancelation agreement in the SOW is extremely important.

———————

CHAPTER 17: SALES CHANNELS

The phrase sales channel refers to a way in which a customer may actually purchase a good or service. These are separate from promotional channels, but do often overlap. A promotional touchpoint, such as an event, may also be a sales channel when sales are made immediately on-site. There is a vast array of sales channels available today. In this chapter we will review several of the most common.

17.1 Physical location

A consistent location where customers may physically come to purchase the good or service.

Direct or branded location

A location that is branded specifically for the business that is run out of the location. These locations may be leased or owned space such as a storefront located in a mall.

Third-party retailer

A highly common selling channel, these third-party retailers are stores such as supercenter chains, grocery store chains, or department store chains. Manufacturers of goods are sold in a business to business transaction to the retailer, and then sold by the third-party retailer in a business to consumer transaction. This relationship offers manufacturers the advantage of wide distribution, but at the loss of controlling the business to consumer sales process.

Consignment

A store that is run by a third party that acts as an intermediary between the customer and the product seller. These differ from third-party retailers in that consignment stores never pay for or take ownership of the product. Consignment stores keep the product available for sale and handle the transaction with the customer. Following the sale, the store will take a commission and give the remainder of the proceeds to the original owner. In an effort to reduce inventory costs, some third-party retailers may use consignment selling for certain products, such as seasonal or perishable items.

Cooperative (Co-op)

A store that is owned and managed by members who invest the funds to maintain the store and then share the profits. As a member, there is partial ownership and control over operations and the sale of goods and services.

17.2 Personal

Absent a consistent physical location, in-person selling is also a primary form of sales for many industries. The sellers are commonly paid commissions or spiffs to incentivize performance.

Multi-level marketing (MLM)

Also known as network marketing. This is a business model where a network of salespeople sells and distributes a product or service. These salespeople are not employed by the company. They act independently and are paid a commission for the products they sell.

Salespeople are compensated for selling products as well as for referring additional salespeople to the network. On an ongoing basis, the referrer receives compensation for the revenue generated by the salespeople they had referred in. This compensation strategy is used with the intent to exponentially grow the network of salespeople.

Events or Markets

Can offer an opportunity to promote a brand or solution and immediately close a sale. Events may provide very targeted and eager customer segments. They also commonly offer a great opportunity to gain customer feedback. These are some of the top event types:

- Concerts / shows
- Farmers markets
- Flea markets
- Trade shows
- Conferences
- Demonstrations (Demos)
- Conferences

Business to business (B2B)

Describes the sales process of one business selling products or services to another business. These transactions often require in-person interaction where negotiations and a relationship are established over the course of the sales process. In the online selling section we will see how B2B sales may occur without the in-person interaction.

Door-to-door

A classic form of selling where salespeople go from home to home to pitch a solution and close a sale.

Mobile

Mobile sales can be exemplified by the food truck industry. The salesperson and experience come to where you are in order to maximize convenience.

17.3 Online selling

Website

Business websites with e-commerce functionality have become increasingly accessible and popular over the last several years. Creating a website allows a company to control the full customer experience and share information that may be limited when selling via a third-party online marketplace.

Marketplaces

Marketplaces are third-party online stores that allow marketers to list their products for sale. These may offer a good way for a marketer to gain access to a large set of buyers, but there are likely competitive items competing for good placement and sales. Marketplaces typically allow for less brand ownership and listing customization in comparison to a custom website. Some examples of popular online marketplaces include:

- Amazon
- Etsy
- eBay
- Alibaba.com
- Walmart
- Craigslist
- Yelp
- Social (Facebook, Instagram)

Apps

Third-party apps offer another way to reach an online audience. These apps generally feature streamlined experiences with simple product listings that may be limited to only a photo and short description. Some examples of popular selling apps include:

- OfferUp
- Facebook marketplace
- Mercari
- Nextdoor

E-sourcing

A B2B solution, e-sourcing is a method of procurement and sales in which a buyer may post information regarding a product or service they are attempting to source. The information may be submitted in the form of a request for proposal (RFP) or request for quote (RFQ). Suppliers are able to view RFPs, and, if desired, they may respond with a proposal. This method helps buyers gain multiple proposals quickly while also providing sellers access to more buyers.

17.4 Others

Telemarketing

The selling of goods or services over the phone. It is not uncommon for companies to outsource this function to third parties due to the added complexity and overhead cost to maintain a call center.

Auction

An auction is the sales process in which goods or services are made available for sale without a set price. Buyers are able to place bids on the item. In most situations the seller will allow bids for a set period of time and at the end of the time, sell the item to the highest bidder. The seller may set a reserve price where if no bid exceeds the price, the seller is not obligated to sell the item. The seller may also set a sale price, where if a buyer wants to immediately purchase the item, they can pay that price. Auctions may occur online or in-person.

Mail order

The selling of goods or services by taking orders via physical mail.

Distributor

Distributors typically maintain relationships with manufacturers and act as an exclusive buyer from the manufacturer with the agreement to distribute the product to a designated territory. Given the extremely high volume of product, distributors most often sell to wholesalers rather than direct to consumers.

Wholesaler

Wholesalers have purchasing relationships with distributors. They will buy high volumes of product from the distributors for a low per unit price and then sell to third-party retailers. Some wholesalers will also sell directly to consumers either from a physical location or through e-commerce.

Reseller

A reseller is a merchant that will purchase a good or service from a supplier with the intention of selling it to a consumer. Resellers may do so with or without the knowledge of their supplier. In situations where the supplier encourages the reselling of its product, the supplier may support the resellers with marketing collateral. The supplier may also provide versions of the product that are customizable so that the reseller may differentiate or uniquely brand the product.

Franchise

A sales and business model where the franchiser, the parent company, allows a franchisee the right to sell its goods or services under the parent's trademark or trade-name. The franchisee will pay the franchiser fees both upfront and ongoing to utilize these assets. Commonly the franchiser will assist the franchisee with systems and processes to help get set up and become successful. The franchiser will require the franchisee to maintain certain standards that are necessary to deliver a consistent brand experience across all franchises.

Part 4: Leading the business

Part 4 chapters:

CHAPTER 18: UNDERSTANDING FINANCIALS

To effectively analyze and manage your business, understanding basic financial terminology and metrics is vital. In this chapter we will review the definitions of common financial terms, various calculations, profit and loss statements, and other financial statements. We will also discuss company equity and its use as compensation.

18.1 Common metrics & terminology

Term	Definition / Calculation
Debt	Money, goods, or services that a company owes due to an agreement. A company may choose to take on debt in the form of bonds or notes in order to finance expenditures with the intention to repay them over time as cash is generated from the sale of goods and services.
Equity	Equity is ownership interest in a company or corporation and is typically in the form of common stock for publicly traded corporations.
Depreciation	This is the recognition of the reduced value of a capital asset (e.g., plant or equipment) over time as its useful life wears out. Depreciation is an expense that companies report with the benefit of reducing taxable income. There are different methods to calculate the amount of depreciation occurring in each year of an asset's useful life. One common method is straight-line depreciation, where the reduction in value is equal each year. For example, a $500,000 machine may be amortized over the course of 10 years, resulting in a $50,000 expense each year.

Term	Definition / Calculation
Amortization	Depreciation where over the course of time, expenses are captured to reduce the value of an intangible asset such as goodwill, patents, or copyrights. Depreciation differs in that it refers to a capital (tangible) asset. For example, a patent has a set time period before it expires. That patent carries value with it, but as the expiration approaches, the value of the patent will decrease. This decrease in value can be divided or amortized over time. From an accounting perspective, amortization is shown as an expense thus reducing a company's taxable income.
Variable cost	An expense that changes in proportion to increases or decreases in production volume within a given production schedule. For example, product inputs such as raw materials, packaging, and hourly labor.
Fixed cost	An expense that does not increase or decrease with changes to production volume. For example, costs such as lease payments, property taxes, and depreciation.
Cost of goods sold (COGS)	The costs directly related to the production of goods sold by a firm. It includes direct costs such as raw materials and direct labor as well as other production costs such as factory overhead.
Selling, general & administrative expenses (SG&A) or Operating expenses (OPEX)	The sum of all direct and indirect selling expenses, R&D expenses, and all general and administrative expenses. SG&A includes all costs not directly attributed to the production of a product or the rendering of a service. It's the cost to sell and deliver goods or services, plus the cost of managing the company.
Capital expenditure (CAPEX)	An investment of cash to purchase or upgrade a capital asset such as machinery, equipment, or buildings.
Sunk cost	An expense that has already been incurred with no way to recoup. The term is commonly used in situations where the subject of the expense, such as a piece of equipment, becomes unneeded. A sunk cost should not be factored into future decisions.

Term	Definition / Calculation
Impairment	A situation in which a company asset has lost value, so much that it has become significantly lower than its asset value to the extent that it cannot be recovered. For example, a brand was purchased by a company for $200 million. The brand reputation quickly declined and could only be reasonably valued at $50 million. The necessary adjustment to the asset's value is known as an impairment cost.
Foreign exchange (FX)	Refers to the impact created by the fluctuation in currency values relative to each other. A firm will report its financials in a single currency. Transactions that occur in other currencies must be converted. These conversions may have a positive or negative effect on financial metrics.
Gross sales	The sum of sales made.
Revenue or Net sales	The income a business generates from typical business activities such as the sale of goods or services. • Net sales = Gross sales - Customer discounts - Returns - Allowances
Gross margin or Gross profit or Gross profit margin	The revenue retained after incurring the direct costs of producing the goods or rendering the services. This may be calculated as number or as a percentage. • Gross margin = Net sales - COGS • Gross margin % = (Net sales - COGS) / Net sales
Operating profit	The remaining income after accounting for the costs of operating the business. • Operating profit = Gross profit - Operating expenses
Net income or Net profit or Bottom line	The remaining income after accounting for all of the accounting flows to and from the business. • Net income = Operating profit - Taxes - Interest or • Net income = Net sales - COGS - Operating expense - Taxes - Interest

Term	Definition / Calculation
Contribution margin	A measure of the profit contributed to the firm from the sale of products or services. Contribution margin may be thought of as the per unit sold profit that helps to offset fixed costs. • Contribution margin = Revenue - Variable costs or • Contribution margin per unit = (Revenue - Variable costs) / Number of units sold
Return on investment (ROI)	A measure of the level of growth for an investment. The higher the ROI, the better. • ROI = (Current value of the investment - Original investment) / Original investment
Earnings before interest, taxes, depreciation, and amortization (EBITDA)	This is a measure to understand a firm's operating profitability as well as act as an indication of cash flow. A negative EBITDA indicates a firm may have issues with generating cash and profit. A positive EBITDA is not a guarantee of a firm's health due to the omission of working capital, capital expenses, taxes, and interest. • EBITDA = Net income + Interest + Taxes - Depreciation and Amortization
Earnings before interest and taxes (EBIT)	This is a measure to understand a firm's earning power. It gives managers a view of the success of the core operating business without the noise created by taxes and capital considerations. • EBIT = Net income + Interest + Taxes or • EBIT = Revenue - COGS - SG&A
Working capital	A measure of a company's operating liquidity. The importance of liquidity is the ability for the firm to turn assets into cash if needed. • Working capital = Current assets - Current liabilities or • Working capital = Cash and cash equivalents + Accounts receivable + Inventory - Accounts payable

Term	Definition / Calculation
Free cash flow (FCF)	The amount of cash a company keeps available to pay debts, dividends, or interest to investors. It helps managers and investors determine how successful the company is at strengthening its balance sheet. FCF is seen as the main driver of a company's valuation. • FCF = EBIT * (1 - Tax rate) + Depreciation and Amortization - Change in working capital - CAPEX or • FCF = Operating cash flow - CAPEX
Cash conversion cycle	The cash conversion cycle is the amount of time it takes from investing cash in raw materials or goods to receiving cash from the sale of a finished good. The cash that is invested is referred to as working capital. Cash conversion cycle is usually measured in days, and the goal of a company is to reduce that conversion cycle to the fewest days possible. In some cases, companies are successful in achieving a negative conversion cycle in which they are able to sell their goods before they are required to pay their suppliers.

18.2 Standard calculations

In this section we will review some of the most common calculations that you are expected to understand and utilize on a daily basis.

Convert decimal to percent

When doing calculations, often you are left with a decimal number that is better communicated as a percentage. To convert the decimal to a percent, multiply it by 100%.

Example: 25 of the 80 units sold were refunded, what was the percent refund rate?

- Refund rate = 25 / 80

- Refund rate = 0.3125

- Percent refund rate = 0.3125 * 100%

- Percent refund rate = 31.25%

Percent growth

When comparing a metric over two periods of time, percent growth is used to calculate the relative growth or decline.

Example: Revenue of a product this year was $175,000, last year its revenue was $125,000. What is the percent year over year growth?

- Percent growth = (Ending value / Beginning value) - 1
- Percent growth = ($175,000 / $125,000) - 1
- Percent growth = 40%

Compound annual growth rate (CAGR)

Compound annual growth rate is a metric that provides a measure of compounded multi-year growth. To illustrate its importance, a product line has grown 80% over the course of the last four years. It may be a first inclination to think the product line grew 20% each year, but that is incorrect. Twenty percent growth each year would result in a total growth of 107.4% = [120% * 120% * 120% * 120% - 1]. Use the CAGR formula to find the correct answer.

Example: Sales increased from $100,000 to $180,000 or 80% over the last four years. Over that period of time, how much did sales grow annually?

- CAGR = (Ending value / Beginning value) ^ (1 / Number of years) - 1
- CAGR = ($180,000 / $100,000) ^ (1 / 4) - 1
- CAGR = 15.8292%

or

- CAGR = (1 + Total growth percentage) ^ (1 / Number of years) - 1
- CAGR = (1 + 80%) ^ (1 / Number of years) - 1
- CAGR = (1.8) ^ (1 / 4) - 1
- CAGR = 15.8292%

The reason why the answer is not simply 20% is due to the compounding effect of growth occurring in each of the four years. The 15.8292% growth in year 1 will increase the year 2 sales number from $100,000 to $115,829. The growth of 15.8929% in year 2 will be multiplied by the new number that includes the year 1 growth, $115,829. The compounding will continue in the same way each additional year.

Example: The annual growth schedule for a sales increase from $100,000 to $180,000 over four years.

- Year 0 = $100,000

- Year 1 = $115,829 = (Prior year amount * (1 + CAGR)) = ($100,000 * 1+15.8292%)

- Year 2 = $134,164 = ($115,829 * (1+15.8292%))

- Year 3 = $155,401 = ($134,164 * (1+15.8292%))

- Year 4 = $180,000 = ($155,401 * (1+15.8292%))

The weakness of the CAGR metric is the inability to understand changes in trends. For instance, the growth after four years was 80% or $80,000, which seems like a fantastic result. But what isn't apparent is that in year 1 the product line grew $60,000, and in year 2 it grew $35,000. In year 3 the product line growth slowed to only $5,000, and in year 4 it declined by $20,000. Looking at CAGR in isolation may give a false impression regarding the health of the business.

Product margin or Product profit or Contribution margin

Product margin is a measure of how much profit is made on a per unit sales basis. This measure focuses only on the variable costs that are incurred to produce or source the item.

Calculate profit margin per unit

- Profit margin per unit = Selling price - Cost per unit

or

- Profit margin per unit = Revenue - Variable costs

Calculate percent profit margin

- Percent profit margin = (Selling price - Cost per unit) / Selling price

or

- Percent profit margin = (Revenue - Variable costs) / Number of units sold

Retail margin and markup

When third-party retailers sell a product, they will often demand a certain amount of margin or markup in order to be interested in selling a product. Margin is based on the price that the item is sold for, whereas markup is based on the cost of the item sold.

Calculate retailer margin and markup

- Retail margin = (Retail price - Cost per unit) / Retail price

- Retail markup = (Retail price - Cost per unit) / Cost per unit

Basis points (bps)

Basis points are a way to communicate percentages and provide a way to calculate the change in percentages that removes the relative impact created by the amount of the percentages. A basis point is equal to one hundredth of a percent.

How basis points are counted

- 1.0% = 100 basis points

- 0.1% = 10 basis points

- 0.01% = 1 basis point

How to do a calculation using basis points

An analysis found that the control version of a test had a conversion rate of 10%, and the test version had a conversion rate of 12%. What is the change in basis points?

- bps = (Percentage "A" - Percentage "B") * 10,000

- bps = (12% - 10%) * 10,000

- bps = (2%) * 10,000

- bps = 200

Basis points in use

An analysis found that the control version of a test had a conversion rate of 10%, and the test version increased the conversion rate by 20%. This statement leaves ambiguity. It's unclear what 20% growth means. It could mean either of the following:

- Test conversion rate = Control conversion rate * (1 + Percent growth)

- 12% = 10% * (1 + 20%)

or

- Test conversion rate = Control conversion rate + Percent growth

- 30% = 10% + 20%

The use of basis points removes this ambiguity. Basis points would be counted as follows:

If the increase was from 10% to 12%, it would be an increase of 200 bps.

- Change in basis points = (Test conversion rate - Control conversion rate) * 10,000

- 200 bps = (12% - 10%) * 10,000

If the increase was from 10% to 30%, it would be an increase of 2,000 bps.

- Change in basis points = (Test conversion rate - Control conversion rate) * 10,000

- 2,000 bps = (30% - 10%) * 10,000

18.3 Profit & loss statement (P&L)

Profits and loss statements are a financial tool that helps you understand net operating profit or loss. P&Ls may be calculated at various levels from the total company level, down to individual products. For marketers the P&L framework assists with understanding the profitability of products, product lines, brands, etc., as well as delivers insight into where cost imbalances may lie. Lastly, P&L statements can help to understand the amount of marketing investment the brand or product line can profitably sustain.

When building a P&L you may encounter the terms *direct* and *indirect* when referring to product costs.

- **Direct cost** - A cost that is specifically tied to the production of a product such as manufacturing line labor, commissions, and raw materials. In most cases a direct cost will be a variable cost where there is an added cost per incremental unit produced and sold.

- **Indirect expenses** - A cost that is not tied to a specific unit or a product such as a plant supervisor salary, equipment depreciation, electricity, and insurance. In most cases indirect costs are fixed costs that will be consistent whether or not the next unit is produced.

Simple P&L statement structure

Figure 18.3.1 Simple profit and loss statement

Company "A" P&L Statement for 20xx		
1 Revenue	$5,000,000	
2 Direct costs	$2,800,000	
3 Gross profit	$2,200,000	Line 1 - Line 2
4 Indirect expenses	$950,000	
5 Net profit	$1,250,000	Line 3 - Line 4

Profit and loss statements should be evaluated at various actionable levels such as the product level, which may be calculated on a per unit basis. This will provide an understanding of the costs that can be absorbed while maintaining a certain level of profitability. These are particularly useful during innovation projects, where they are used to find the profit that the new product will deliver, as well as how much marketing investment is possible while adhering to a profitability requirement.

The order, categorization, and naming of P&L lines may differ by company, but the following example will give you an insight into how one is structured for a specific product. Note, in the following example corporate overhead not controllable by the business unit, such as tax and general and administrative expenses, are not included as they are allocated at a higher company-wide P&L level. This is common when the per product unit allocation of these expenses is extremely small or in the case of tax expense where there are other significant factors that will affect the overall company's tax liability. Because these items are not included, you will see that line 25 is referred to as gross margin, not net profit.

Product P&L statement example

Figure 18.3.2 Product P&L statement

	Widget "A" unit profit and loss statement		
1	**Retail price**	**$25.00**	
2	**Retail margin**	**30%**	(Line 1 - Line 2) / Line 1
3	**List price**	**$17.50**	
4	**Direct sales costs**	**$3.75**	Line 5 + Line 6 + Line 7
5	Coupons	$1.00	
6	Trade funds	$1.50	
7	Royalties	$1.25	
8	**Net Sales**	**$13.75**	Line 3 - Line 4
9	**Commissions**	**$0.75**	Line 10 + Line 11
10	Standard commissions	$0.50	
11	Spiffs	$0.25	
12	**Transportation**	**$0.75**	
13	**Warehousing**	**$0.20**	
14	**Product costs**	**$9.15**	Line 15 + Line 16 + Line 17 + Line 18
15	Raw materials	$2.45	
16	Packaging	$3.00	
17	Processing	$3.50	
18	Display packaging	$0.20	
19	**Unusual manufacturing**	**$0.02**	
20	**Product margin**	**$2.88**	Line 8 - Line 9 - Line 12 - Line 13 - Line14 - Line 19
21	**Marketing costs**	**$0.70**	Line 22 + Line 23 + Line 24
22	Events	$0.05	
23	Promotional materials	$0.20	
24	Advertising	$0.45	
25	**Gross margin**	**$2.18**	Line 20 - Line 21
	Product margin %	**16.5%**	Line 20 / Line 3
	Gross margin %	**12.5%**	Line 25 / Line 3

P&L statement line items explained

Line item	Description
Line 1: Retail price	The price retailers sell to customers.
Line 3: List price	The price a retailer or distributor pays the manufacturer for the product.
Line 4: Direct sales costs	Costs that can be directly attributed to a particular sale.
Line 5: Coupons	Offer discounts or monetary added value given at the time of purchase directly paid by the manufacturer, not filtered through an entity such as a retailer.
Line 6: Trade funds	An allotment of funds provided by the manufacturer to a third-party seller. These funds may be used for a number of reasons, such as slotting fees, scrap or damage fees, and to fund product offers run by the third party.
Line 7: Royalties	Funds awarded to a third party on a per unit basis. Examples: • The sharing of revenue to obtain the right to use a sports team logo. • Money committed to a charity based on the sales of the product.
Line 8: Net sales	The income a business generates from typical business activities, such as the sale of goods or services.
Line 10: Standard commissions	Normal commissions paid to sales personnel.
Line 11: Spiffs	Additional commissions paid typically for a limited period of time with the intent to increase focus on selling a particular product.
Line 12: Transportation	The cost of moving the product.
Line 13: Warehousing	The cost of storing the product.

Line item	Description
Line 15: Raw materials	The cost inputs and materials purchased that go into the manufacturing of a product.
Line 16: Packaging	The cost of the packaging materials.
Line 17: Processing (tolling)	The cost of processing the raw materials and completing the process of packaging the processed material inputs.
Line 18: Display costs	Additional packaging that may be used for products that require merchandising support.
Line 19: Unusual manufacturing	One-time costs or anticipated waste due to special circumstances.
Line 20: Product margin	The profit / loss achieved on a per product sold basis.
Line 21: Marketing costs	Marketing costs that are specifically related to the product but can't be tied to a particular sale. These overall costs may be estimated on a per unit sold basis by dividing the total cost by the number of units sold.
Line 25: Gross margin	The final profit / loss of the product with all costs factored in.

18.4 Accounting basics

At a minimum there are three financial statements that you should be familiar with that all U.S. corporations are required to file on a quarterly basis.

- Statement of income (Income statement)
- Balance sheet
- Statement of cash flows

Corporations are also required to provide a statement of comprehensive income as well as a statement of stockholders' equity. For our purposes we will focus on the first three as they are most closely tied to the work of marketing professionals.

Statement of income (Income statement)

Income statements may also go by the names profit and loss statement or the statement of operations. This statement provides a view of the revenue or income and the expenses incurred during a period of time. The income statement utilizes the following formula:

- Net income = (Revenue + Gains) - (Expenses + Losses)

Component	Example(s)
Revenue	The income a business generates from typical business activities such as the sale of goods or services
Gains	Sale of a piece of equipment or piece of property
Expenses	<ul><li>Cost of sales</li><li>Product fulfillment</li><li>Marketing expense</li><li>Depreciation expense</li><li>General and administrative expenses</li><li>Interest expense</li><li>Tax expense</li></ul>
Losses	<ul><li>Payout due to lawsuit settlement</li><li>Impairment</li></ul>

At the end of an income statement, publicly traded companies will divide net income by the number of outstanding shares to provide investors a highly followed metric called earnings per share (EPS).

Figure 18.4.1 Income statement - Apple Inc. 2019 Annual report

Apple Inc.

CONSOLIDATED STATEMENTS OF OPERATIONS

(In millions, except number of shares which are reflected in thousands and per share amounts)

	Years ended		
	September 28, 2019	September 29, 2018	September 30, 2017
Net sales:			
Products	$ 213,883	$ 225,847	$ 196,534
Services	46,291	39,748	32,700
Total net sales	260,174	265,595	229,234
Cost of sales:			
Products	144,996	148,164	126,337
Services	16,786	15,592	14,711
Total cost of sales	161,782	163,756	141,048
Gross margin	98,392	101,839	88,186
Operating expenses:			
Research and development	16,217	14,236	11,581
Selling, general and administrative	18,245	16,705	15,261
Total operating expenses	34,462	30,941	26,842
Operating income	63,930	70,898	61,344
Other income/(expense), net	1,807	2,005	2,745
Income before provision for income taxes	65,737	72,903	64,089
Provision for income taxes	10,481	13,372	15,738
Net income	$ 55,256	$ 59,531	$ 48,351
Earnings per share:			
Basic	$ 11.97	$ 12.01	$ 9.27
Diluted	$ 11.89	$ 11.91	$ 9.21
Shares used in computing earnings per share:			
Basic	4,617,834	4,955,377	5,217,242
Diluted	4,648,913	5,000,109	5,251,692

See accompanying Notes to Consolidated Financial Statements.

Apple Inc. | 2019 Form 10-K | 29

Balance sheet

The balance sheet gives managers and investors a look into a company's current financial position. It is a snapshot for a point in time delivering an assessment of what the company owns versus what it owes. This snapshot helps with providing an understanding of a company's health, liquidity, and financial flexibility. A balance sheet is separated into two sections: the first is assets, and the second is liabilities and stockholders' equity. The formula used for the balance sheet is:

- Assets = Liabilities + Shareholders' equity

Component	Definition and examples
Assets	Anything that is owned by a firm with an economic or exchange value. Examples: • Cash and cash equivalents • Inventory • Accounts receivable • Property and equipment • Goodwill
Liabilities	A claim on assets by outside entities. Excluding a claim on equity. Examples: • Accounts payable • Unearned revenue • Long-term debt
Stockholders' equity	The amount of assets remaining, payable to stockholders after liabilities have been paid. Examples: • Preferred stock • Common stock • Retained earnings

Figure 18.4.2 Balance sheet - Apple Inc. 2019 Annual report

Apple Inc.

CONSOLIDATED BALANCE SHEETS

(In millions, except number of shares which are reflected in thousands and par value)

	September 28, 2019	September 29, 2018
ASSETS:		
Current assets:		
Cash and cash equivalents	$ 48,844	$ 25,913
Marketable securities	51,713	40,388
Accounts receivable, net	22,926	23,186
Inventories	4,106	3,956
Vendor non-trade receivables	22,878	25,809
Other current assets	12,352	12,087
Total current assets	162,819	131,339
Non-current assets:		
Marketable securities	105,341	170,799
Property, plant and equipment, net	37,378	41,304
Other non-current assets	32,978	22,283
Total non-current assets	175,697	234,386
Total assets	$ 338,516	$ 365,725
LIABILITIES AND SHAREHOLDERS' EQUITY:		
Current liabilities:		
Accounts payable	$ 46,236	$ 55,888
Other current liabilities	37,720	33,327
Deferred revenue	5,522	5,966
Commercial paper	5,980	11,964
Term debt	10,260	8,784
Total current liabilities	105,718	115,929
Non-current liabilities:		
Term debt	91,807	93,735
Other non-current liabilities	50,503	48,914
Total non-current liabilities	142,310	142,649
Total liabilities	248,028	258,578
Commitments and contingencies		
Shareholders' equity:		
Common stock and additional paid-in capital, $0.00001 par value: 12,600,000 shares authorized; 4,443,236 and 4,754,986 shares issued and outstanding, respectively	45,174	40,201
Retained earnings	45,898	70,400
Accumulated other comprehensive income/(loss)	(584)	(3,454)
Total shareholders' equity	90,488	107,147
Total liabilities and shareholders' equity	$ 338,516	$ 365,725

See accompanying Notes to Consolidated Financial Statements.

Apple Inc. | 2019 Form 10-K | 31

Statement of cash flows

A statement of cash flows provides a summary of the cash and cash equivalents that are entering and leaving a company. It is a tool to measure how successful a company is at generating cash to handle its operating expenses and debt obligations. The statement will begin with the period's starting cash position and show inflows and outflows under the various activities to arrive at an ending cash position.

The statement of cash flows differs from the income statement in that it does not include depreciation or amortization. Cash flow statements are purely concerned with cash inflows and outflows. However, when reviewing a cash flow statement, adjustments for depreciation and amortization may be present to reconcile numbers with those shown in the income statement.

There are three primary components to a cash flow statement and a fourth supplemental component:

Component	Example(s)
Cash from operating activities	• Net income • Adjustments from operating activities such as depreciation, other operating expenses, changes in operating assets and liabilities such as inventory, accounts receivable or accounts payable
Cash from investing activities	Payment or proceeds on property and equipment
Cash from financing activities	• Paid dividends • Payments on long-term debt • Stock buyback
Disclosure of noncash activities (supplemental)	These activities can be wide-ranging, one such example is the exchange of stock for land

Figure 18.4.3 Statement of cash flows - Apple Inc. 2019 Annual report

Apple Inc.

CONSOLIDATED STATEMENTS OF CASH FLOWS

(In millions)

	Years ended		
	September 28, 2019	September 29, 2018	September 30, 2017
Cash, cash equivalents and restricted cash, beginning balances	$ 25,913	$ 20,289	$ 20,484
Operating activities:			
Net income	55,256	59,531	48,351
Adjustments to reconcile net income to cash generated by operating activities:			
Depreciation and amortization	12,547	10,903	10,157
Share-based compensation expense	6,068	5,340	4,840
Deferred income tax expense/(benefit)	(340)	(32,590)	5,966
Other	(652)	(444)	(166)
Changes in operating assets and liabilities:			
Accounts receivable, net	245	(5,322)	(2,093)
Inventories	(289)	828	(2,723)
Vendor non-trade receivables	2,931	(8,010)	(4,254)
Other current and non-current assets	873	(423)	(5,318)
Accounts payable	(1,923)	9,175	8,966
Deferred revenue	(625)	(3)	(593)
Other current and non-current liabilities	(4,700)	38,449	1,092
Cash generated by operating activities	69,391	77,434	64,225
Investing activities:			
Purchases of marketable securities	(39,630)	(71,356)	(159,486)
Proceeds from maturities of marketable securities	40,102	55,881	31,775
Proceeds from sales of marketable securities	56,988	47,838	94,564
Payments for acquisition of property, plant and equipment	(10,495)	(13,313)	(12,451)
Payments made in connection with business acquisitions, net	(624)	(721)	(329)
Purchases of non-marketable securities	(1,001)	(1,871)	(521)
Proceeds from non-marketable securities	1,634	353	126
Other	(1,078)	(745)	(124)
Cash generated by/(used in) investing activities	45,896	16,066	(46,446)
Financing activities:			
Proceeds from issuance of common stock	781	669	555
Payments for taxes related to net share settlement of equity awards	(2,817)	(2,527)	(1,874)
Payments for dividends and dividend equivalents	(14,119)	(13,712)	(12,769)
Repurchases of common stock	(66,897)	(72,738)	(32,900)
Proceeds from issuance of term debt, net	6,963	6,969	28,662
Repayments of term debt	(8,805)	(6,500)	(3,500)
Proceeds from/(Repayments of) commercial paper, net	(5,977)	(37)	3,852
Other	(105)	—	—
Cash used in financing activities	(90,976)	(87,876)	(17,974)
Increase/(Decrease) in cash, cash equivalents and restricted cash	24,311	5,624	(195)
Cash, cash equivalents and restricted cash, ending balances	$ 50,224	$ 25,913	$ 20,289
Supplemental cash flow disclosure:			
Cash paid for income taxes, net	$ 15,263	$ 10,417	$ 11,591
Cash paid for interest	$ 3,423	$ 3,022	$ 2,092

See accompanying Notes to Consolidated Financial Statements.

Apple Inc. | 2019 Form 10-K | 33

18.5 Equity basics

It is highly likely that during the course of your career you will work for a publicly traded company or a company that is private but uses equity as a way to fund activities and compensate individuals. This chapter will discuss some basics regarding equity in an effort to lay a foundational understanding for why leaders of a company take certain actions or decisions. This will help you understand how a company may use equity as a method for compensation. We will review common terminology and some basic information regarding company equity.

Company equity

Company equity refers to an ownership stake in a company, the most common of which are stock held by publicly traded company shareholders. These stocks are bought and sold on market exchanges, which in the U.S. are primarily the New York Stock Exchange (NYSE) and the NASDAQ. The following is a list of basic terms that you should be familiar with when discussing equity.

Term	Definition
Earnings date	Every three months corporations are required to submit an earnings report to the Securities and Exchange Commission (SEC). These are public reports that disclose financial statements as well as disclosures about the business results.
Shares outstanding	The number of stock shares that are held by stockholders as shown on the corporate balance sheet.
Market capitalization or Market cap	The dollar value of a corporation as determined by the value of its outstanding shares. • Market cap = Number of outstanding shares * Price per share
Initial public offering (IPO)	A corporation's first offering of ownership to the public through the sale of stock.
Earnings per share (EPS)	Earnings per share is a commonly followed metric that indicates the financial health of a corporation. It is listed on the income statement. • EPS = Net income / Number of shares outstanding
Price to earnings ratio (P/E ratio)	A metric that provides insight into a corporation's stock price in relation to its ability to generate earnings. High-growth companies typically have higher P/E ratios. • P/E ratio = Stock price / Earnings per share

Term	Definition
Insider	An individual who is a senior manager, officer, board of directors member, or shareholder with more than 10% equity in the company. Individuals who possess material information that has not been made public, such as an impending merger, are also considered insiders. Insiders are required to adhere to strict regulations regarding the purchase or sale of company stock.

Organization valuation

As an employee of a publicly traded company, you may often wonder what causes the value of your company to move up or down. There are countless reasons why investors and traders choose to buy or sell stock in a company. Here's a list of some of the most notable reasons:

Common factors that affect a company's valuation

- A change in the company's valuation and growth relative to the industry and rest of the market, using metrics such as FCF, P/E ratio, and EPS

- A quarterly report exceeds or falls below analysts' expectations

- Stability and consistency of company's financial performance

- Future expectations communicated by management

- A major announcement such as restructuring or acquisition

- An analyst upgrade or downgrade

- Speculation or hype

- Macro-economic factors that cause a broader bull or bear market movement

Employee equity compensation

Some companies award employees equity ownership as a form of compensation. Equity compensation is primarily done in a few ways:

- **Share plans** - These plans may operate in many different manners. In most cases the company will allow you the opportunity to purchase company stock at a discounted price.

- **Restricted stock** - A company may award you stock as compensation. Restricted stock is given to you and held in an account for you, but before you gain ownership of the stock, certain criteria must be met. A common criterion is to complete a certain period of employment with the company.

- **Options** - There are several different types of options. Generally, a stock option is awarded to an employee with a designated strike price. The strike price never changes, so if the value of the stock increases above the strike price, the employee has the option to purchase the stock at the strike price, which instantly results in a capital gain. If the stock price is below the strike price, the employee is not obligated to purchase the stock.

Most often equity awards are subject to vesting. Vesting refers to a minimum period of time that you must be employed by the company prior to giving you ownership of the equity. For example, a company may award you $20,000 in equity but stipulate that there is a four-year vesting period in which 25% of the value is released each year. Therefore the $20,000 is set aside for you. It is important to note that the value may increase or decrease over that time, but you may not access the funds until they are vested. Assuming the value stays at $20,000, at the end of year 1 you have ownership of $5,000 of the $20,000. After year 2 you will have ownership of an additional $5,000 of the total $20,000, and so forth.

Awards of equity may be taxed as income. A company may or may not cover that tax liability when they award you the equity, so talk to your human resources representative, accountant or financial advisor to understand more. If you are an investor in your company or in stocks, any realized gain will be subject to capital gains tax. The tax rate on capital gains differs based on the length of time you own the stock prior to selling. Short-term capital gains are when a stock is owned for less than a year prior to the sale. These gains are taxed at your income tax rate. Long-term capital gains are when a stock is owned for more than a year prior to the sale. This tax rate is usually significantly lower than your income tax rate, but the specific rate you pay will depend on your income.

Note: This chapter is not intended to serve as investment, financial, or tax advice. Tax rates are subject to change at any time.

CHAPTER 19: LEADERSHIP & BUSINESS ETIQUETTE

The manner in which you present yourself, communicate, and lead will play a determining factor in your ability to ascend within an organization. This chapter is devoted to providing best practices to help you succeed and be more efficient. It will help you think deeper about how to influence your perception and understand methods to strengthen that perception. Every organization has its own culture, norms, and nuances; the information in this chapter is designed to transcend these and benefit you regardless of the organization you are in.

19.1 Presentations

Mastering how to deliver a presentation and learning how to build an effective slideshow takes time and practice. Most may never "master" presenting, and those who are great presenters can always work to improve. Here are the steps and best practices to help you command the room and deliver a knockout presentation.

1) Preliminary planning

Set your goal for the presentation. Create a set of key points that will align to and support the attainment of the goal. For example, if your goal is to get management to agree to invest marketing dollars into a product launch, a key point could be to communicate the added revenue potential created by the investment. The key points and goal must align in order to create a logical and cohesive story that the audience can follow.

Choose and analyze your audience. Based on the goal and key points of the presentation, the audience for your presentation may vary. Think through considerations such as:

- **Decision-making ability** - Have the right people in the room

- **Values and interests** - Make the information easily relatable

- **Level of background knowledge** - Determine the level of detail and level-setting that is required to ensure the entire group has enough understanding to feel comfortable in making a decision

- **Preconceptions related to the topic** - Anticipate how much convincing will be required to achieve your goal

- **Preferred communication style, such as:**
  - > Conversational vs. lecture
  - > Professional vs. personal
  - > Formal vs. lighthearted
  - > High vs. low number of visuals

2) Building and organizing

A presentation is a story. It should give background information, build through a logical flow, and culminate with a final conclusion with the intent to achieve the goal.

- **Create the storyline** - Separate the presentation into distinct sections, and at the conclusion of a section, succinctly recap key points that you want the audience to recall. Keep the number of key points manageable. At the conclusion of the presentation, the points from the various sections should tie together to tell the story in support of your goal. They should culminate on a summary slide that also serves as the final push to align on the goal. In some formats it may be preferred to have an executive summary slide at the beginning of the presentation that will likely resemble the summary slide at the conclusion of the presentation.

- **Maintain focus** - Keep the content relevant to the topic and audience. Avoid tangential information. A presentation is not a forum to show how much you know; it's a forum to show how effectively you can communicate information in the effort to achieve a goal. Practice discipline. As you develop the presentation and list key points at the end of a section, ensure they support the objectives and goal. If they don't, remove them, because they act as noise and risk reducing the effectiveness of your message.

- **Use variety and emphasis** - Presentations can become monotonous, especially those which are chart and data centric. Find ways to break up the presentation to add emphasis. For instance, the use of a video, quote, or key visual may re-engage the audience and create a memorable moment in the presentation.

- **Slides support the presentation** - Don't have the slides do the talking. They should utilize short bulleted statements that summarize the points that you will narrate. You are delivering a presentation, not sharing a report. Add an appendix to your presentation as the place to provide larger sets of information and data.

- **Show don't tell** - When possible, utilize images and visuals. They are more memorable and powerful than words on a screen.

- **Handouts** - Decide whether or not to provide handouts for the presentation. If you plan to provide the handouts prior to or at the beginning of the presentation, expect the audience to flip through and look ahead. If this is not desired, do not deliver handouts ahead of time.

- **Build effective slides** - Some do's and don'ts:
  - > Don't overwhelm the audience with information on a slide.
  - > Don't ever present a slide that you plan to introduce as an "eye chart." It means the slide is unreadable and ineffective.

> Don't target a certain number of slides and cram information onto a slide in order to reduce the number of slides. This may cause a slide to become crowded and be a distraction from your presentation as the audience attempts to decipher the information. Whether the information is clearly displayed on three slides versus crammed onto one slide, the amount of information remains the same.

> Don't be captain obvious and use bullet points to re-state what is glaringly obvious from a chart or other visual on a slide.

> Do have a clear point or takeaway from each slide.

> Do keep information spaced and legible.

> Do follow similar formats and layouts throughout. The familiarity among slides will help the audience quickly absorb the information.

> Do use high contrast. Colors on a computer screen often are more vibrant and distinguishable than those on projection screens.

> Do make the slides transferable. They should be understandable without your narrative, and do not use animation that renders the slide unreadable if the presentation is printed or viewed outside of presentation mode.

> Do include your sources of information.

> Do include an appendix for "eye chart" data, or tangential information for those who are interested. Often presentations are met with tangential questions. The appendix may serve as a resource to show that you have anticipated those questions and have the information available.

3) Preparation and delivery

- **Learn your style** - People can differ greatly in their approach to presenting, and you will need to learn what works best for you. Some presenters can build the presentation and immediately be ready to go, while others need to practice and even memorize lines to nail the presentation. If you are memorizing lines, maintain authenticity and passion. Try to avoid the trap of sounding robotic as you recite your prepared words. Regardless of preparation style, speak clearly, project your voice, pace yourself, and address the audience, not your computer or presentation screen.

- **Set participation guidelines** - Tell the audience whether you'd like the presentation to be interactive with questions throughout or would like to save questions until the end. If you request that the audience hold questions until the end, fully anticipate that you will still receive some questions as you go through the content. Embrace the questions as they can provide a terrific opportunity to create a memorable moment.

- **Prepare for questions** - Anticipate questions and have answers prepared, particularly on any assertions or conclusions, especially those that may be controversial or counter to conventional wisdom. If you don't have an answer to a question, take a quick note and let the audience know that you will follow up. If you need a minute to think through an answer, let the person know that it is a great question and take a minute to consider how to best answer.

- **Audience participation styles** - The audience may consist of many types of participants, including supporters, quiet observers, detractors, and challengers. Encourage supporters and accept challengers as key contributors who may become ardent supporters if successfully answered.

- **Lead the discussion** - Control the room. If questions and comments begin to derail the presentation, ask the group to save them for a break in the content, such as at the end of a section.

- **Manage the time** - Plan appropriately to hit your time limit. Don't run out of time or rush. Rushing through a presentation will degrade the content and detract from the effectiveness of the presentation.

- **Espouse confidence** - Try not to be nervous. Remember that the people in the room, your manager, and leadership want to see you do well and be impressed.

4) Post-presentation follow-up

- **Share documents** - Send out any supporting documents immediately following the presentation.

- **Follow-up on open questions** - If you commit to following up on a question or topic, follow up and do so in a timely manner.

- **Get feedback** - Don't be afraid to ask for feedback and ensure you ask someone who will be honest with you.

- **Focus and improve** - As you develop as a presenter, practice and consciously work to avoid superfluous gestures or words such as "uh" or "umm." To help remove these words, focus on pacing your speech to afford you the time to deliberately choose your words.

19.2 Leading meetings

Running effective meetings can set you apart from your peers. This is a fantastic opportunity to establish your reputation as decision maker, critical thinker, organizer, collaborator, and most importantly, a leader.

Meeting setup and preparation

- **Invite the right people** - Be mindful of meeting attendees. Only invite colleagues who need to be in the meeting. Meetings with bloated lists of attendees can cost companies millions of dollars in wasted time. Extraneous attendees may feel the need to participate and may trigger tangential discussions. It may also hurt your reputation, particularly as a leader, if colleagues begin to consider your meetings useless.

- **Be focused and organized** - Set a meeting goal and an agenda. The agenda does not need to be extensive, but you as the host should have a path for the meeting to follow in order to prevent it from going off topic. Try to avoid tackling too many topics in a single meeting as fatigue may set in and interest may erode over time.

- **Get the time right** - Schedule the correct amount of time. Meetings that are scheduled for more time than needed can unnecessarily block calendars. The extra time may lead to meandering conversations and unproductive discussion as attendees see an opportunity to exploit the time. Underestimating the amount of time a meeting requires may cause significant issues. If the meeting is cut short, the goal may not be attained, requiring an additional meeting where the participants will need to gather again and be reintroduced to the topic. If the meeting continues past the allotted time, it creates significant inconvenience for the participants who are then late to their following meetings or have lost time in their day for other scheduled work.

- **Be ready** - Be prepared to start the meeting on time and keep the meeting moving without unnecessary interruption. If presenting, make sure the room's audio / visual equipment is ready to go. If you are planning to share your computer screen, have files and presentations open and ready to show. Be conscientious about screen sharing, close potentially confidential files or windows, and exit your email and chat to avoid potentially sensitive or embarrassing notifications.

Running the meeting

- **Get on the same page** - State the goal and the agenda at the beginning of the meeting. Ensure that the group is aligned and prepared to discuss. If the group is not prepared, close the meeting and reschedule. Without appropriate data, information and preparation meetings can devolve into conjecture that may lead to misguided conclusions.

- **Familiarize the team** - Introduce meeting participants if needed.

- **Keep records** - Either delegate a participant or personally take notes during the meeting. Notes should include attendees, key information, decisions, and action items discussed during the meeting.

- **Maintain focus** - Manage the meeting, keep the discussion on task and linear, and avoid tangents and rehashing discussions. If the conversation deviates from the agenda, politely interrupt the discussion and get it back on topic. This may be done by letting the group know that you noticed the discussion has moved off topic and you would like to realign the conversation because you value their time and would like to ensure that the goal of the meeting is achieved. If desired, you may suggest that the tangential topic be taken offline or be the topic of a different meeting.

- **Build rapport** - Display empathy as you engage with the various meeting participants. Ask for their perspective and priorities to help yourself and the group understand each other's position.

Closing a meeting

- **Confirm alignment** - Begin to adjourn the meeting by clearly stating how the goal was reached and by confirming alignment. Not all members may agree but should be aligned on the path forward.

- **State the action plan** - State the action items and their respective owners. Time commitments should be established and noted.

- **Last chance to be heard** - Ask the participants if there is "anything else" that needs to be discussed prior to adjourning the meeting.

- **Send a recap** - Shortly after the meeting, send a recap. The recap should include notes from the meeting, the aligned decisions, and the action items with their respective owners and timing. Invite comments to ensure the participants can respond if there is a misalignment.

The silent meeting

Often, meetings will have the goal to discuss a topic that requires background research, data, or other information. It's common for the information to be presented to the group. The pace at which the information is presented and the way it is presented may cause insights to be missed and can limit the thoughtfulness of the discussion. In this scenario, presenters can fully control the conversation. They may foster groupthink, emphasize or deemphasize information, or inject bias, all with the potential to result in bad decisions.

The concept of the silent meeting was notably utilized by the company Square. The silent meeting allows the group to take time at the beginning of a meeting to individually and silently review the information pertinent to the discussion (Py, 2018). This allows the members of the group to hone in on different aspects of the information and create their own conclusions, free of bias. After a certain amount of time, the group will discuss the information and move toward achieving the meeting's goal.

19.3 Meeting etiquette

Your ability to be a valued contributor in meetings can go a long way in solidifying your perception as a high performer and advancing your career. Here are some best practices to follow:

- **Prepare** - Review agenda prior to the meeting and be prepared to contribute.

- **Be on-time** - Based on the culture or your company, the definition of "on-time" may differ. Ensure you are in line with the cultural norms. If you suspect that you will be late, give the leader of the meeting advanced notice.

- **Be selective** - If you join a meeting, have a reason to be there. If you attend meetings and consistently remain silent, colleagues may question what level of contribution you can make both in and outside of meetings.

- **Selectively contribute** - When you choose to contribute to a meeting, do so with purpose, not for the sake of talking. Help bring new information and perspective. Move the conversation forward. Avoid repeating or "echoing" statements, and avoid tangents.

- **Confidently contribute** - Espouse confidence when you speak, and never begin a statement with the phrase, "This may be dumb, but...."

- **Embrace the team dynamic** - Display understanding and empathy for your teammates. Ask others about their needs and how you can help, just as you would in your role as the leader of a meeting.

- **Understand the audience** - When you contribute to a meeting, keep in mind that you likely have more expertise or intimate knowledge regarding the subject of your comment. Others in the meeting may not have the same level of background knowledge, so be sure to provide context but do so succinctly. Avoid rambling and causing others to lose focus on your primary point. If someone wants additional detail that won't clearly benefit the group, you may suggest that you both connect outside of the meeting.

- **Be respectful** - Do not fall asleep and do not audibly yawn. It is extremely rude and a great way to find yourself on a precarious career path. If you are struggling to focus, stand up along a wall or behind your seat.

19.4 Email etiquette

The dependence of email in business communications is astounding and has become the primary method of communication for many. To help you effectively communicate via email, here are some best practices to follow:

- **Be concise** - Keep emails short and try to limit yourself to five sentences at most. As the length of your email increases, the likelihood of it getting read decreases. Use bullet points and spacing when possible to avoid heavy blocks of text.

- **Be focused** - Stick to the subject of the email and ensure the subject of the email is descriptive. The receiver of the email should be able to understand the topic of the email without prior context.

- **Convenience is important** - Put key information, such as a chart, in the email body rather than as an attachment. The likelihood of people opening attachments or clicking links is drastically lower than them viewing the information in the body of the email.

- **Help them navigate** - Mindfully limit the number of attachments and their file size. In your email describe what is in each attachment. It is helpful to note whether the attachment is intended to be immediately reviewed or is attached as supporting information that may be reviewed if desired.

- **Know the device** - Consider the type of device the recipient of the email typically uses. If the person is on-the-go and uses their phone to view 95% of emails, attempt to present the information in a format that will be easily viewed on a phone. For emails to mobile device users, the use of attachments is precarious. They are easy to overlook and often ignored because of unneeded images, such as headers and signature lines that are shown as attachments.

- **Use an appropriate signature** - Evaluate how necessary it is to have an image in your signature. Does that approach add value or does it annoy your audience, when the images are transformed into attachments?

- **Don't cry wolf** - Only use a high priority flag when it is truly a high priority. Remember that the recipient of your email is receiving emails from many other people. Does your email really take priority over the others received by the recipient?

- **Avoid ambiguity** - Direct questions to a specific person, or two at most. Messages that ask a broad group to respond often get no reply because there is no ownership and people will wait for others to respond.

- **Email is not for discussions** - Avoid open questions that may be subject to interpretation or a matter of opinion. The outcome of such a question can be a seemingly endless chain of emails that wastes time and annoys recipients. For a question of that nature, schedule a meeting. If you find yourself in a situation where an email thread is growing out of control, propose a stop to the thread and organize a meeting to discuss.

  Additionally, don't rely on email to conduct discussions that could be more efficiently completed via discussion in-person or by phone / video. Not only may email be less efficient, it may also detract from your ability to build rapport with the other party.

- **Don't SPAM** - Only copy (cc) those who need or want to be cc'd. Do not SPAM your co-workers.

- **Be responsive** - A common rule of thumb is to respond to emails within 24 hours. If you are unable to fully respond within that time frame, simply send a quick reply acknowledging their email and set an expectation for when they may get a response.

19.5 A note on leadership

For those who are interested in advancement and career growth, becoming widely recognized as a leader and as a great teammate is essential. In this section we will discuss several ways to approach your work in a manner that promotes your perception as a leader.

Project confidence in your work but not cockiness. When making assertions, particularly those counter to common belief, be overly prepared to explain your rationale. Even if you don't get alignment with your view, your ability to demonstrate knowledge and the ability to think critically can go a long way.

Be stoic. Have emotional control and composure. Great lessons can be learned by watching the actions of some of the most successful coaches of all-time, such as Bill Belichick, the head coach of the National Football League's team the New England Patriots. If you observe his demeanor on the sideline, he exemplifies stoicism. This does three things:

- Demonstrates to the team that he is in control

- Eliminates distractions caused by overreactions, so he can focus on the next move

- When an emotional reaction is made, it is calculated and carries greater impact

Passion for your business and its mission does not equate to the need for emotional outbursts. It can be manifested through dedicated, strategic work performed in a professional manner. And while stoicism and control are important, bear in mind that a balance is needed. A complete absence of sentiment may make you appear robotic and unrelatable to a fault.

Reassure yourself and go into situations knowing that people you encounter want you to succeed. Managers and senior leaders want to be impressed by the team they've built. It is a reflection on them as hiring managers and mentors. They want to feel confident that their team will be able to handle delegated tasks. Use this knowledge to inspire confidence in your work and your presentations.

Collaboration across cross-functional teams is essential, particularly in a world where many companies value 360-degree feedback. To facilitate that collaboration, understand and value the fact that any person you work with has competing priorities. The work you ask of a person will need to be weighed against their other tasks, and your request will likely not be their first priority. Understand this and attempt to help where possible so that both of your needs are met.

When working with colleagues, attempt to build a connection and reciprocate efforts. Use various forms of communication to build rapport. It's not uncommon for written correspondence to be mistakenly interpreted as negative. Prior to sending, read and re-read emails to minimize that possibility. Foster relationships with video or phone calls, as well as in-person contact.

Be pragmatic and focus on what matters. The ability to effectively prioritize cannot be understated. Often, bright shiny projects become opportunities, but many times they distract from focusing on the core business that carries greater impact. Insist on and create a business case for work that needs to be prioritized. Be honest and consider the realistic potential of the project and the level of effort required to complete the project.

Regardless of your level within the company, understand and communicate the vision. Connect the day-to-day work that you and your teams do as progress toward achieving that vision. Think strategically, long term, and anticipate actions (game theory). This will demonstrate your ability to think strategically and to successfully lead the business. Lastly, take time to recognize the accomplishments of your teams and those around you. Give credit and celebrate wins.

References

Badenhausen, K. (2019, May 22). The World's Most Valuable Brands 2019: Apple On Top At $206 Billion. Retrieved from Forbes: https://www.forbes.com/sites/kurtbadenhausen/2019/05/22/the-worlds-most-valuable-brands-2019-apple-on-top-at-206-billion/#fff7b8537c2d

Baker, G. (2017, October 15). National anthem controversy hurting the NFL's brand. Retrieved from The Seattle Times: https://www.seattletimes.com/sports/seahawks/national-anthem-controversy-hurting-the-nfls-brand/

Berr, J. (2018, February 21). Facebook's younger users are abandoning ship. Retrieved from CBS NEWS: https://www.cbsnews.com/news/facebooks-younger-users-are-abandoning-ship/#targetTextAccording-20to20a20recent20reportdrop20by20nearly20620percent

Brtnická, M. (2021, 06 25). Brtnicka martina case_study_heartbrands. Retrieved from Slideshare: https://www.slideshare.net/MartinaBrtnick/brtnicka-martina-casestudyheartbrands

Budds, D. (2015, September 18). How Pantone Became The Definitive Language Of Color. Retrieved from Fast Company: https://www.fastcompany.com/3050240/how-pantone-became-the-definitive-language-of-color

Burton, Gollins, McNeely, & Walls, a. (2019). Revisiting the relationship between ad frequency and purchase intentions: How affect and cognition mediate outcomes at different levels of advertising frequency. Journal of Advertising Research.

Business Wire. (2021, 04 15). "Helllllooo Again Ladies and Gents". Retrieved from Business Wire: https://www.businesswire.com/news/home/20200122005416/en/%E2%80%9CHelllllooo-Again-Ladies-and-Gents%E2%80%9D

Butschli, J. (2021, 04 15). Brawny uses packaging to continue Wounded Warrior Project partnership. Retrieved from Packaging World: https://www.packworld.com/design/flexible-packaging/article/13362892/brawny-uses-packaging-to-continue-wounded-warrior-project-partnership

Chierotti, L. (2019, March 26). Harvard Professor Says 95% of Purchasing Decisions Are Subconscious - When marketing a product to a consumer, it's most effective to target the subconscious mind. Retrieved from Inc: https://www.inc.com/logan-chierotti/harvard-professor-says-95-of-purchasing-decisions-are-subconscious.html#:~:text=Emotion%20is%20what%20really%20drives,are%20incapable%20of%20making%20decisions.

Court, D., Elzinga, D., Mulder, S., & Vetvik, O. J. (2020, March 9). The consumer decision journey. Retrieved from McKinsey & Company: https://www.mckinsey.com/business-functions/marketing-and-sales/our-insights/the-consumer-decision-journey

Dr. Johnson, T. A. (2018, May). What is 20/20 vision? Retrieved from University of Iowa Hospitals & Clinics: https://uihc.org/health-topics/what-2020-vision#:~:text=How%20common%20is%2020%2F20,t%20 see%20very%20well%2C%20Dr.

emarts, e. (2021, 06 19). Screen printing. Retrieved from Unsplash: https://unsplash.com/photos/ZCTh-4f4mv18

Facebook IQ. (2016, July 16). Effective Frequency: Reaching Full Campaign Potential. Retrieved from Facebook: https://www.facebook.com/business/news/insights/effective-frequency-reaching-full-campaign-potential

Federal Trade Commission. (2020, July 20). CAN-SPAM ACT: A COMPLIANCE GUIDE FOR BUSINESS. Retrieved from Federal Trade Commission: https://www.ftc.gov/tips-advice/business-center/guidance/can-spam-act-compliance-guide-business

GDPR. (2020, July 20). FAQ. Retrieved from GDPR: https://gdpr.eu/faq/

Google LLC. (2011, April). The zero moment of truth macro study. Retrieved from Think with Google: https://www.thinkwithgoogle.com/consumer-insights/the-zero-moment-of-truth-macro-study/

Hanbury, M. (2018, July 19). Gymboree is back from the dead, but furious parents say its new look 'is complete garbage. Retrieved from Business Insider: https://www.businessinsider.com/gymboree-new-clothes-anger-parents-2018-7

Hooker, L. (2016, June 21). How to Create a Distinct Color Palette for Your Brand. Retrieved from Elle & Company: https://www.elleandcompanydesign.com/blog/color-palette

IKEA. (2020, March 4). IKEA VISION, CULTURE AND VALUES. Retrieved from IKEA: https://ikea.jobs.cz/en/vision-culture-and-values/

Johnson, K. (2020, January 8). Ford F-Series is America's Best-Selling Truck for 43rd Year. Retrieved from The News Wheel: https://thenewswheel.com/ford-2019-sales-results-united-states/

Keller, K. (2012). Strategic Brand Management: Building, Measuring, and Managing Brand Equity. New York, New York: Pearson.

Kotler, P. a. (2006). Marketing Management (12th ed.). Upper Saddle River, New Jersey: Prentice Hall.

Lanning, M. J. (2000). Delivering Profitable Value. A Revolutionary Framework to Accelerate Growth, Generate Wealth, and Rediscover the Heart of Business. New York, New York: Perseus Book Group.

Maslow, A. H. (1970). Motivation and Personality. New York, New York: Harper and Row.

Maynard, W. (2010, September 22). Old Spice Guy Brings 107% Increase in Sales. Retrieved from kinesis: https://www.kinesisinc.com/old-spice-guy-brings-107-increase-in-sales/

Moore, G. (1991). Crossing the Chasm. New York, New York: Harper Business Essentials.

Nielsen. (2012, April 11). CONSUMER TRUST IN ONLINE, SOCIAL AND MOBILE ADVERTISING GROWS. Retrieved from Nielsen: https://www.nielsen.com/us/en/insights/article/2012/consumer-trust-in-online-social-and-mobile-advertising-grows/

Okadar, G. (2017, July 30). How frequency of exposure can maximise the resonance of your digital campaigns. Retrieved from Nielsen: https://www.nielsen.com/au/en/insights/article/2017/how-frequency-of-exposure-can-maximise-the-resonance-of-your-digital-campaigns/

Osterwalder, A. P. (2014). Value Proposition Design: How to Create Products and Services Customers Want. Hoboken, New Jersey: John Wiley & Sons.

Pine II, J., & Gilmore, J. (1998, July-August). Welcome to the Experience Economy. Harvard Business Review.

Porter, M. E. (1980). Competitive Strategy: Techniques for analyzing industries and competitiors. New York, New York: Simon & Schuster Inc.

Power Reviews. (2019, June 14). 12 of the Best Brand Promise Examples We've Seen. Retrieved from Power

Reviews: https://www.powerreviews.com/blog/brand-promise-examples/

Py. (2018, September 4). A silent meeting is worth a thousand words. Retrieved from Medium: https://medium.com/square-corner-blog/a-silent-meeting-is-worth-a-thousand-words-2c7213b12fb6

Rogers, D. E. (1962). Diffusion of Innovations. New York, New York: Free Press Simon & Schuster.

Seaney, R. (2017, August 23). History of Airline Fees: Bags, Food & More. Retrieved from farecompare: https://www.farecompare.com/travel-advice/airline-fees-bags-history/

Smith, K. (2019, December 30). 126 Amazing Social Media Statistics and Facts. Retrieved from Brandwatch: https://www.brandwatch.com/blog/amazing-social-media-statistics-and-facts/

State of California Department of Justice. (2020, July 20). California Consumer Privacy Act (CCPA). Retrieved from State of California Department of Justice: https://oag.ca.gov/privacy/ccpa

Sterling, G. (2019, June 17). Almost 70% of digital ad spending going to Google, Facebook, Amazon, says analyst firm. Retrieved from Marketing Land: https://marketingland.com/almost-70-of-digital-ad-spending-going-to-google-facebook-amazon-says-analyst-firm-262565#:~:text=However%2C%20eMarketer%20revised%20downward%20its,nearly%2050%25%20to%2038%25.&text=Google%2C%20Facebook%20and%20Amazon%20are,dolla

Target. (2021, 04 15). Tide + Febreze Spring Renewal. Retrieved from Target.com: https://www.target.com/p/tide-plus-febreze-spring-renewal-high-efficiency-liquid-laundry-detergent-92-fl-oz/-/A-15043040

The Home Depot. (2021, 04 15). Newsroom. Retrieved from The Home Depot: https://corporate.homedepot.com/newsroom/home-depot-announces-strategic-priorities

Thomas, L. (2019, October 15). Gymboree brand will stage a comeback in 2020 thanks to Children's Place. Retrieved from CNBC: https://www.cnbc.com/2019/10/15/gymboree-will-stage-a-comeback-in-2020-thanks-to-childrens-place.html

Thomas, L. (2019, Oct 15). Gymboree brand will stage a comeback in 2020 thanks to Children's Place. Retrieved from CNBC: https://www.cnbc.com/2019/10/15/gymboree-will-stage-a-comeback-in-2020-thanks-to-childrens-place.html

Unilever. (2020, October 16). Dove. Retrieved from Dove: https://www.dove.com/us/en/home.html

Unilever. (2020, March 3). Dove Men+Care. Retrieved from Dove: https://www.dove.com/us/en/men-care.html

UX User Experience. (2014, 02 18). What's the reason some places use milk bags instead of milk jugs or other means? Retrieved from UX User Experience: https://ux.stackexchange.com/questions/53184/whats-the-reason-some-places-use-milk-bags-instead-of-milk-jugs-or-other-means

von Neumann, J., & Morgenstern, O. (1944). The Theory of Games and Economic Behavior. Princeton, NJ: Princeton University Press.

Williams, J. (2015, December 15). Infographic: 17 B2B Referral Statistics You Should Know (But Probably Don't). Retrieved from influitive: https://influitive.com/blog/infographic-17-stats-about-b2b-referrals-you-should-know-but-probably-dont/

Zhang, B. (2018, November 27). The glorious history of the Ford F-Series truck, America's best selling vehicle for 36 years. Retrieved from Business Insider: https://www.businessinsider.com/ford-f-series-f150-truck-sales-record-history-2017-1

Index